Jim Lee, *Editorial Director*
John Nee, *Senior VP—Business Development*
Ben Abernathy, *Editor*
Kristy Quinn, *Assistant Editor*
Ed Roeder, *Art Director*
Paul Levitz, *President & Publisher*
Georg Brewer, *VP—Design & DC Direct Creative*
Richard Bruning, *Senior VP—Creative Director*
Patrick Caldon, *Executive VP—Finance & Operations*
Chris Caramalis, *VP—Finance*
John Cunningham, *VP—Marketing*
Terri Cunningham, *VP—Managing Editor*
Alison Gill, *VP—Manufacturing*
David Hyde, *VP—Publicity*
Hank Kanalz, *VP—General Manager, WildStorm*
Paula Lowitt, *Senior VP—Business & Legal Affairs*
MaryEllen McLaughlin, *VP—Advertising & Custom Publishing*
Gregory Noveck, *Senior VP—Creative Affairs*
Sue Pohja, *VP—Book Trade Sales*
Steve Rotterdam, *Senior VP—Sales & Marketing*
Cheryl Rubin, *Senior VP—Brand Management*
Jeff Trojan, *VP—Business Development, DC Direct*
Bob Wayne, *VP—Sales*

EX MACHINA: POWER DOWN. Published by WildStorm Productions, an imprint of DC Comics. 888 Prospect St. #240, La Jolla, CA 92037. Cover, compilation copyright © 2008 Brian K. Vaughan and Tony Harris. All Rights Reserved. EX MACHINA is ™ Brian K. Vaughan and Tony Harris. Originally published in single magazine form as EX MACHINA #26-29, EX MACHINA: INSIDE THE MACHINE © 2007 Brian K. Vaughan and Tony Harris. EX MACHINA #23 © 2006, Cover #1 © 2004, Cover #4 © 2004, Cover #5 © 2004, Cover #12 © 2005, Specials covers © 2006, Tag TPB cover © 2005, Fact v. Fiction TPB cover © 2006 Smoke Smoke TPB cover © 2007 Brian K. Vaughan and Tony Harris.

DC Comics, a Warner Bros. Entertainment Company.

ISBN: 978-1-4012-1498-2

Chapter 1 Power Down part 1

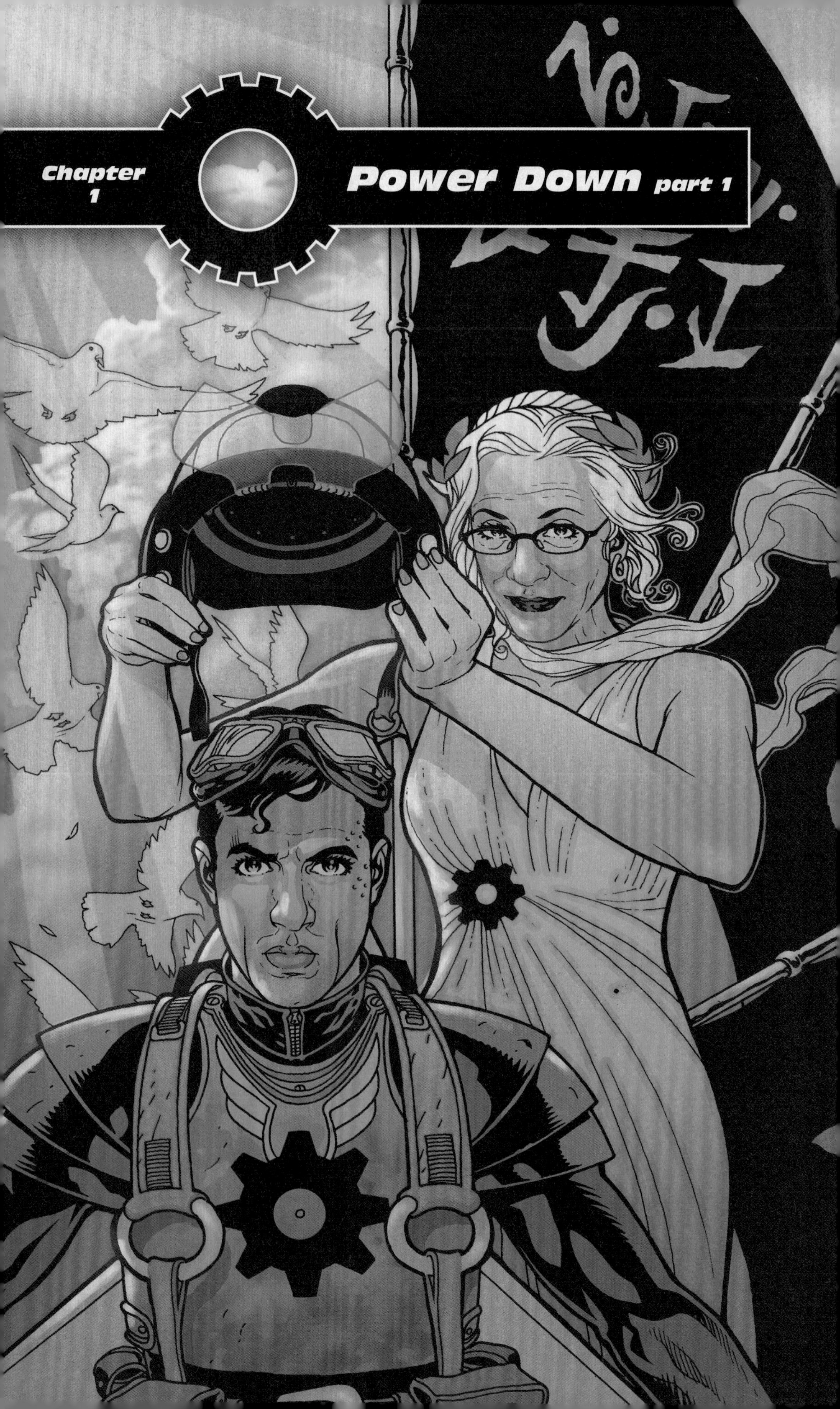

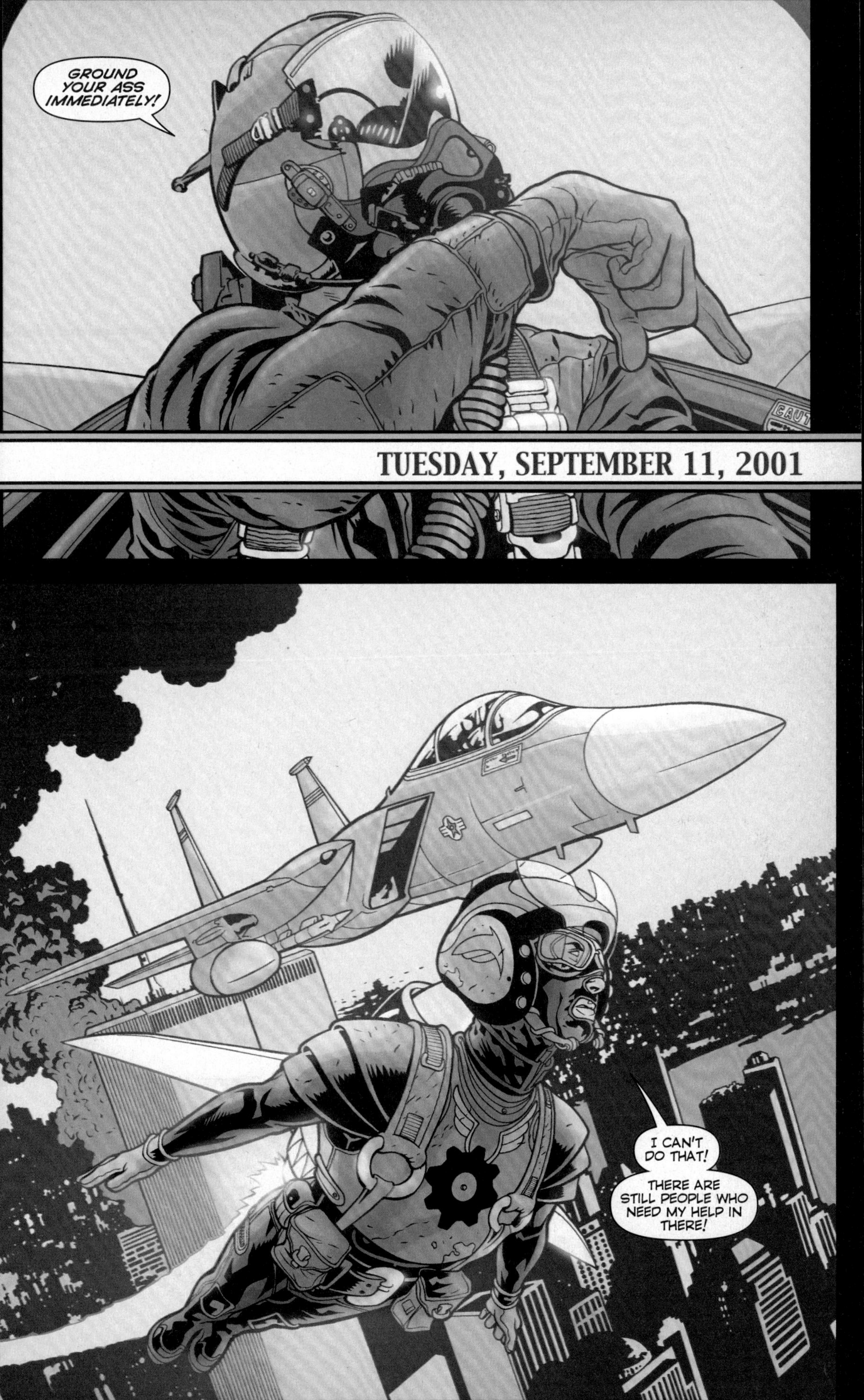
GROUND YOUR ASS IMMEDIATELY!
TUESDAY, SEPTEMBER 11, 2001
I CAN'T DO THAT! THERE ARE STILL PEOPLE WHO NEED MY HELP IN THERE!

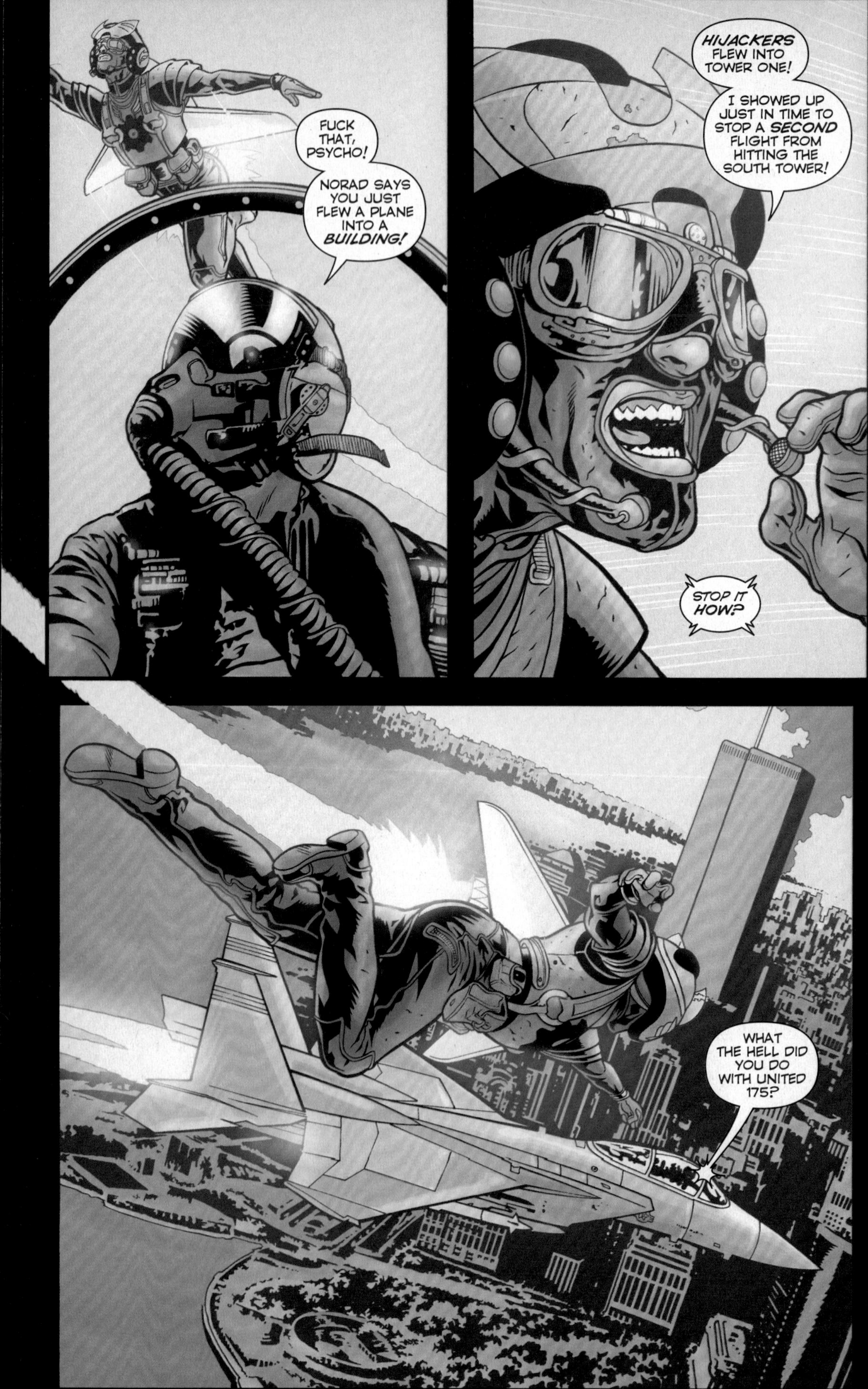
FUCK THAT, PSYCHO!
NORAD SAYS YOU JUST FLEW A PLANE INTO A BUILDING!
HIJACKERS FLEW INTO TOWER ONE!
I SHOWED UP JUST IN TIME TO STOP A SECOND FLIGHT FROM HITTING THE SOUTH TOWER!
STOP IT HOW?
WHAT THE HELL DID YOU DO WITH UNITED 175?

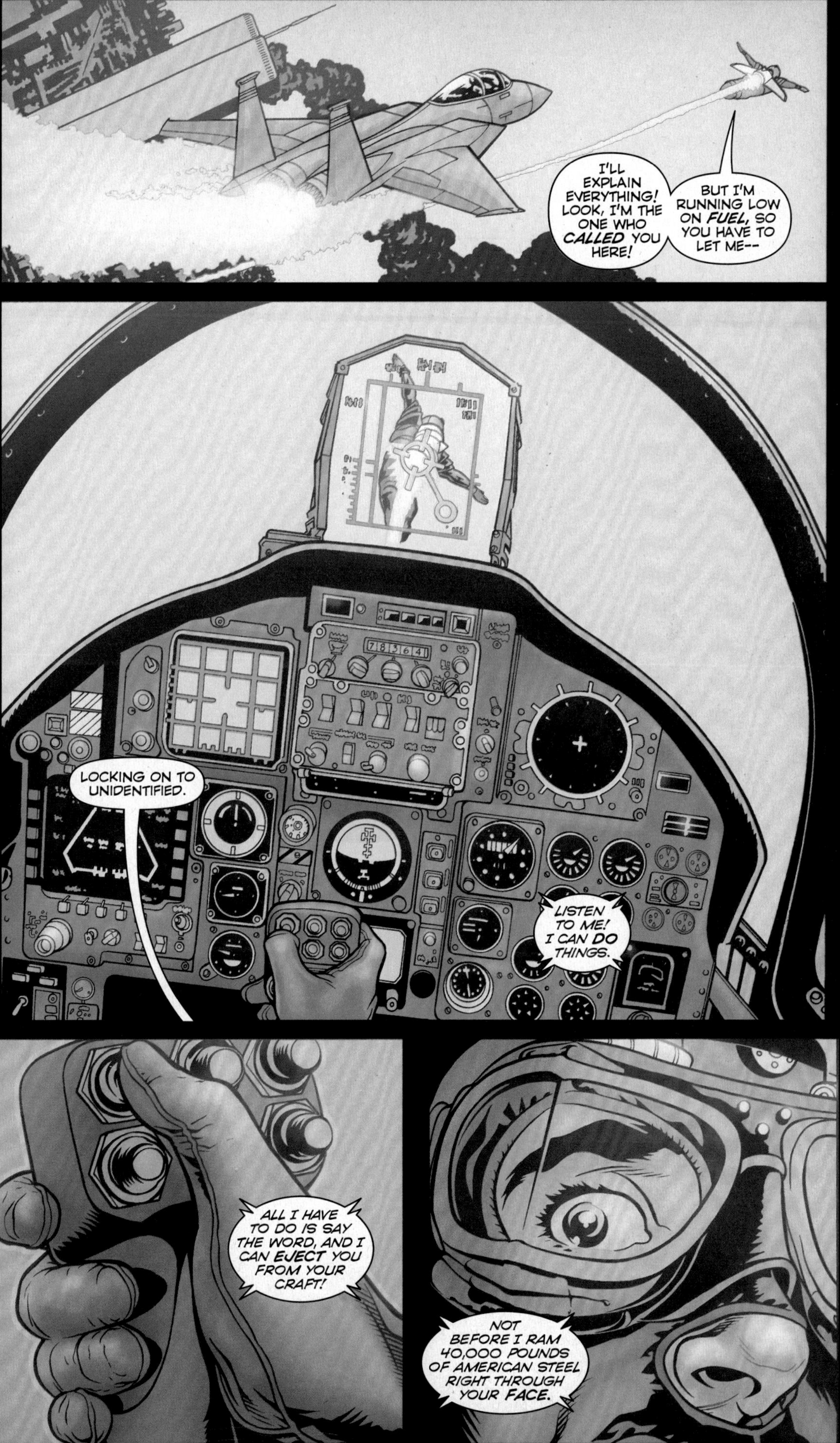
I'LL EXPLAIN EVERYTHING! LOOK, I'M THE ONE WHO CALLED YOU HERE!
BUT I'M RUNNING LOW ON FUEL, SO YOU HAVE TO LET ME--
LOCKING ON TO UNIDENTIFIED.
LISTEN TO ME! I CAN DO THINGS.
ALL I HAVE TO DO IS SAY THE WORD, AND I CAN EJECT YOU FROM YOUR CRAFT!
NOT BEFORE I RAM 40,000 POUNDS OF AMERICAN STEEL RIGHT THROUGH YOUR FACE.

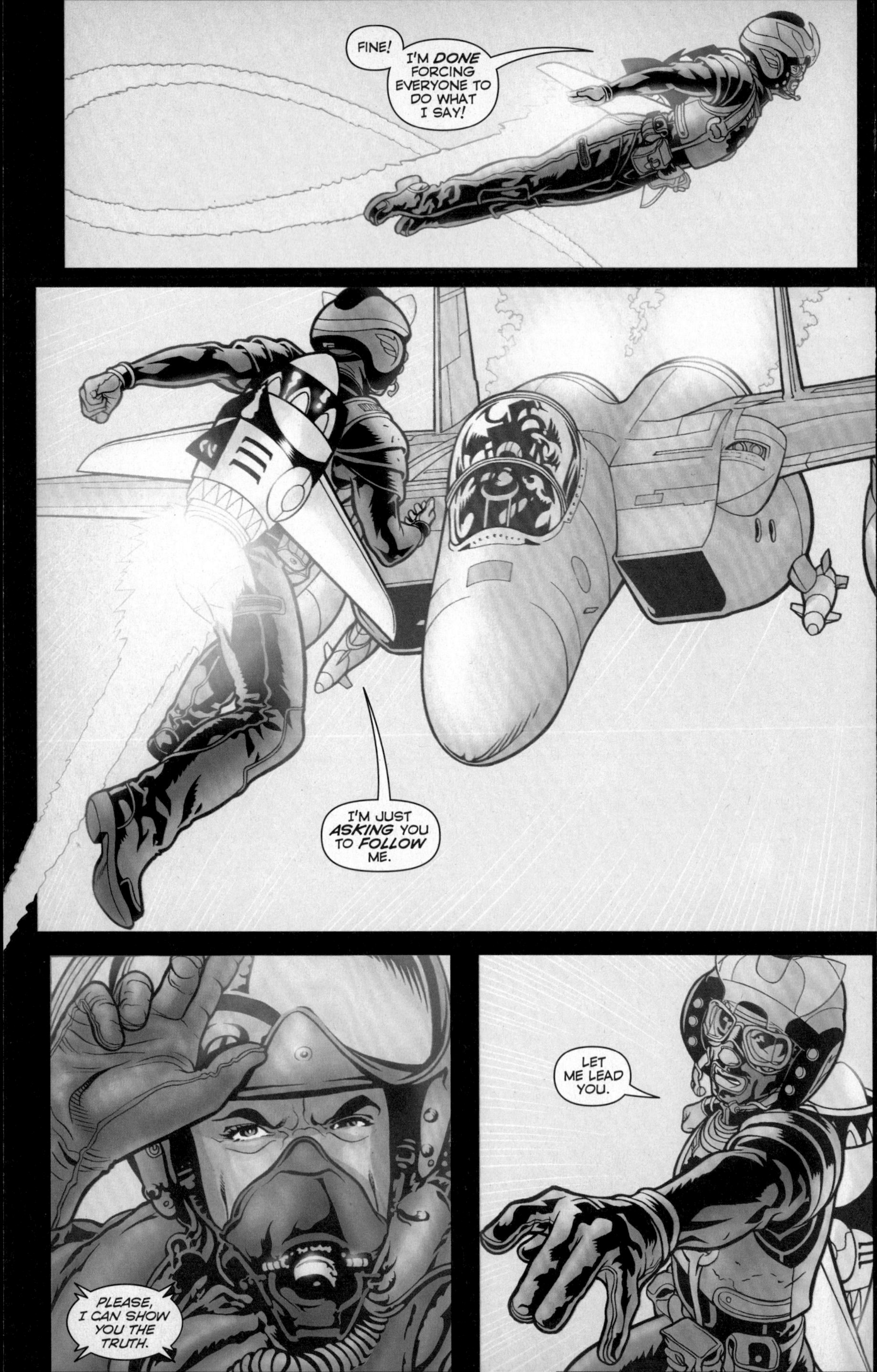
FINE!
I'M DONE FORCING EVERYONE TO DO WHAT I SAY!
I'M JUST ASKING YOU TO FOLLOW ME.
PLEASE, I CAN SHOW YOU THE TRUTH.
LET ME LEAD YOU.

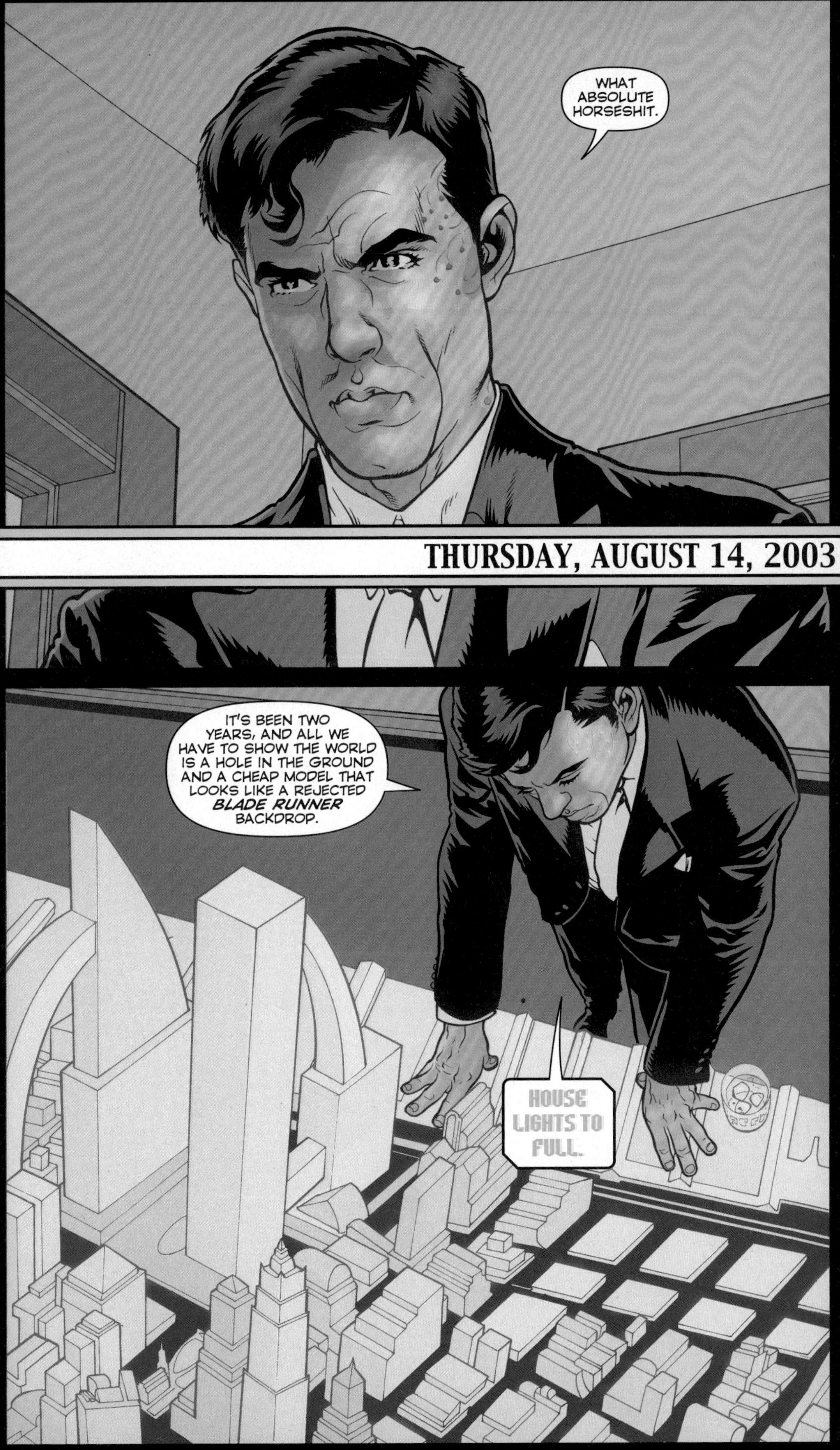
WHAT ABSOLUTE HORSESHIT.
THURSDAY, AUGUST 14, 2003
IT'S BEEN TWO YEARS, AND ALL WE HAVE TO SHOW THE WORLD IS A HOLE IN THE GROUND AND A CHEAP MODEL THAT LOOKS LIKE A REJECTED *BLADE RUNNER* BACKDROP.
HOUSE LIGHTS TO FULL.

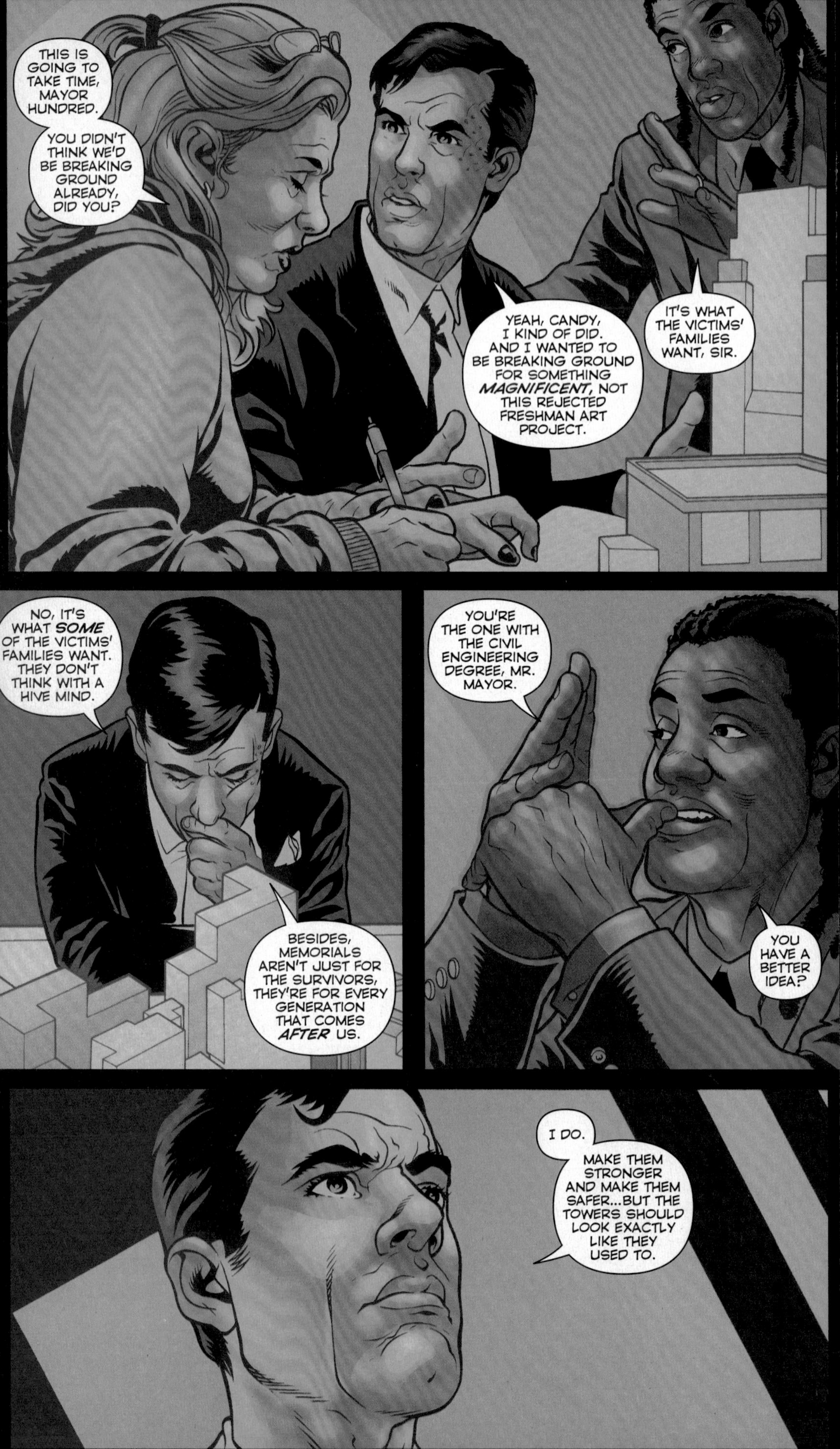
THIS IS GOING TO TAKE TIME, MAYOR HUNDRED.
YOU DIDN'T THINK WE'D BE BREAKING GROUND ALREADY, DID YOU?
YEAH, CANDY, I KIND OF DID. AND I WANTED TO BE BREAKING GROUND FOR SOMETHING *MAGNIFICENT*, NOT THIS REJECTED FRESHMAN ART PROJECT.
IT'S WHAT THE VICTIMS' FAMILIES WANT, SIR.
NO, IT'S WHAT **SOME** OF THE VICTIMS' FAMILIES WANT. THEY DON'T THINK WITH A HIVE MIND.
BESIDES, MEMORIALS AREN'T JUST FOR THE SURVIVORS, THEY'RE FOR EVERY GENERATION THAT COMES ***AFTER*** US.
YOU'RE THE ONE WITH THE CIVIL ENGINEERING DEGREE, MR. MAYOR.
YOU HAVE A BETTER IDEA?
I DO.
MAKE THEM STRONGER AND MAKE THEM SAFER...BUT THE TOWERS SHOULD LOOK EXACTLY LIKE THEY USED TO.

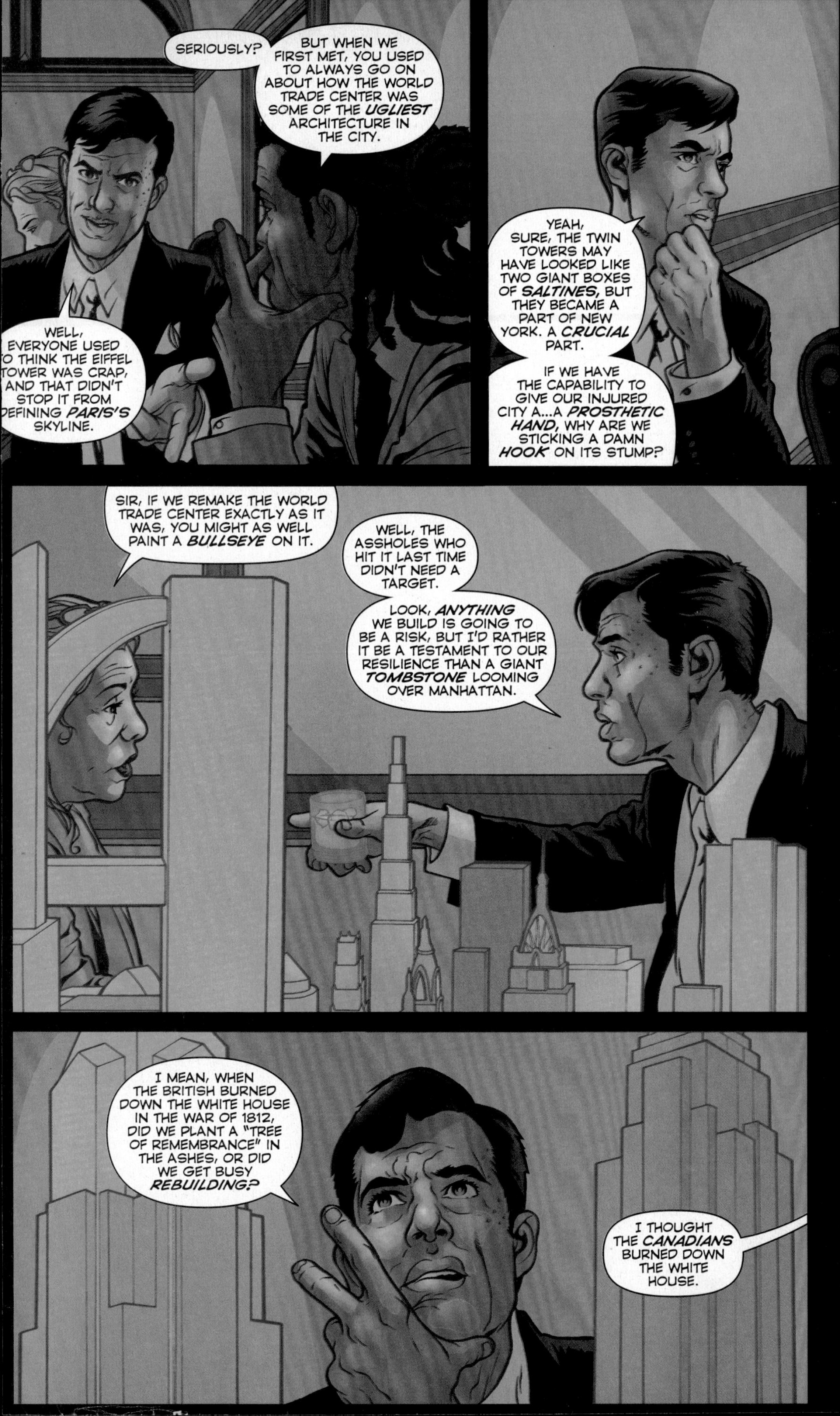
SERIOUSLY?
BUT WHEN WE FIRST MET, YOU USED TO ALWAYS GO ON ABOUT HOW THE WORLD TRADE CENTER WAS SOME OF THE UGLIEST ARCHITECTURE IN THE CITY.
WELL, EVERYONE USED TO THINK THE EIFFEL TOWER WAS CRAP, AND THAT DIDN'T STOP IT FROM DEFINING PARIS'S SKYLINE.
YEAH, SURE, THE TWIN TOWERS MAY HAVE LOOKED LIKE TWO GIANT BOXES OF SALTINES, BUT THEY BECAME A PART OF NEW YORK. A CRUCIAL PART.
IF WE HAVE THE CAPABILITY TO GIVE OUR INJURED CITY A...A PROSTHETIC HAND, WHY ARE WE STICKING A DAMN HOOK ON ITS STUMP?
SIR, IF WE REMAKE THE WORLD TRADE CENTER EXACTLY AS IT WAS, YOU MIGHT AS WELL PAINT A BULLSEYE ON IT.
WELL, THE ASSHOLES WHO HIT IT LAST TIME DIDN'T NEED A TARGET.
LOOK, ANYTHING WE BUILD IS GOING TO BE A RISK, BUT I'D RATHER IT BE A TESTAMENT TO OUR RESILIENCE THAN A GIANT TOMBSTONE LOOMING OVER MANHATTAN.
I MEAN, WHEN THE BRITISH BURNED DOWN THE WHITE HOUSE IN THE WAR OF 1812, DID WE PLANT A "TREE OF REMEMBRANCE" IN THE ASHES, OR DID WE GET BUSY REBUILDING?
I THOUGHT THE CANADIANS BURNED DOWN THE WHITE HOUSE.

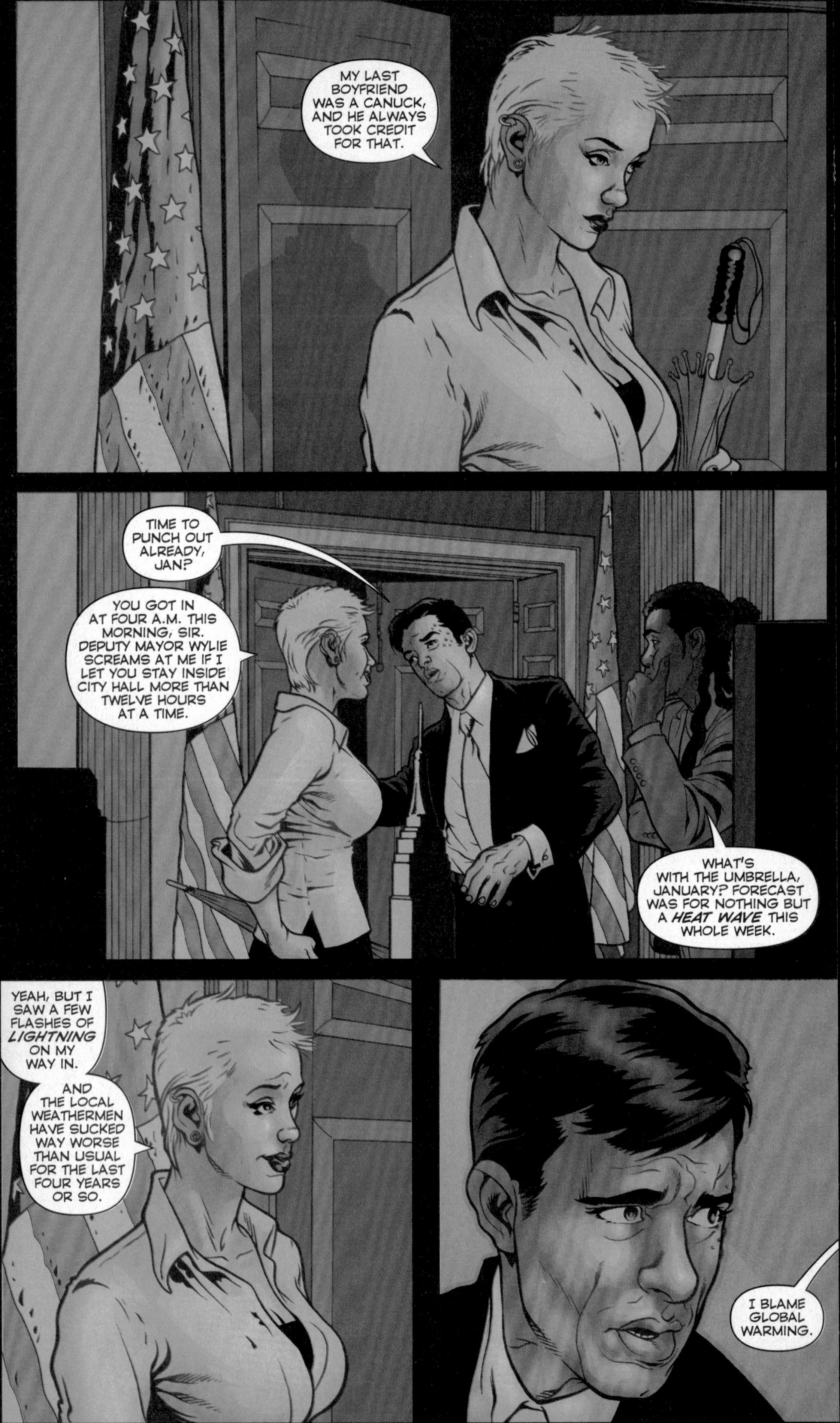
MY LAST BOYFRIEND WAS A CANUCK, AND HE ALWAYS TOOK CREDIT FOR THAT.
TIME TO PUNCH OUT ALREADY, JAN?
YOU GOT IN AT FOUR A.M. THIS MORNING, SIR. DEPUTY MAYOR WYLIE SCREAMS AT ME IF I LET YOU STAY INSIDE CITY HALL MORE THAN TWELVE HOURS AT A TIME.
WHAT'S WITH THE UMBRELLA, JANUARY? FORECAST WAS FOR NOTHING BUT A ***HEAT WAVE*** THIS WHOLE WEEK.
YEAH, BUT I SAW A FEW FLASHES OF ***LIGHTNING*** ON MY WAY IN.
AND THE LOCAL WEATHERMEN HAVE SUCKED WAY WORSE THAN USUAL FOR THE LAST FOUR YEARS OR SO.
I BLAME GLOBAL WARMING.

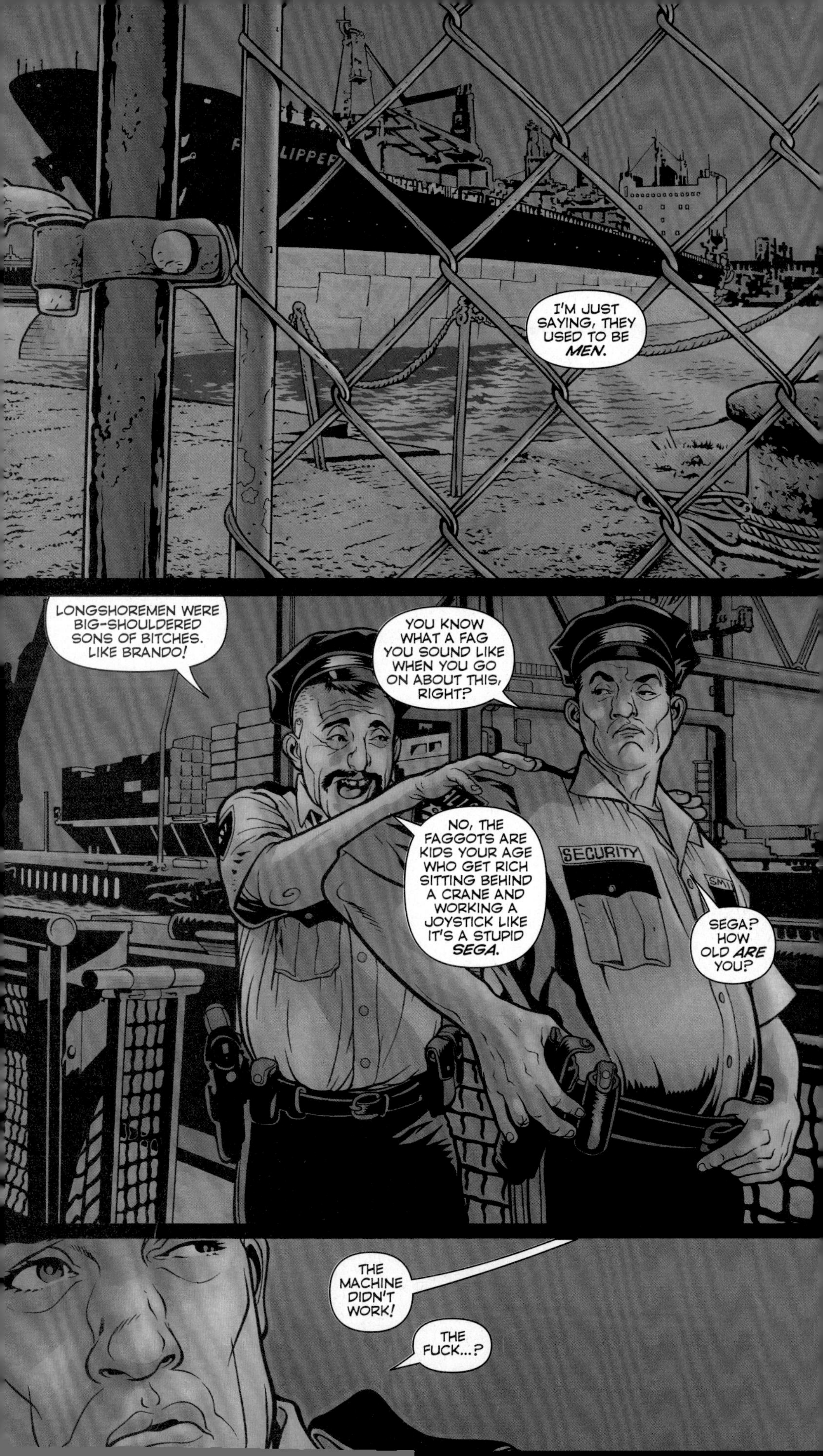
I'M JUST SAYING, THEY USED TO BE *MEN*.
LONGSHOREMEN WERE BIG-SHOULDERED SONS OF BITCHES. LIKE BRANDO!
YOU KNOW WHAT A FAG YOU SOUND LIKE WHEN YOU GO ON ABOUT THIS, RIGHT?
NO, THE FAGGOTS ARE KIDS YOUR AGE WHO GET RICH SITTING BEHIND A CRANE AND WORKING A JOYSTICK LIKE IT'S A STUPID *SEGA*.
SECURITY
SEGA? HOW OLD *ARE* YOU?
THE MACHINE DIDN'T WORK!
THE FUCK...?

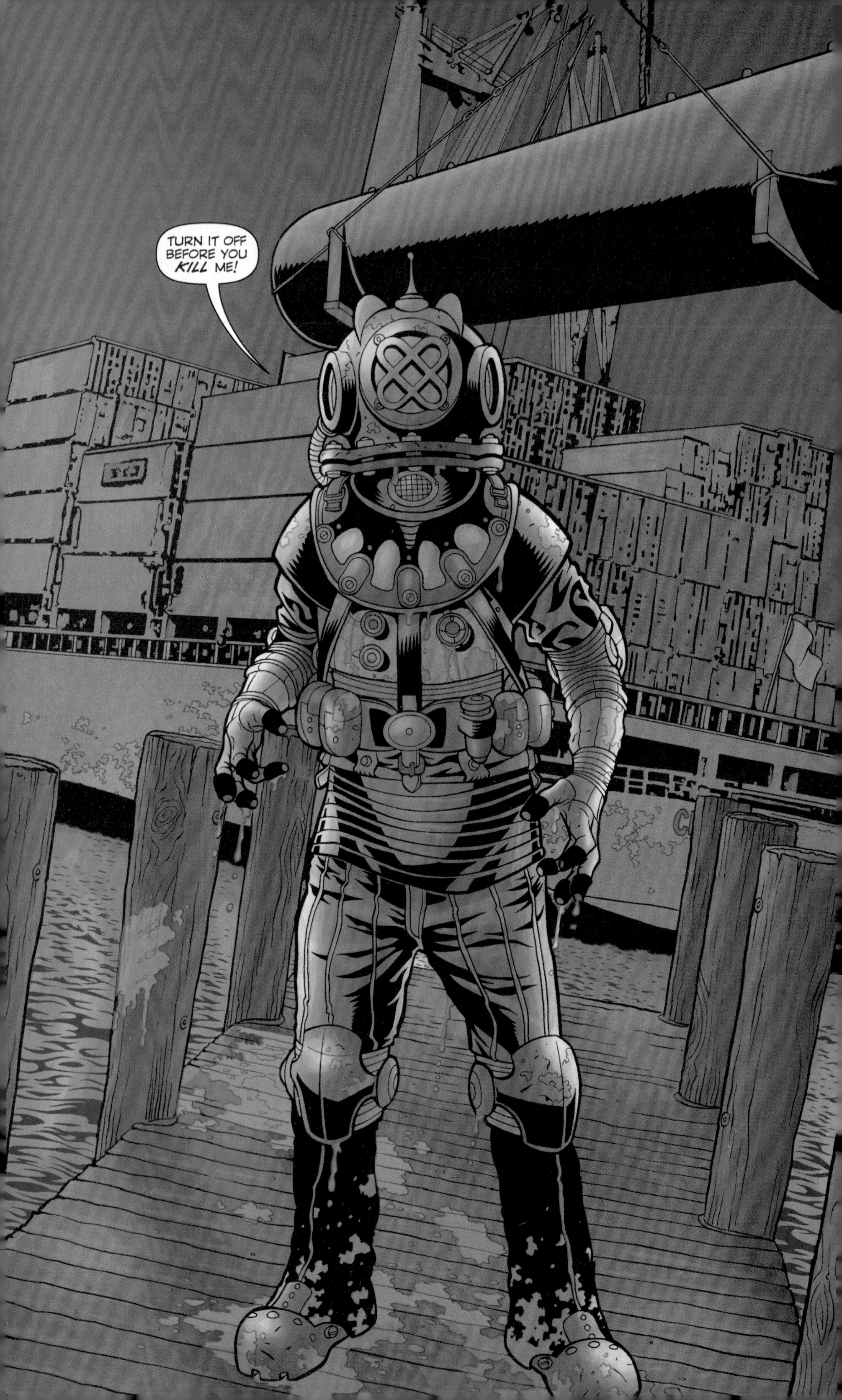
TURN IT OFF BEFORE YOU KILL ME!

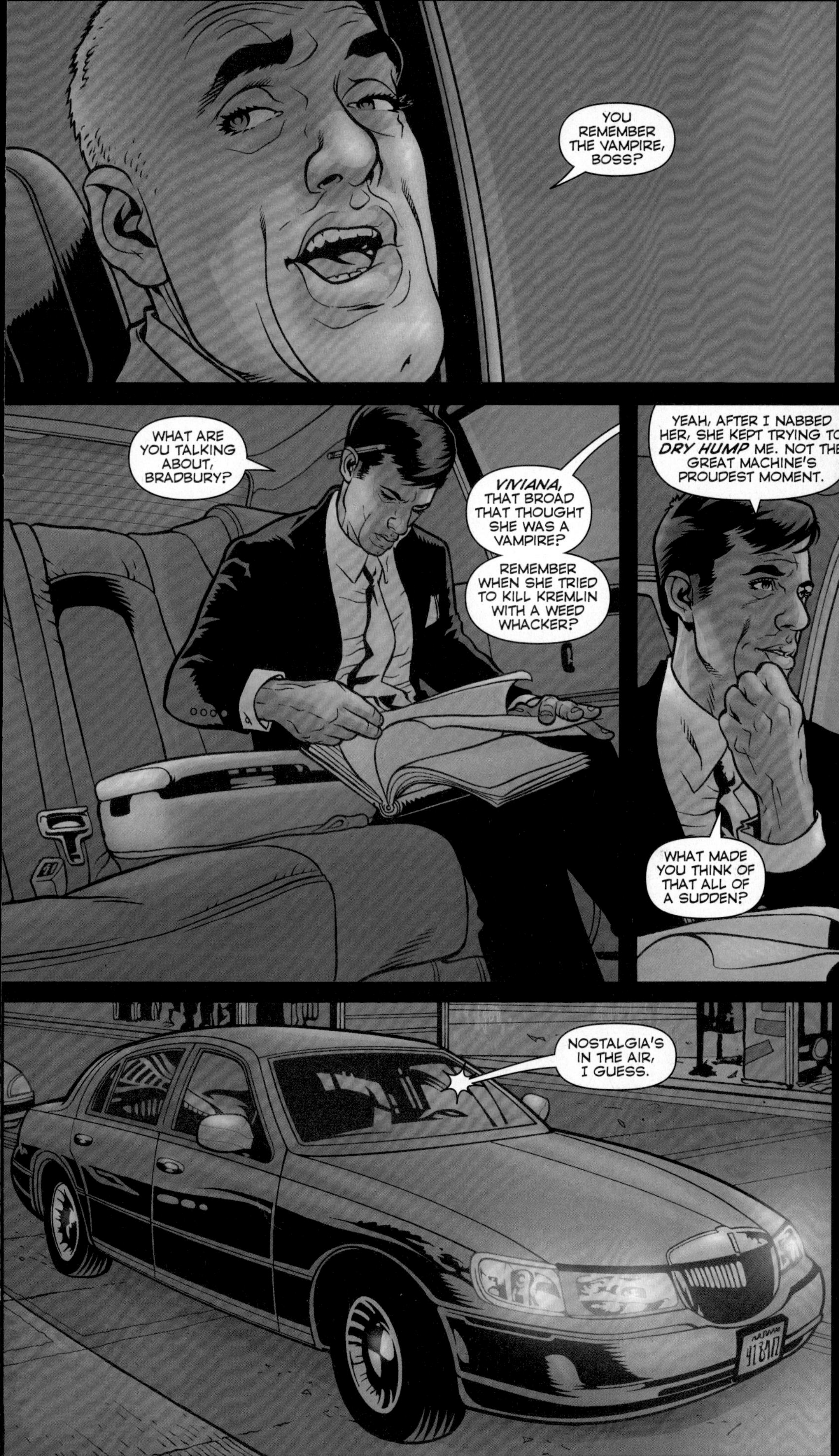
YOU REMEMBER THE VAMPIRE, BOSS?
WHAT ARE YOU TALKING ABOUT, BRADBURY?
VIVIANA, THAT BROAD THAT THOUGHT SHE WAS A VAMPIRE?
REMEMBER WHEN SHE TRIED TO KILL KREMLIN WITH A WEED WHACKER?
YEAH, AFTER I NABBED HER, SHE KEPT TRYING TO DRY HUMP ME. NOT THE GREAT MACHINE'S PROUDEST MOMENT.
WHAT MADE YOU THINK OF THAT ALL OF A SUDDEN?
NOSTALGIA'S IN THE AIR, I GUESS.

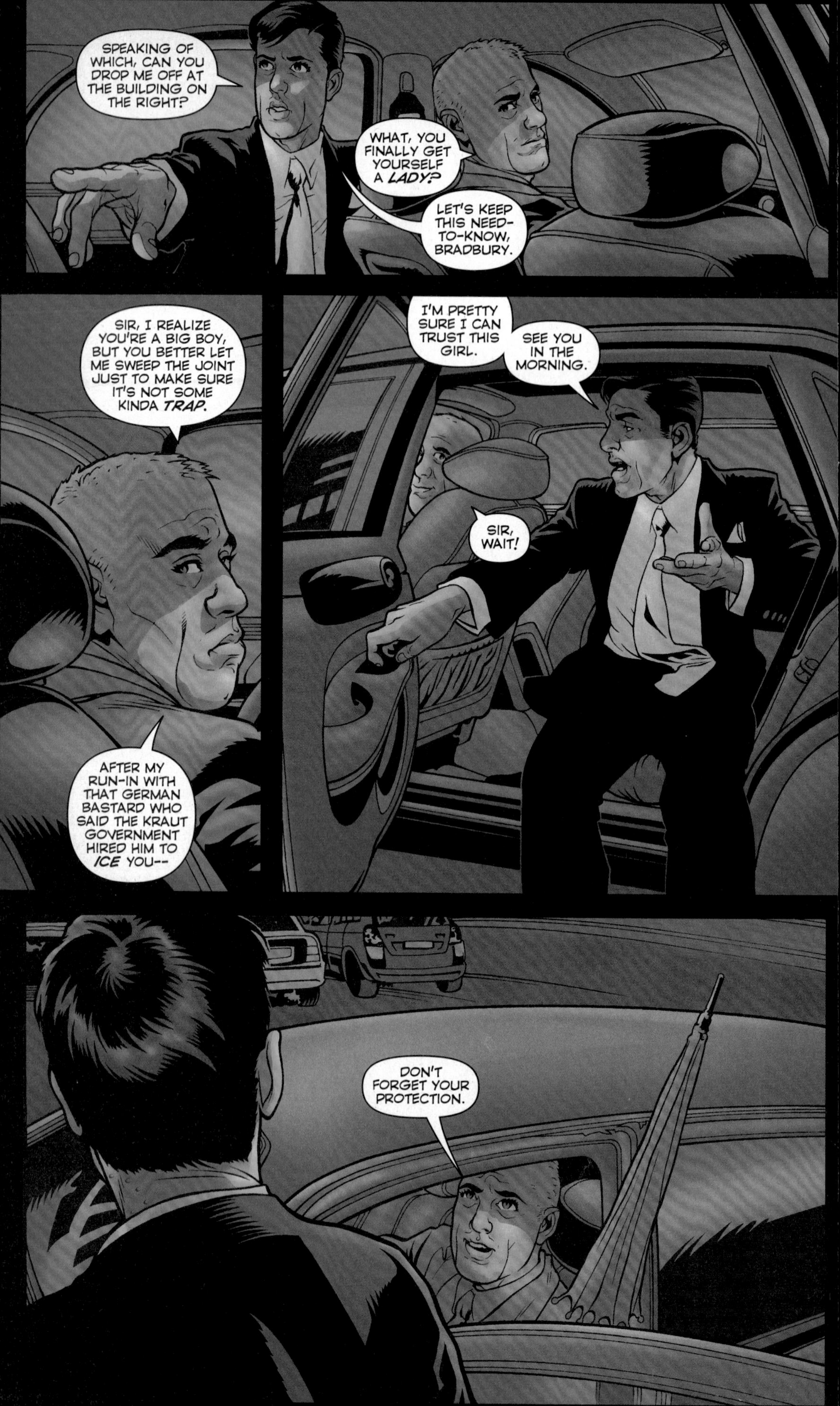
SPEAKING OF WHICH, CAN YOU DROP ME OFF AT THE BUILDING ON THE RIGHT?
WHAT, YOU FINALLY GET YOURSELF A *LADY?*
LET'S KEEP THIS NEED-TO-KNOW, BRADBURY.
SIR, I REALIZE YOU'RE A BIG BOY, BUT YOU BETTER LET ME SWEEP THE JOINT JUST TO MAKE SURE IT'S NOT SOME KINDA *TRAP*.
AFTER MY RUN-IN WITH THAT GERMAN BASTARD WHO SAID THE KRAUT GOVERNMENT HIRED HIM TO *ICE* YOU--
I'M PRETTY SURE I CAN TRUST THIS GIRL.
SEE YOU IN THE MORNING.
SIR, WAIT!
DON'T FORGET YOUR PROTECTION.

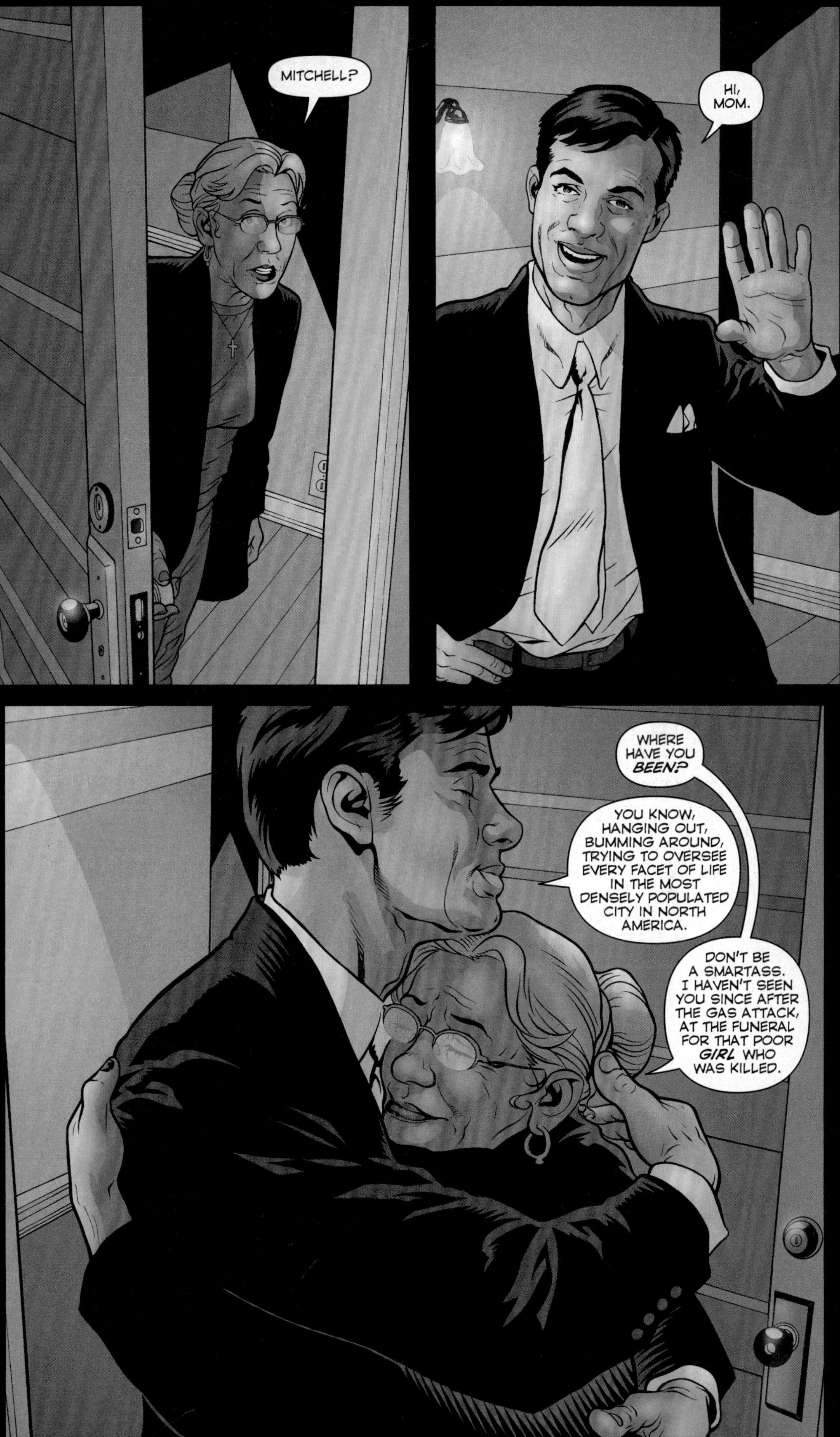
MITCHELL?
HI, MOM.
WHERE HAVE YOU *BEEN?*
YOU KNOW, HANGING OUT, BUMMING AROUND, TRYING TO OVERSEE EVERY FACET OF LIFE IN THE MOST DENSELY POPULATED CITY IN NORTH AMERICA.
DON'T BE A SMARTASS. I HAVEN'T SEEN YOU SINCE AFTER THE GAS ATTACK, AT THE FUNERAL FOR THAT POOR *GIRL* WHO WAS KILLED.

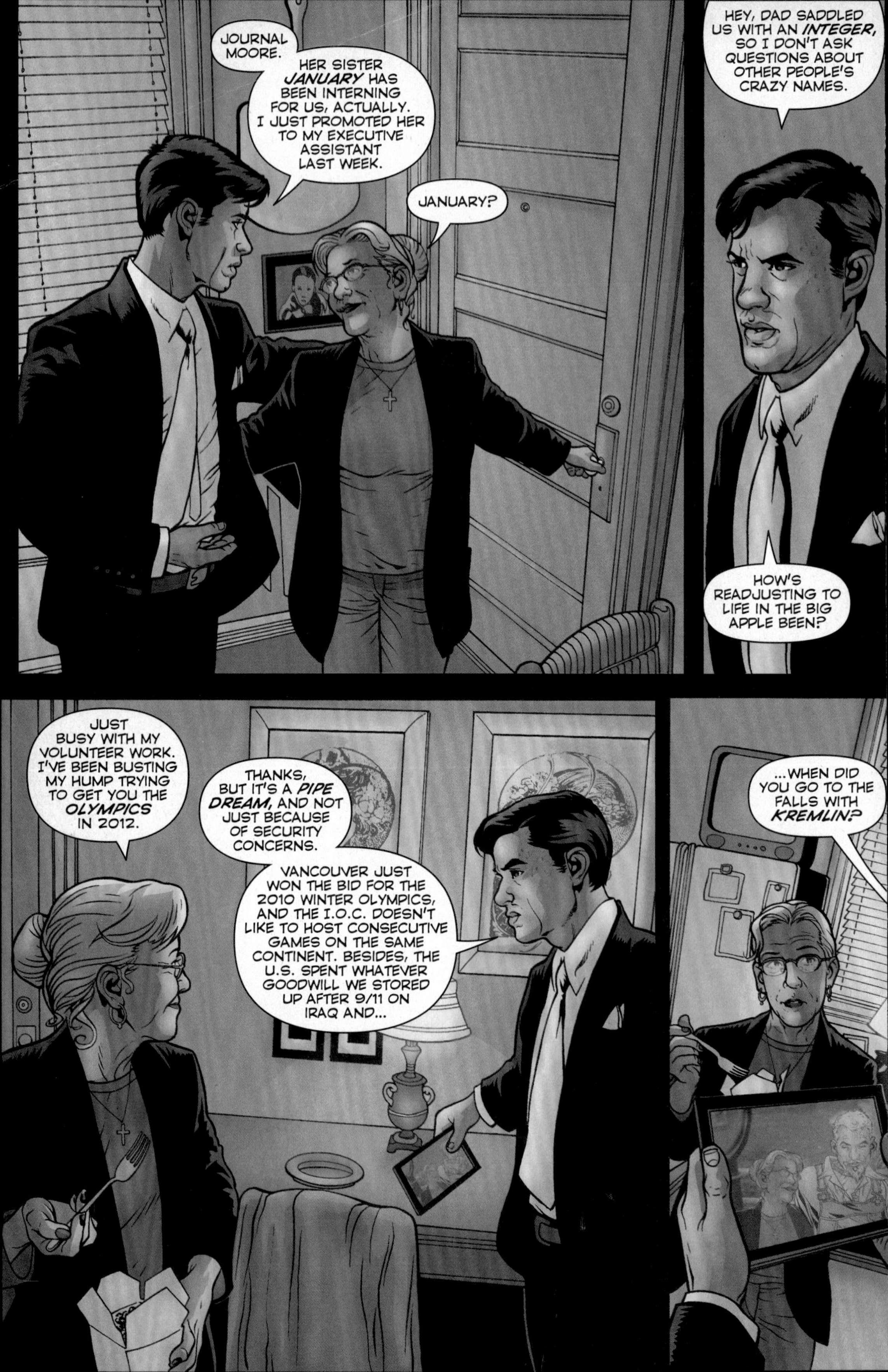
JOURNAL MOORE.
HER SISTER JANUARY HAS BEEN INTERNING FOR US, ACTUALLY. I JUST PROMOTED HER TO MY EXECUTIVE ASSISTANT LAST WEEK.
JANUARY?
HEY, DAD SADDLED US WITH AN INTEGER, SO I DON'T ASK QUESTIONS ABOUT OTHER PEOPLE'S CRAZY NAMES.
HOW'S READJUSTING TO LIFE IN THE BIG APPLE BEEN?
JUST BUSY WITH MY VOLUNTEER WORK. I'VE BEEN BUSTING MY HUMP TRYING TO GET YOU THE OLYMPICS IN 2012.
THANKS, BUT IT'S A PIPE DREAM, AND NOT JUST BECAUSE OF SECURITY CONCERNS.
VANCOUVER JUST WON THE BID FOR THE 2010 WINTER OLYMPICS, AND THE I.O.C. DOESN'T LIKE TO HOST CONSECUTIVE GAMES ON THE SAME CONTINENT. BESIDES, THE U.S. SPENT WHATEVER GOODWILL WE STORED UP AFTER 9/11 ON IRAQ AND...
...WHEN DID YOU GO TO THE FALLS WITH KREMLIN?

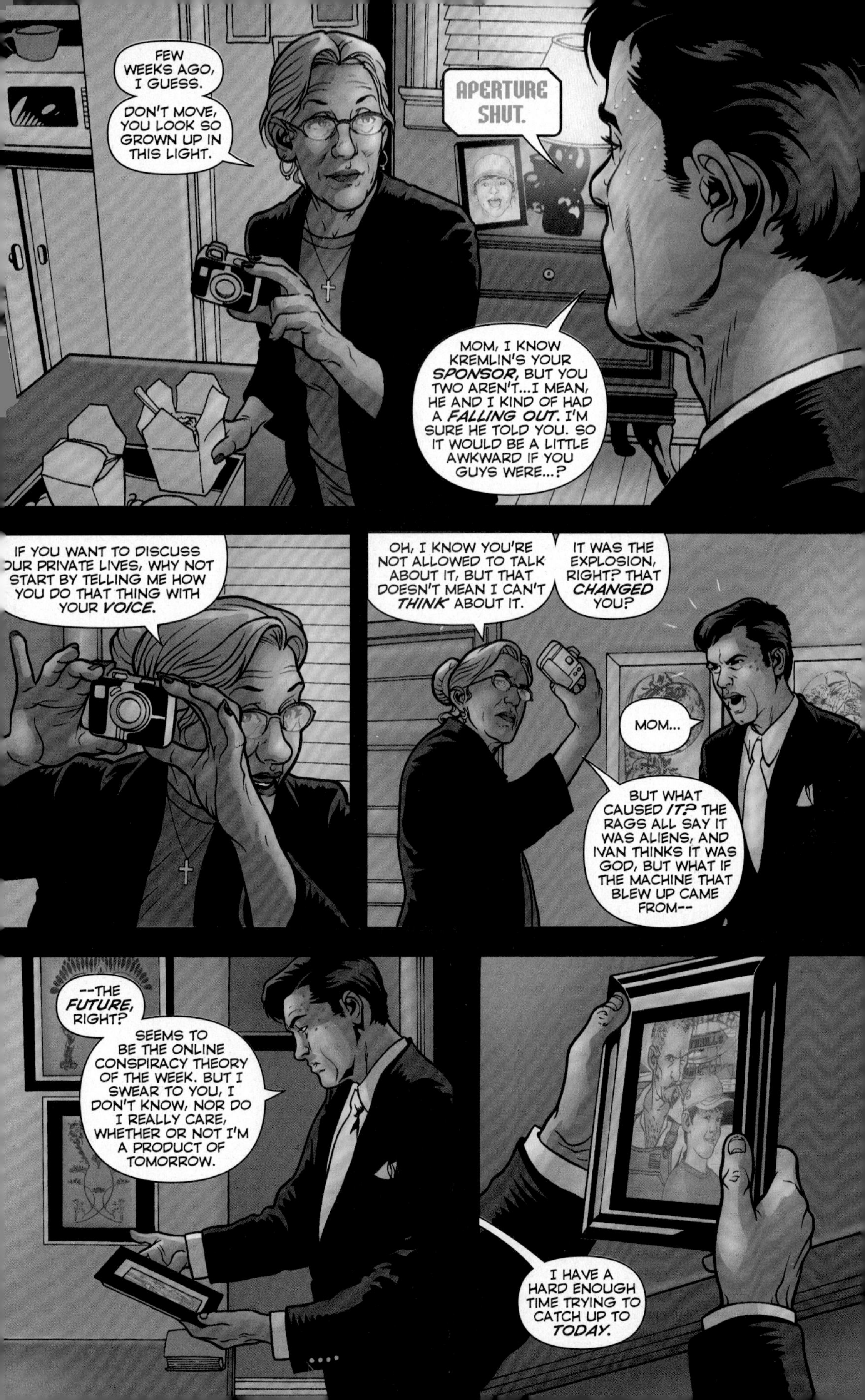
FEW WEEKS AGO, I GUESS.
DON'T MOVE, YOU LOOK SO GROWN UP IN THIS LIGHT.
APERTURE SHUT.
MOM, I KNOW KREMLIN'S YOUR *SPONSOR,* BUT YOU TWO AREN'T...I MEAN, HE AND I KIND OF HAD A *FALLING OUT*. I'M SURE HE TOLD YOU. SO IT WOULD BE A LITTLE AWKWARD IF YOU GUYS WERE...?
IF YOU WANT TO DISCUSS OUR PRIVATE LIVES, WHY NOT START BY TELLING ME HOW YOU DO THAT THING WITH YOUR *VOICE*.
OH, I KNOW YOU'RE NOT ALLOWED TO TALK ABOUT IT, BUT THAT DOESN'T MEAN I CAN'T *THINK* ABOUT IT.
IT WAS THE EXPLOSION, RIGHT? THAT *CHANGED* YOU?
MOM...
BUT WHAT CAUSED *IT?* THE RAGS ALL SAY IT WAS ALIENS, AND IVAN THINKS IT WAS GOD, BUT WHAT IF THE MACHINE THAT BLEW UP CAME FROM--
--THE *FUTURE,* RIGHT?
SEEMS TO BE THE ONLINE CONSPIRACY THEORY OF THE WEEK. BUT I SWEAR TO YOU, I DON'T KNOW, NOR DO I REALLY CARE, WHETHER OR NOT I'M A PRODUCT OF TOMORROW.
I HAVE A HARD ENOUGH TIME TRYING TO CATCH UP TO *TODAY*.

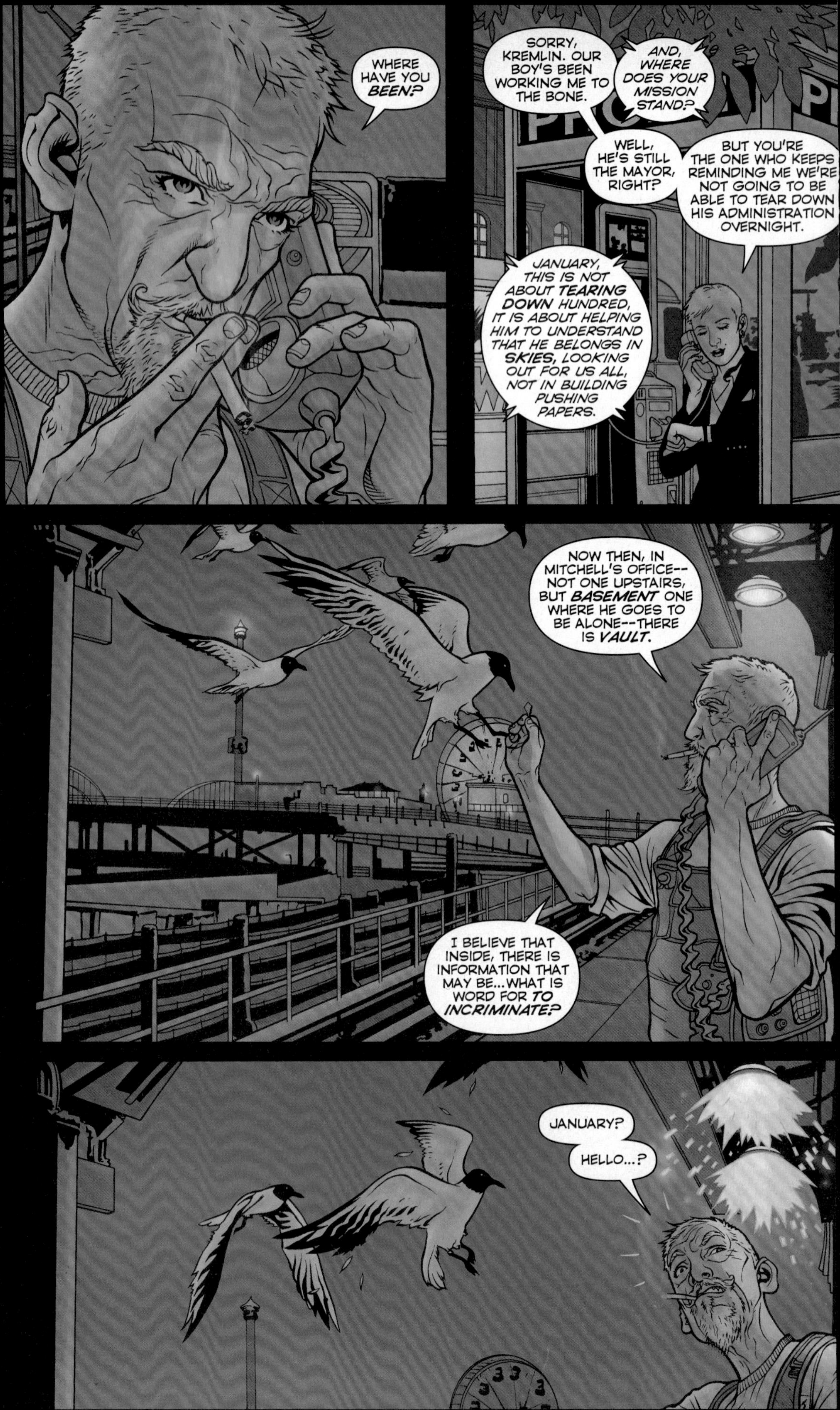
WHERE HAVE YOU *BEEN?*
SORRY, KREMLIN. OUR BOY'S BEEN WORKING ME TO THE BONE.
AND, WHERE DOES YOUR MISSION STAND?
WELL, HE'S STILL THE MAYOR, RIGHT?
BUT YOU'RE THE ONE WHO KEEPS REMINDING ME WE'RE NOT GOING TO BE ABLE TO TEAR DOWN HIS ADMINISTRATION OVERNIGHT.
*JANUARY, THIS IS NOT ABOUT **TEARING DOWN** HUNDRED, IT IS ABOUT HELPING HIM TO UNDERSTAND THAT HE BELONGS IN **SKIES,** LOOKING OUT FOR US ALL, NOT IN BUILDING PUSHING PAPERS.*
NOW THEN, IN MITCHELL'S OFFICE--NOT ONE UPSTAIRS, BUT ***BASEMENT*** ONE WHERE HE GOES TO BE ALONE--THERE IS ***VAULT.***
I BELIEVE THAT INSIDE, THERE IS INFORMATION THAT MAY BE...WHAT IS WORD FOR ***TO INCRIMINATE?***
JANUARY?
HELLO...?

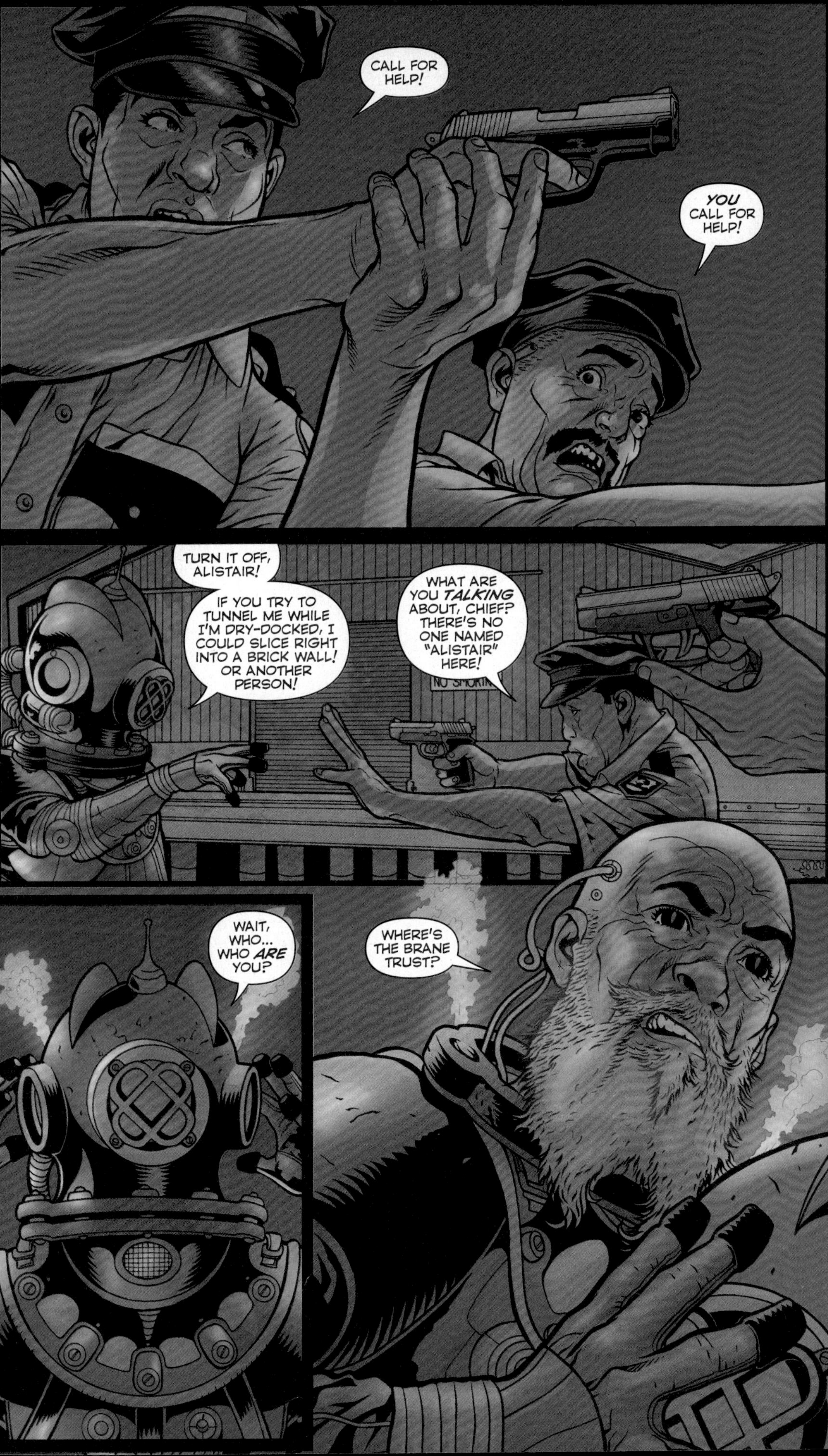
CALL FOR HELP!
YOU CALL FOR HELP!
TURN IT OFF, ALISTAIR!
IF YOU TRY TO TUNNEL ME WHILE I'M DRY-DOCKED, I COULD SLICE RIGHT INTO A BRICK WALL! OR ANOTHER PERSON!
WHAT ARE YOU TALKING ABOUT, CHIEF? THERE'S NO ONE NAMED "ALISTAIR" HERE!
WAIT, WHO... WHO ARE YOU?
WHERE'S THE BRANE TRUST?

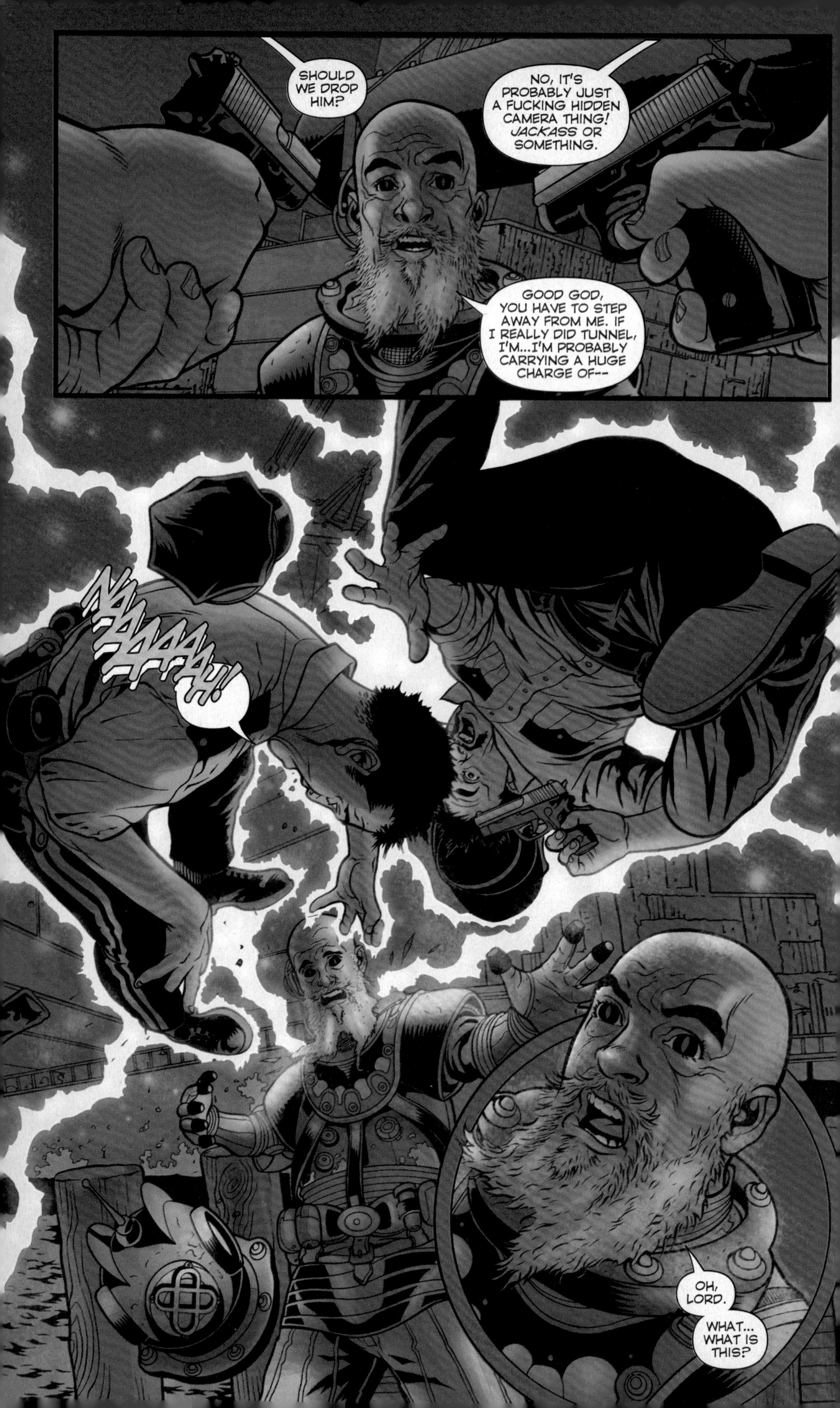
SHOULD WE DROP HIM?
NO, IT'S PROBABLY JUST A FUCKING HIDDEN CAMERA THING! JACKASS OR SOMETHING.
GOOD GOD, YOU HAVE TO STEP AWAY FROM ME. IF I REALLY DID TUNNEL, I'M...I'M PROBABLY CARRYING A HUGE CHARGE OF--
NAAAAAAH!
OH, LORD.
WHAT... WHAT IS THIS?

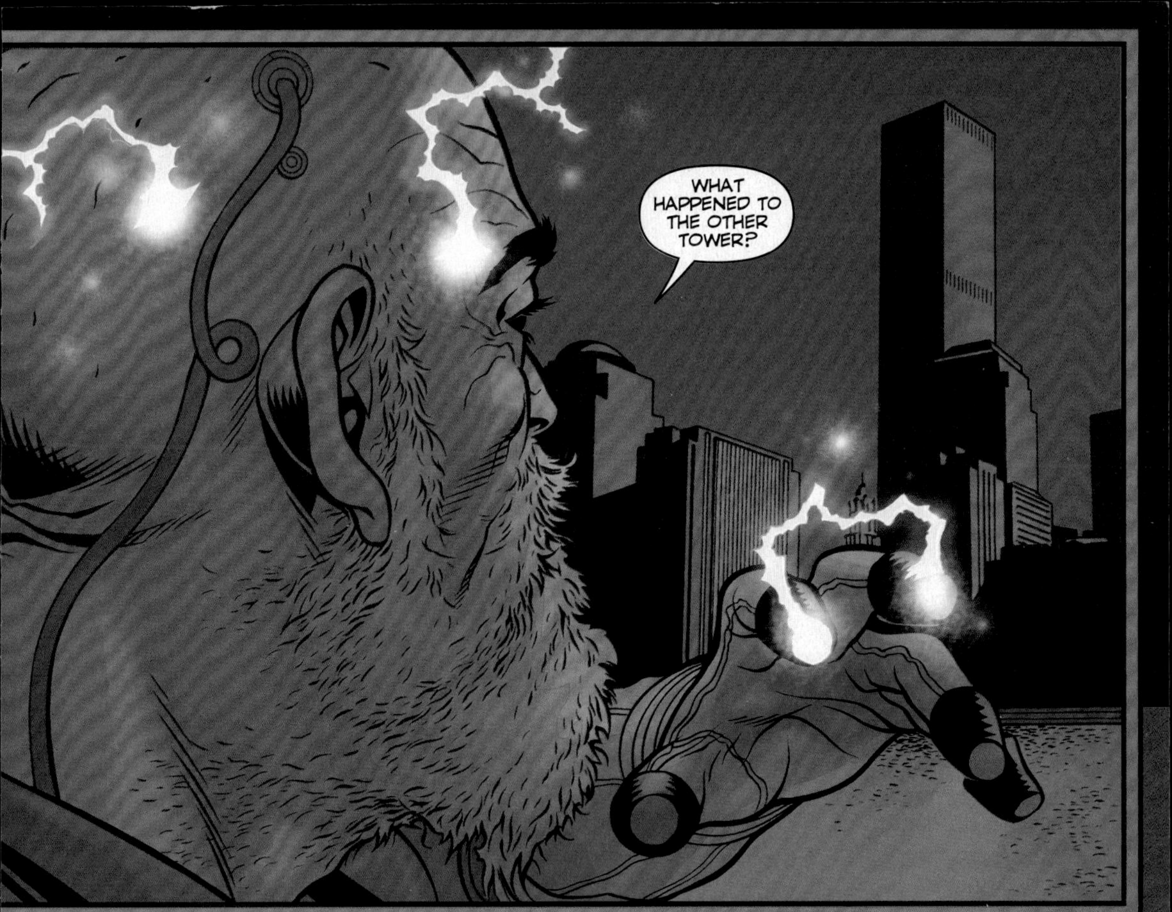
WHAT HAPPENED TO THE OTHER TOWER?
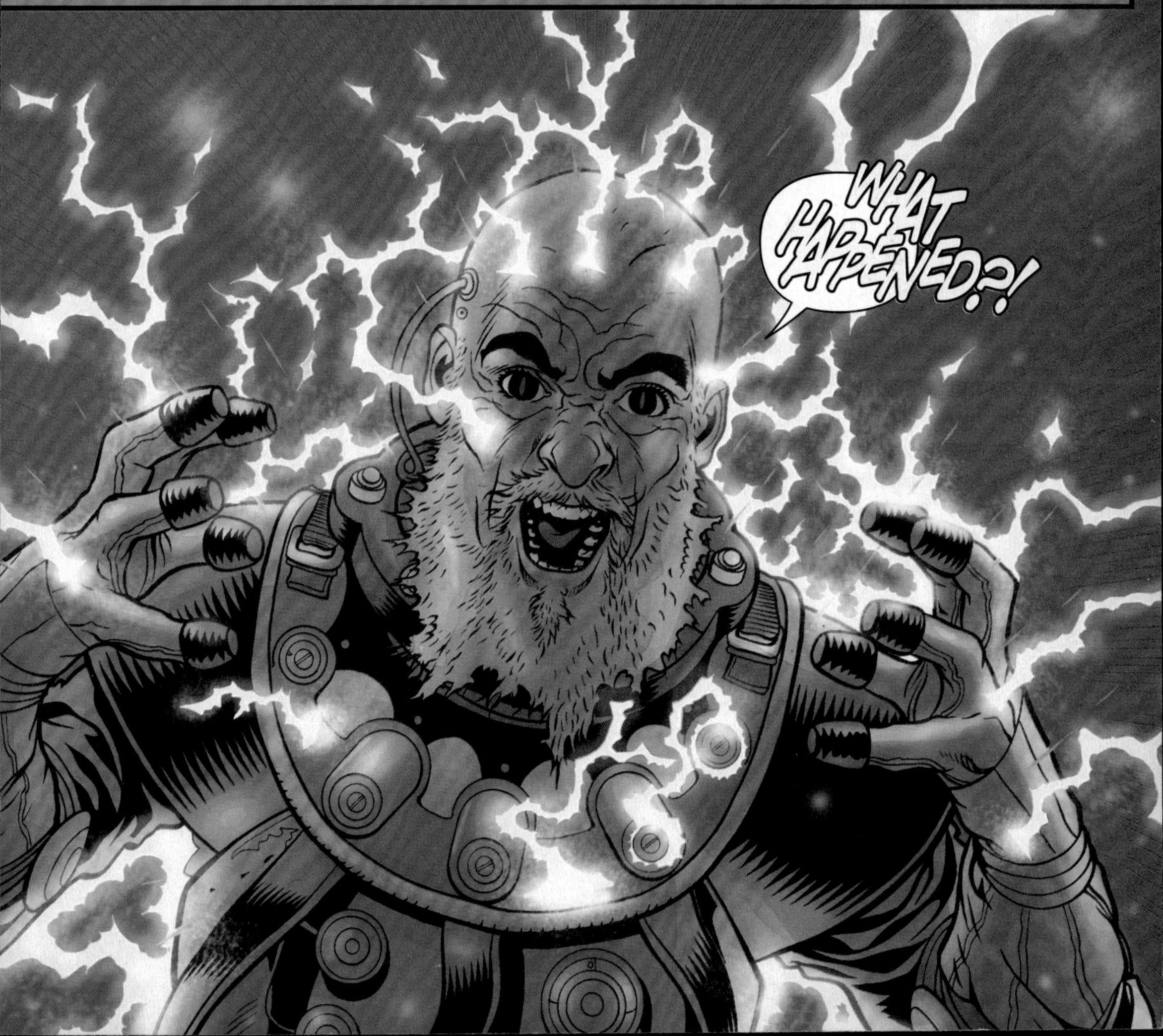
WHAT HAPPENED?!

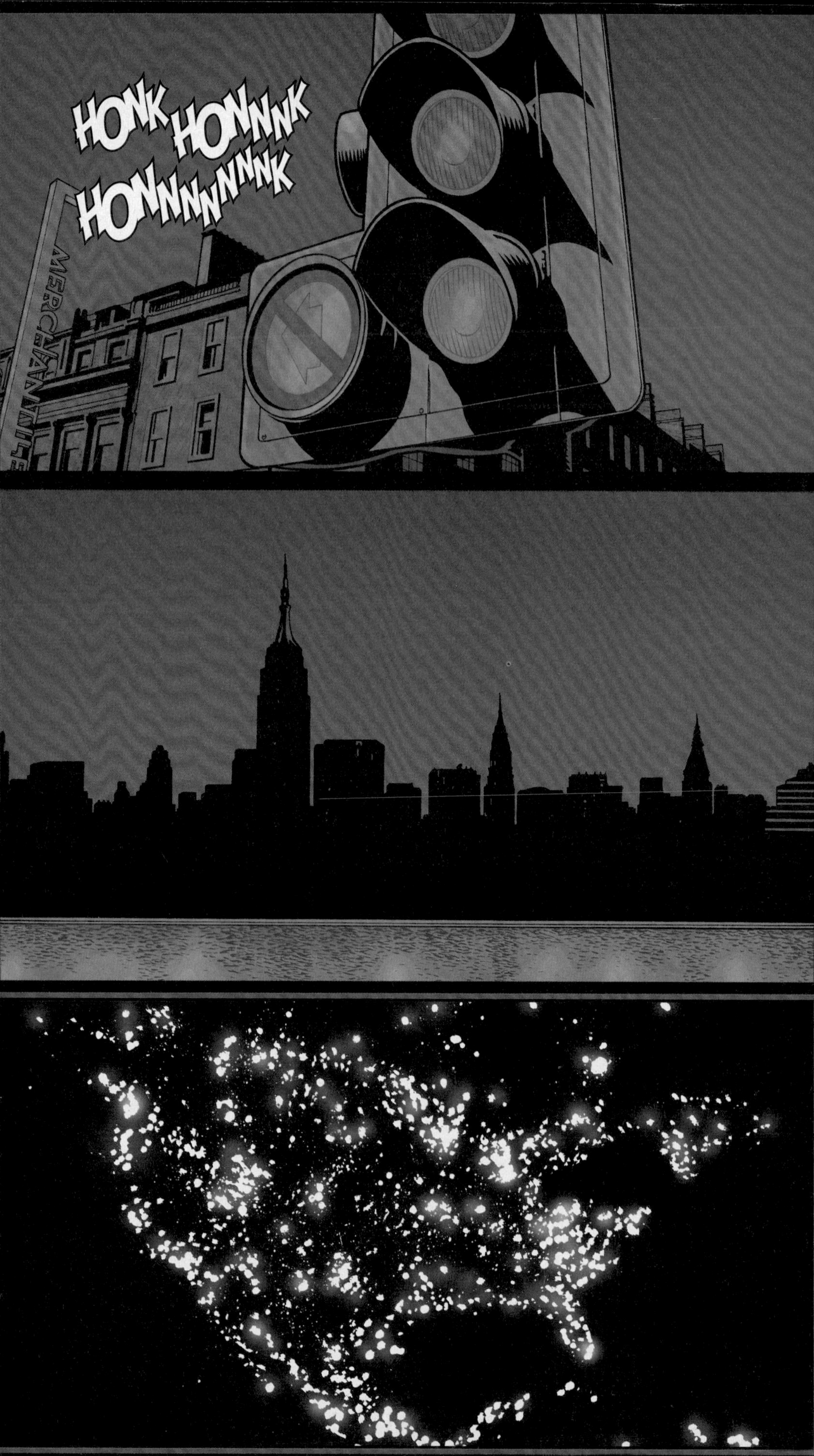
HONK HONNNK
HONNNNNNNK

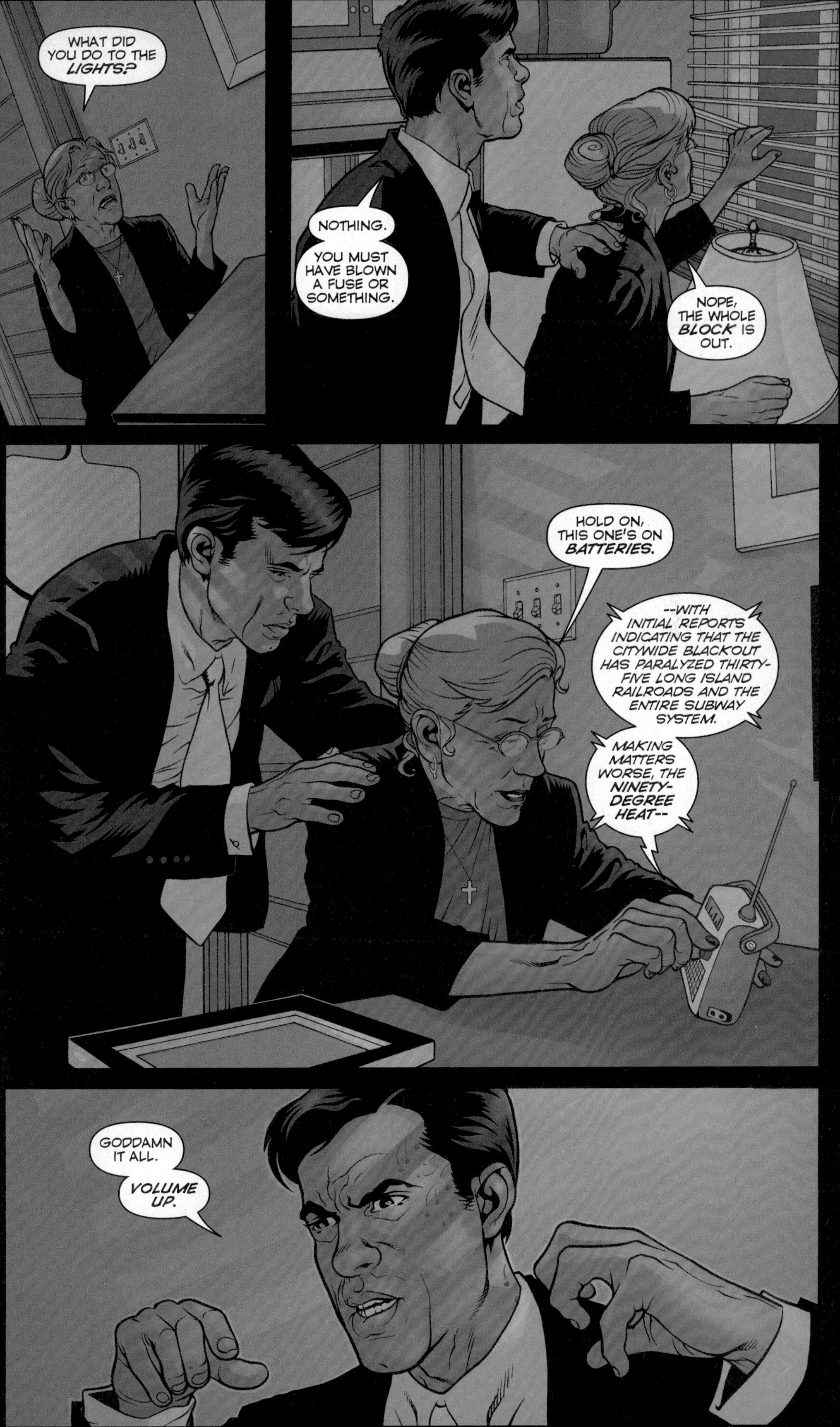

WHAT DID YOU DO TO THE *LIGHTS?*
NOTHING.
YOU MUST HAVE BLOWN A FUSE OR SOMETHING.
NOPE, THE WHOLE *BLOCK* IS OUT.
HOLD ON, THIS ONE'S ON *BATTERIES.*
--WITH INITIAL REPORTS INDICATING THAT THE CITYWIDE BLACKOUT HAS PARALYZED THIRTY-FIVE LONG ISLAND RAILROADS AND THE ENTIRE SUBWAY SYSTEM.
MAKING MATTERS WORSE, THE *NINETY-DEGREE HEAT--*
GODDAMN IT ALL.
VOLUME UP.

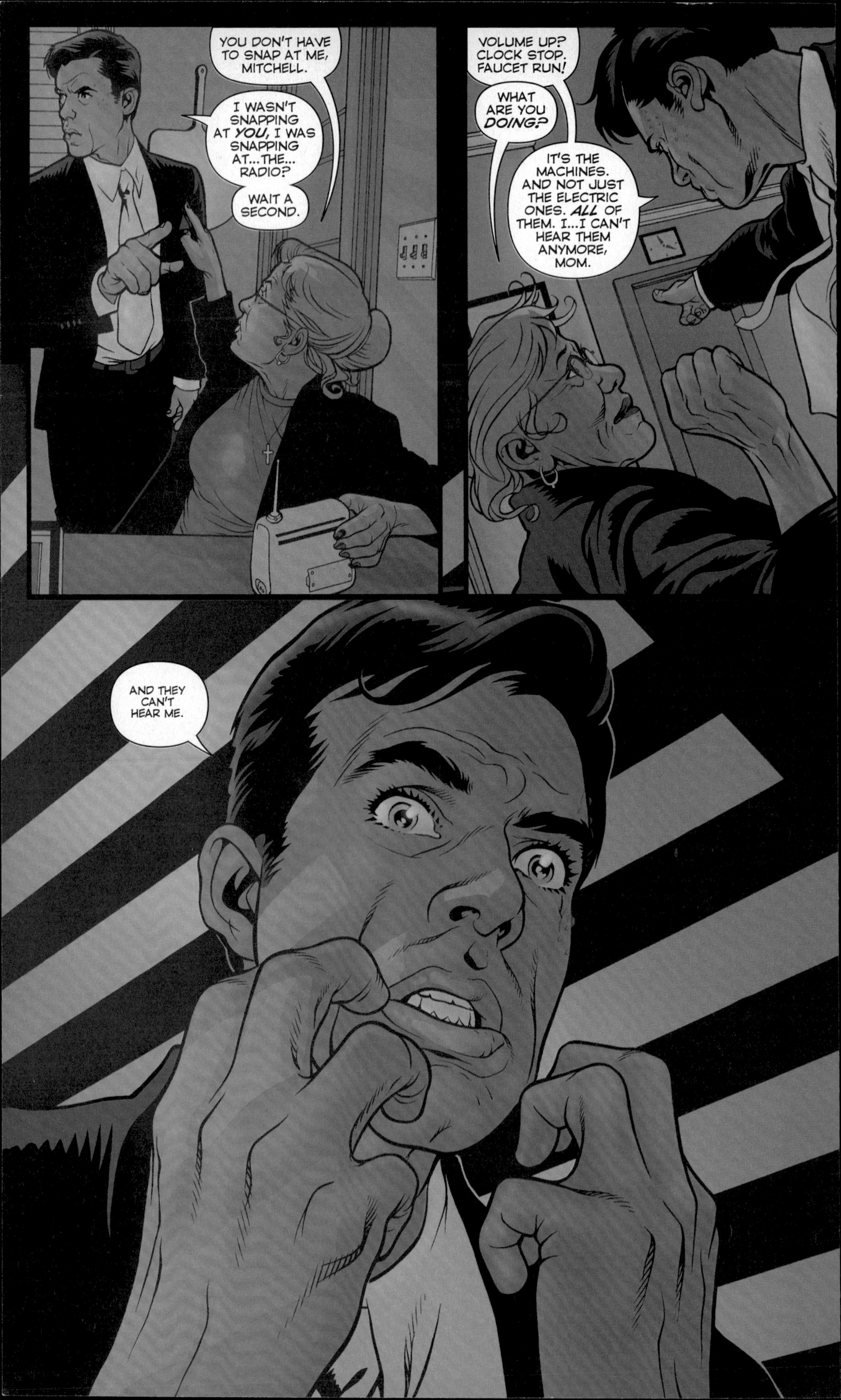
YOU DON'T HAVE TO SNAP AT ME, MITCHELL.
I WASN'T SNAPPING AT *YOU*, I WAS SNAPPING AT...THE... RADIO?
WAIT A SECOND.
VOLUME UP? CLOCK STOP. FAUCET RUN!
WHAT ARE YOU *DOING?*
IT'S THE MACHINES. AND NOT JUST THE ELECTRIC ONES. *ALL* OF THEM. I...I CAN'T HEAR THEM ANYMORE, MOM.
AND THEY CAN'T HEAR ME.

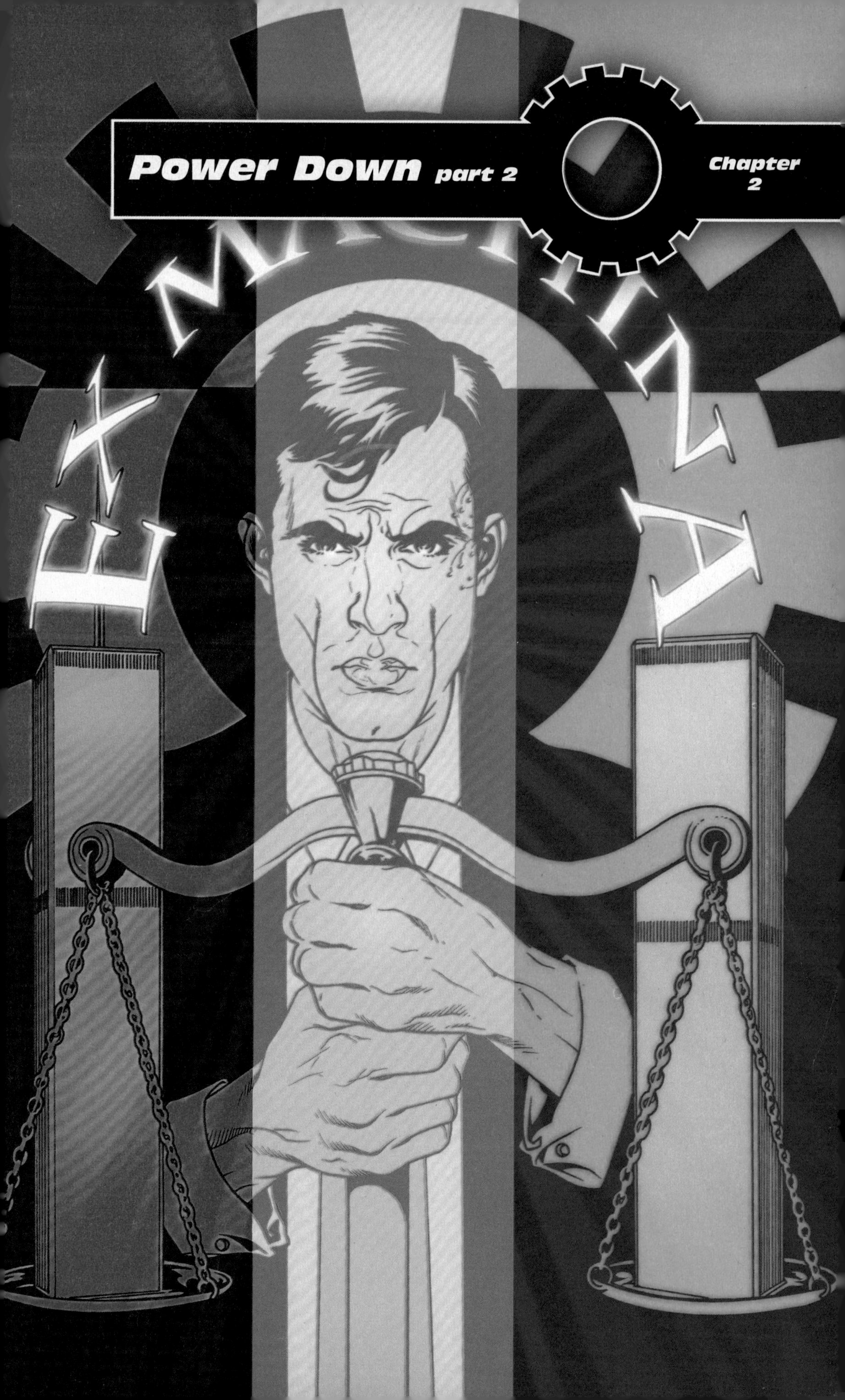
Power Down part 2
Chapter
2

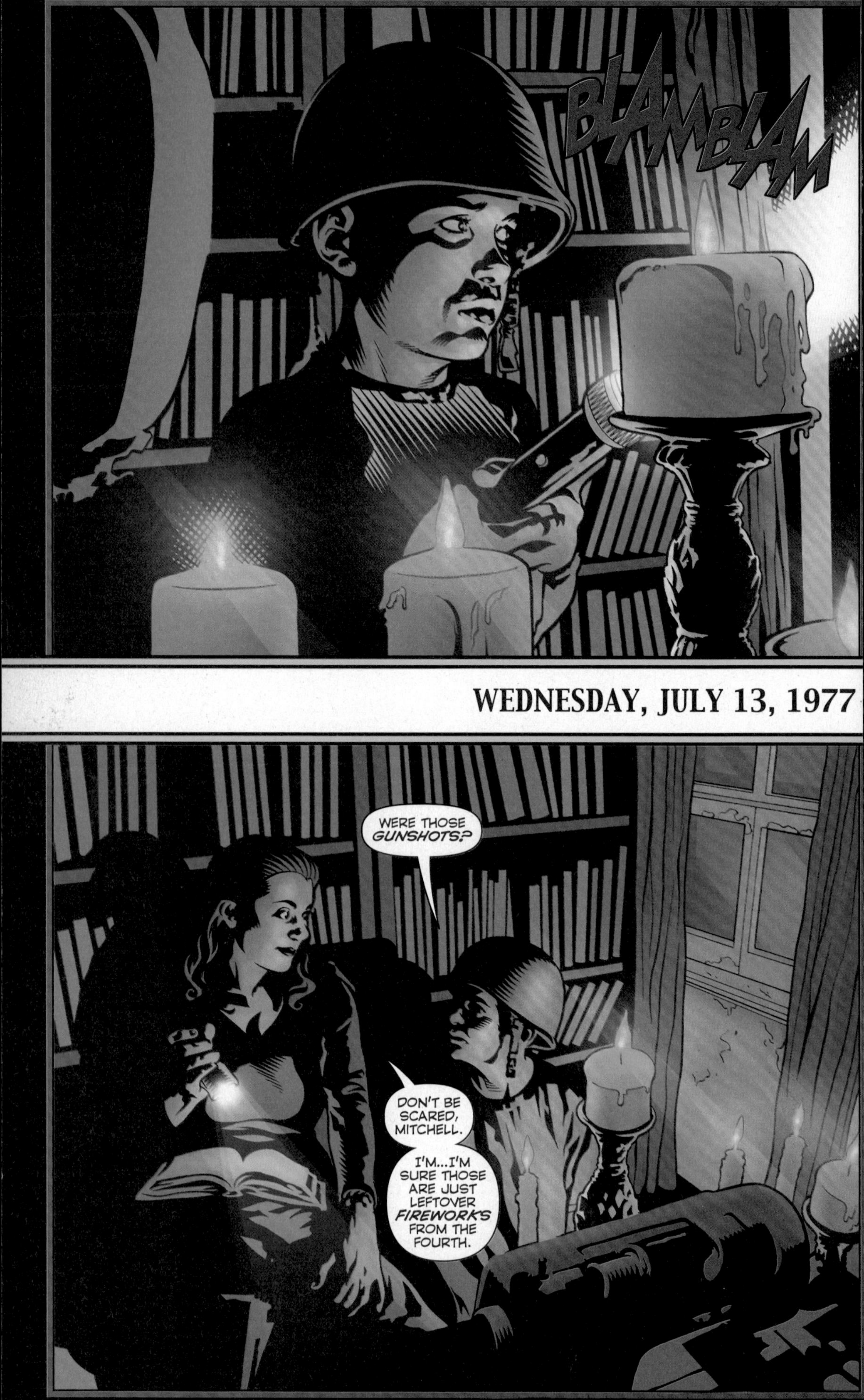
BLAMBLAM
WEDNESDAY, JULY 13, 1977
WERE THOSE GUNSHOTS?
DON'T BE SCARED, MITCHELL.
I'M...I'M SURE THOSE ARE JUST LEFTOVER FIREWORKS FROM THE FOURTH.

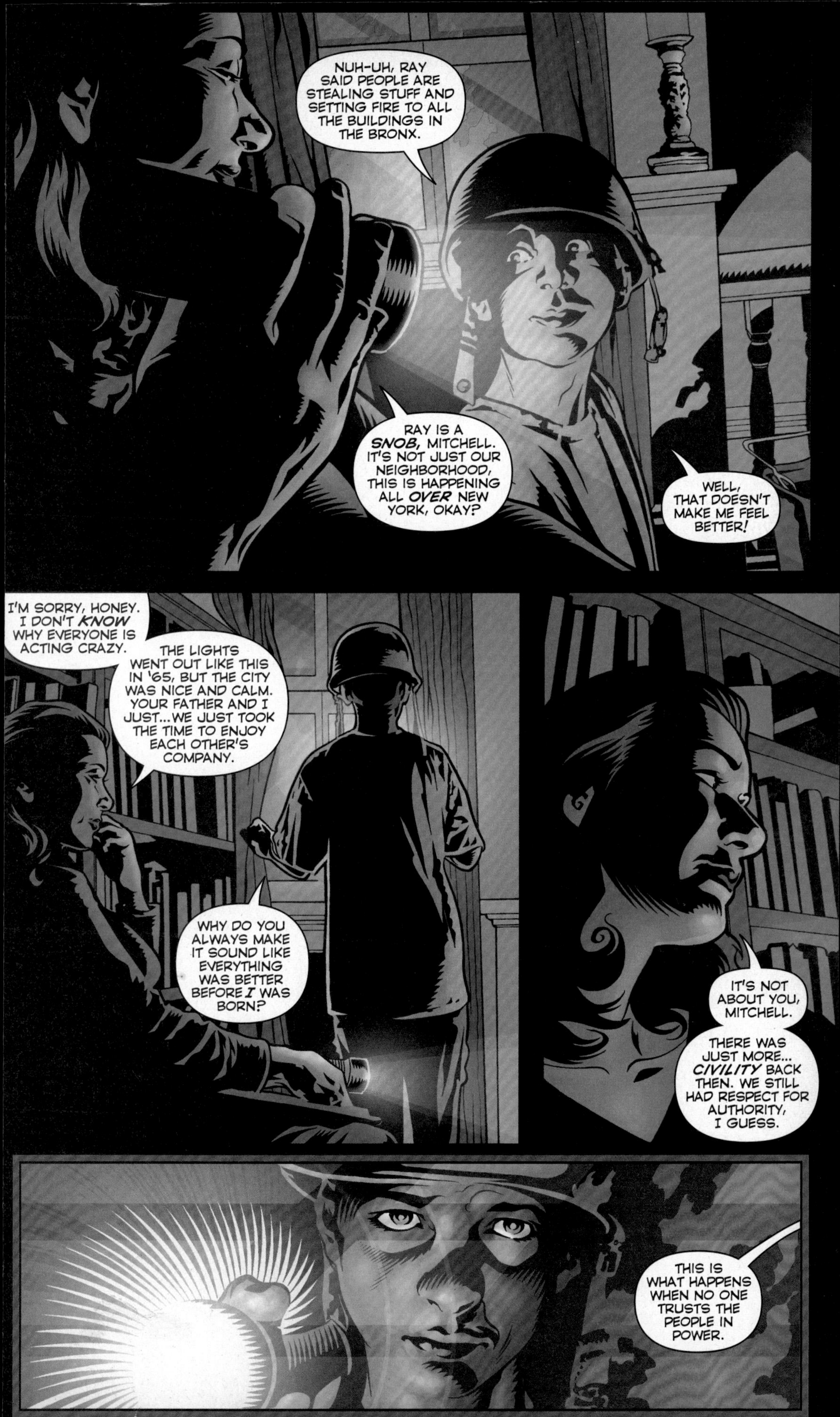
NUH-UH, RAY SAID PEOPLE ARE STEALING STUFF AND SETTING FIRE TO ALL THE BUILDINGS IN THE BRONX.
RAY IS A *SNOB,* MITCHELL. IT'S NOT JUST OUR NEIGHBORHOOD, THIS IS HAPPENING ALL *OVER* NEW YORK, OKAY?
WELL, THAT DOESN'T MAKE ME FEEL BETTER!
I'M SORRY, HONEY. I DON'T *KNOW* WHY EVERYONE IS ACTING CRAZY.
THE LIGHTS WENT OUT LIKE THIS IN '65, BUT THE CITY WAS NICE AND CALM. YOUR FATHER AND I JUST...WE JUST TOOK THE TIME TO ENJOY EACH OTHER'S COMPANY.
WHY DO YOU ALWAYS MAKE IT SOUND LIKE EVERYTHING WAS BETTER BEFORE *I* WAS BORN?
IT'S NOT ABOUT YOU, MITCHELL.
THERE WAS JUST MORE... *CIVILITY* BACK THEN. WE STILL HAD RESPECT FOR AUTHORITY, I GUESS.
THIS IS WHAT HAPPENS WHEN NO ONE TRUSTS THE PEOPLE IN POWER.

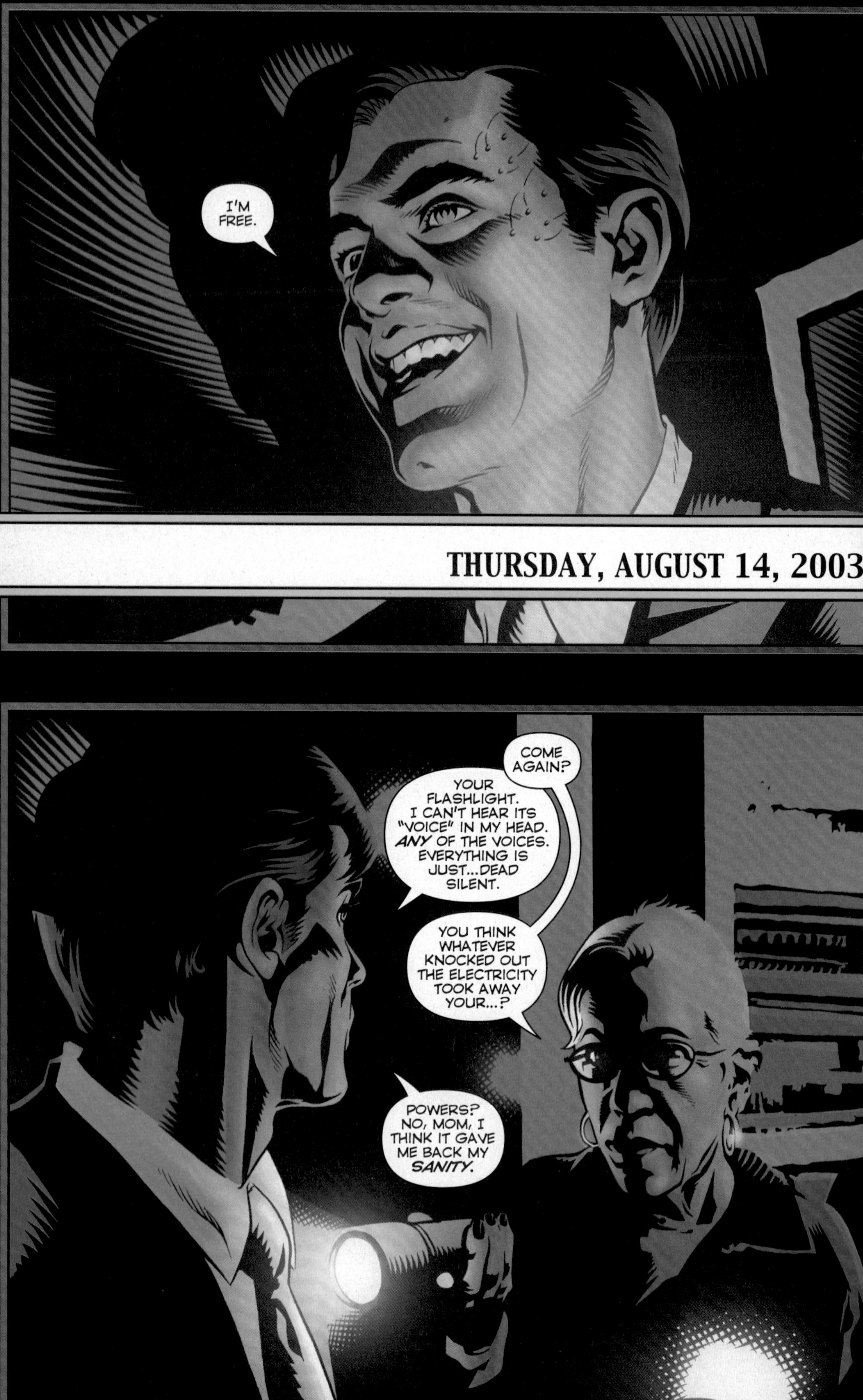
I'M FREE.
THURSDAY, AUGUST 14, 2003
COME AGAIN?
YOUR FLASHLIGHT. I CAN'T HEAR ITS "VOICE" IN MY HEAD. *ANY* OF THE VOICES. EVERYTHING IS JUST...DEAD SILENT.
YOU THINK WHATEVER KNOCKED OUT THE ELECTRICITY TOOK AWAY YOUR...?
POWERS? NO, MOM, I THINK IT GAVE ME BACK MY *SANITY*.

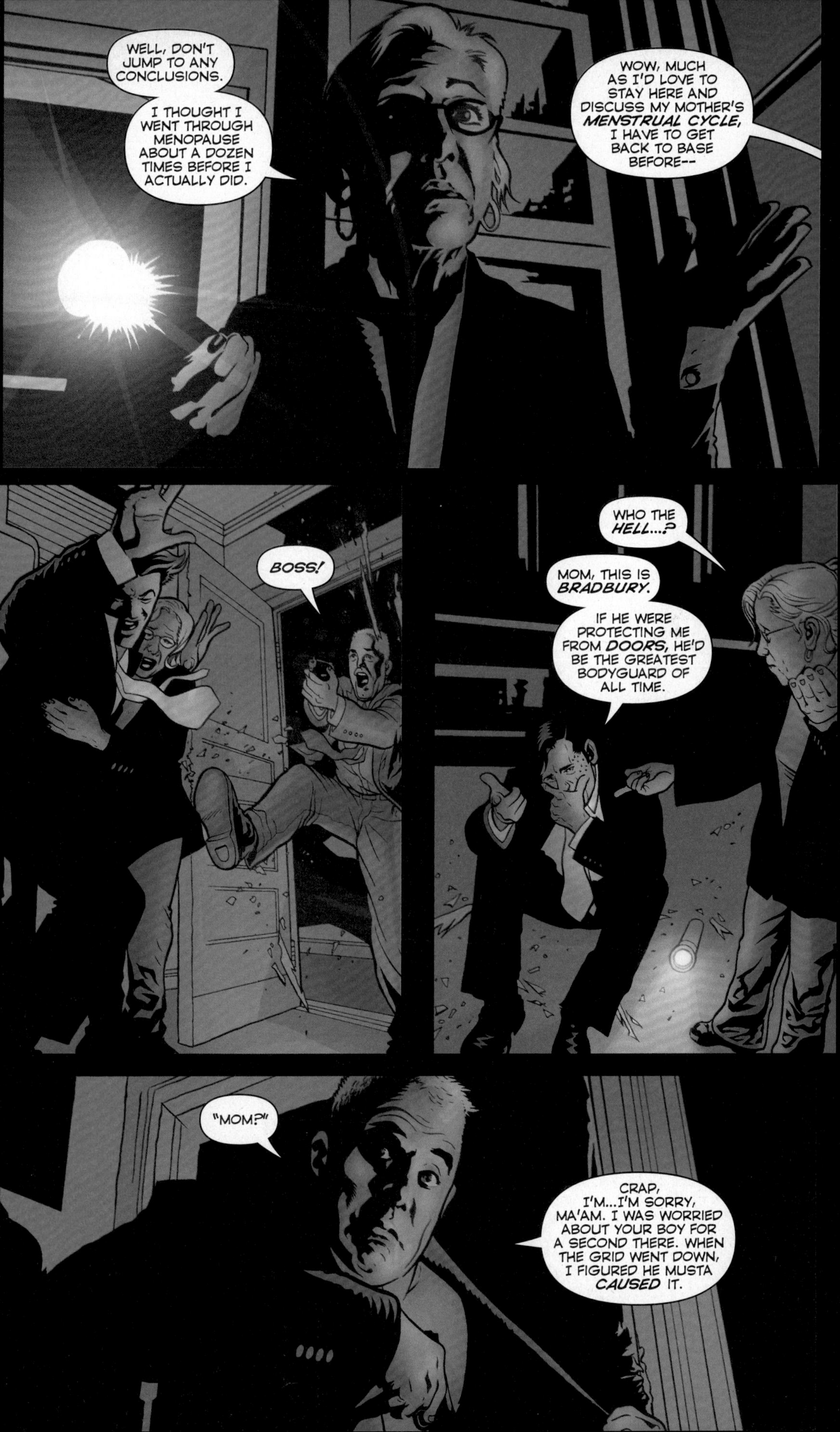

WELL, DON'T JUMP TO ANY CONCLUSIONS.
I THOUGHT I WENT THROUGH MENOPAUSE ABOUT A DOZEN TIMES BEFORE I ACTUALLY DID.
WOW, MUCH AS I'D LOVE TO STAY HERE AND DISCUSS MY MOTHER'S MENSTRUAL CYCLE, I HAVE TO GET BACK TO BASE BEFORE--
BOSS!
WHO THE HELL...?
MOM, THIS IS BRADBURY.
IF HE WERE PROTECTING ME FROM DOORS, HE'D BE THE GREATEST BODYGUARD OF ALL TIME.
"MOM?"
CRAP, I'M...I'M SORRY, MA'AM. I WAS WORRIED ABOUT YOUR BOY FOR A SECOND THERE. WHEN THE GRID WENT DOWN, I FIGURED HE MUSTA CAUSED IT.

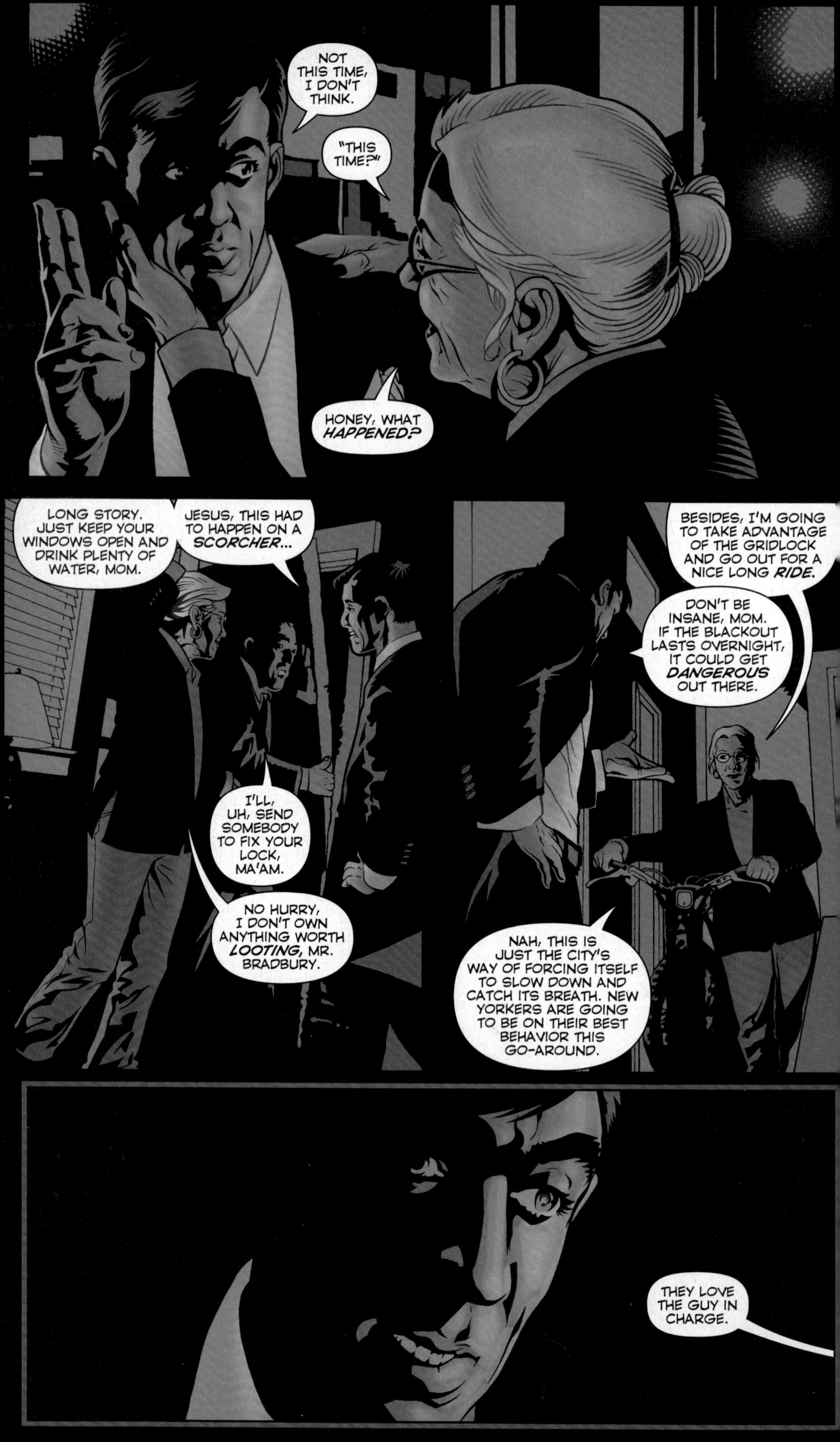
NOT THIS TIME, I DON'T THINK.
"THIS TIME?"
HONEY, WHAT HAPPENED?
LONG STORY. JUST KEEP YOUR WINDOWS OPEN AND DRINK PLENTY OF WATER, MOM.
JESUS, THIS HAD TO HAPPEN ON A SCORCHER...
I'LL, UH, SEND SOMEBODY TO FIX YOUR LOCK, MA'AM.
NO HURRY, I DON'T OWN ANYTHING WORTH LOOTING, MR. BRADBURY.
BESIDES, I'M GOING TO TAKE ADVANTAGE OF THE GRIDLOCK AND GO OUT FOR A NICE LONG RIDE.
DON'T BE INSANE, MOM. IF THE BLACKOUT LASTS OVERNIGHT, IT COULD GET DANGEROUS OUT THERE.
NAH, THIS IS JUST THE CITY'S WAY OF FORCING ITSELF TO SLOW DOWN AND CATCH ITS BREATH. NEW YORKERS ARE GOING TO BE ON THEIR BEST BEHAVIOR THIS GO-AROUND.
THEY LOVE THE GUY IN CHARGE.

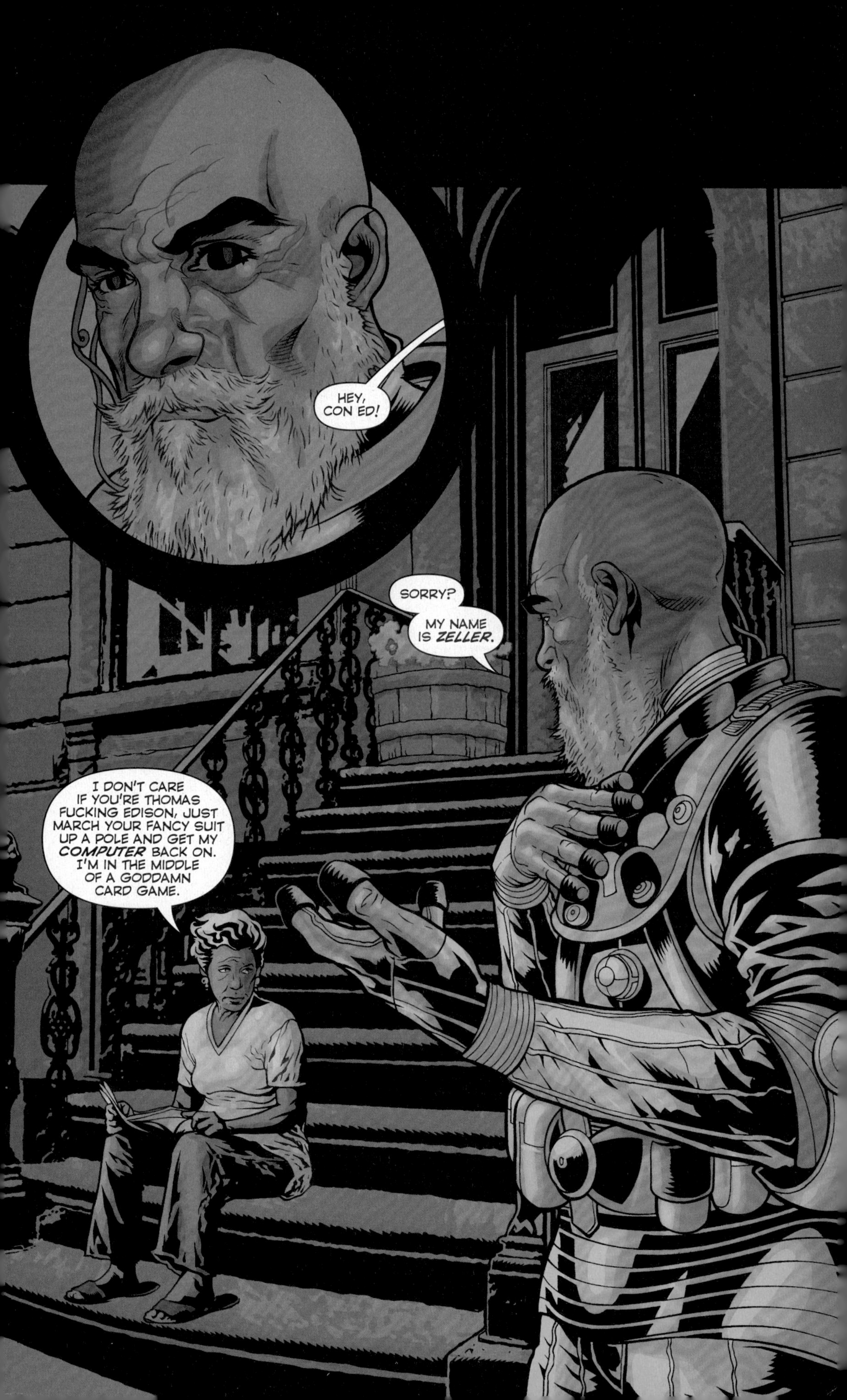

HEY, CON ED!
SORRY?
MY NAME IS ZELLER.
I DON'T CARE IF YOU'RE THOMAS FUCKING EDISON, JUST MARCH YOUR FANCY SUIT UP A POLE AND GET MY COMPUTER BACK ON. I'M IN THE MIDDLE OF A GODDAMN CARD GAME.

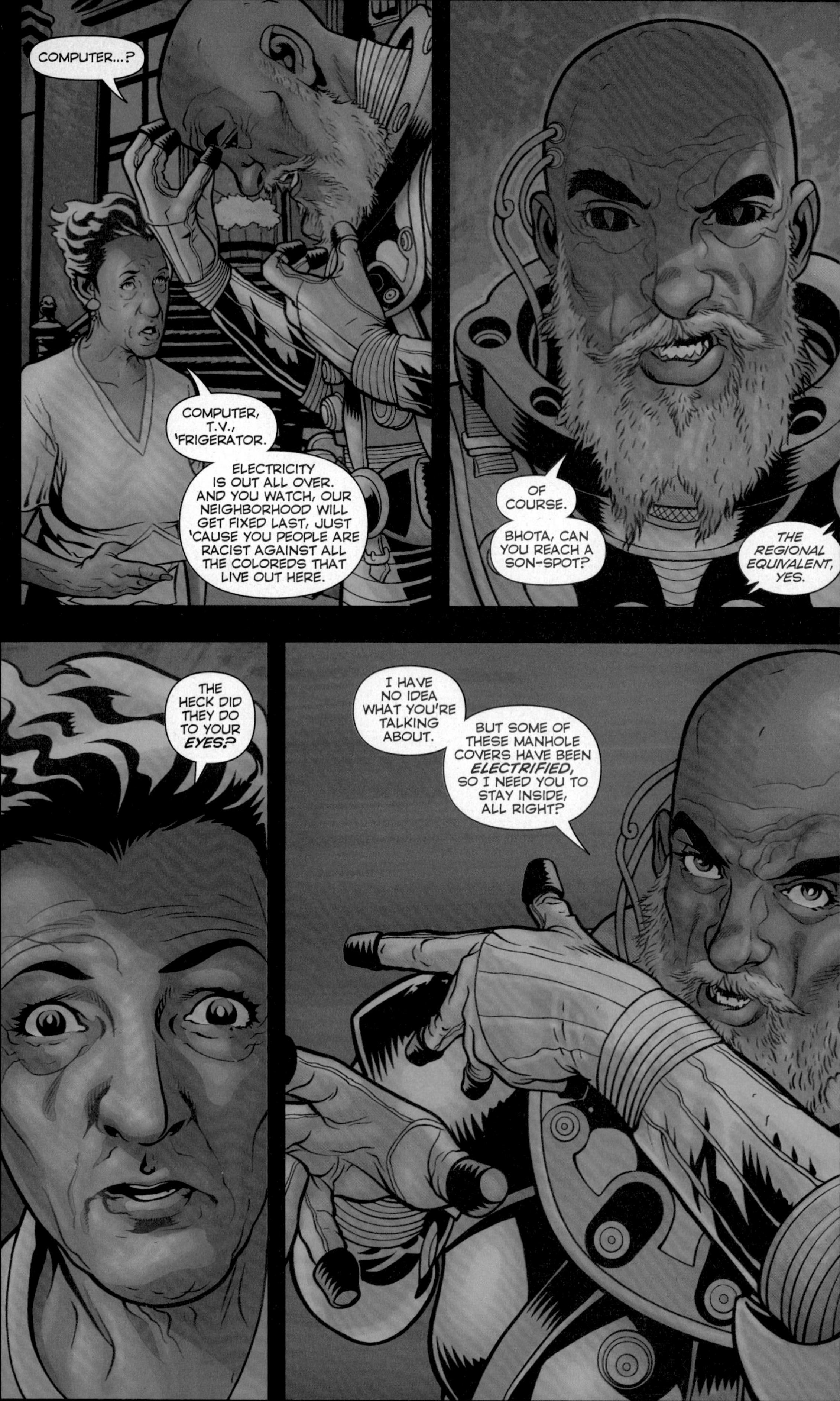
COMPUTER...?
COMPUTER, T.V., 'FRIGERATOR.
ELECTRICITY IS OUT ALL OVER. AND YOU WATCH, OUR NEIGHBORHOOD WILL GET FIXED LAST, JUST 'CAUSE YOU PEOPLE ARE RACIST AGAINST ALL THE COLOREDS THAT LIVE OUT HERE.
OF COURSE.
BHOTA, CAN YOU REACH A SON-SPOT?
THE REGIONAL EQUIVALENT, YES.
THE HECK DID THEY DO TO YOUR EYES?
I HAVE NO IDEA WHAT YOU'RE TALKING ABOUT.
BUT SOME OF THESE MANHOLE COVERS HAVE BEEN ELECTRIFIED, SO I NEED YOU TO STAY INSIDE, ALL RIGHT?

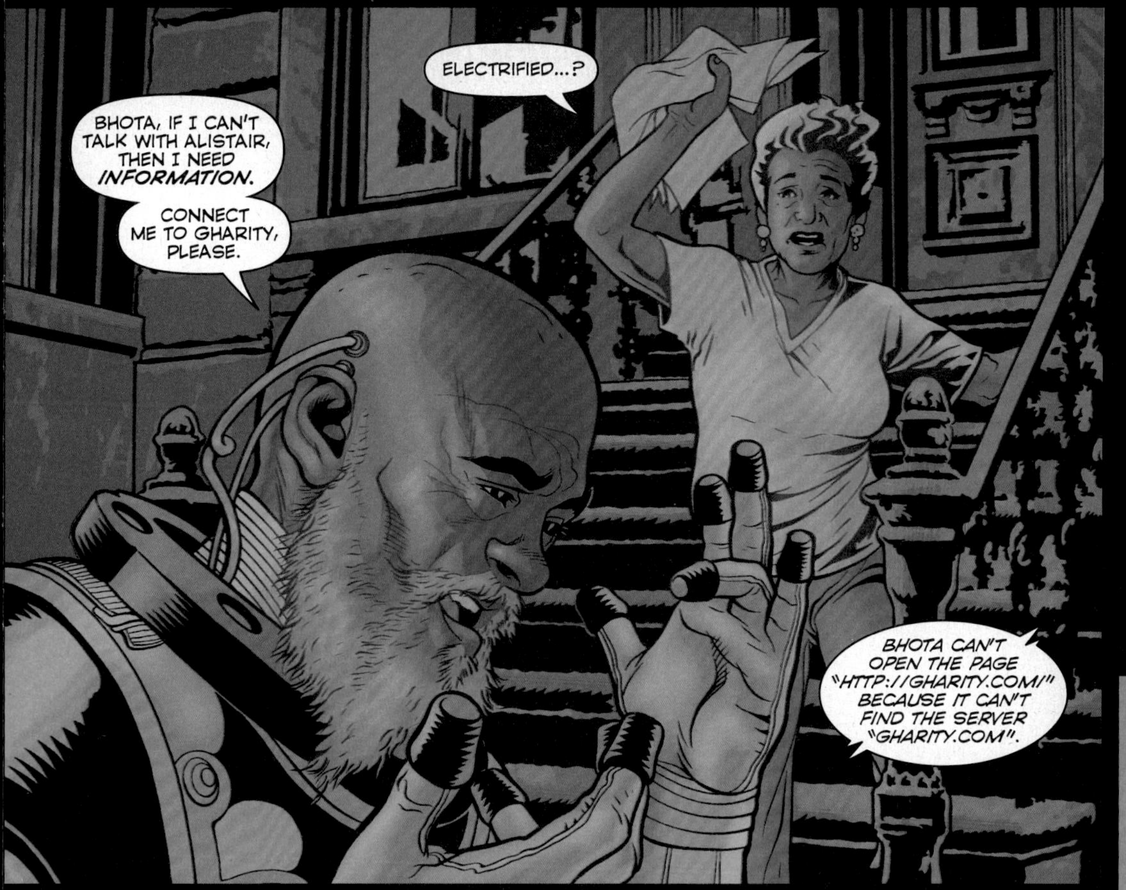
BHOTA, IF I CAN'T TALK WITH ALISTAIR, THEN I NEED ***INFORMATION.***
CONNECT ME TO GHARITY, PLEASE.
ELECTRIFIED...?
BHOTA CAN'T OPEN THE PAGE "HTTP://GHARITY.COM/" BECAUSE IT CAN'T FIND THE SERVER "GHARITY.COM".

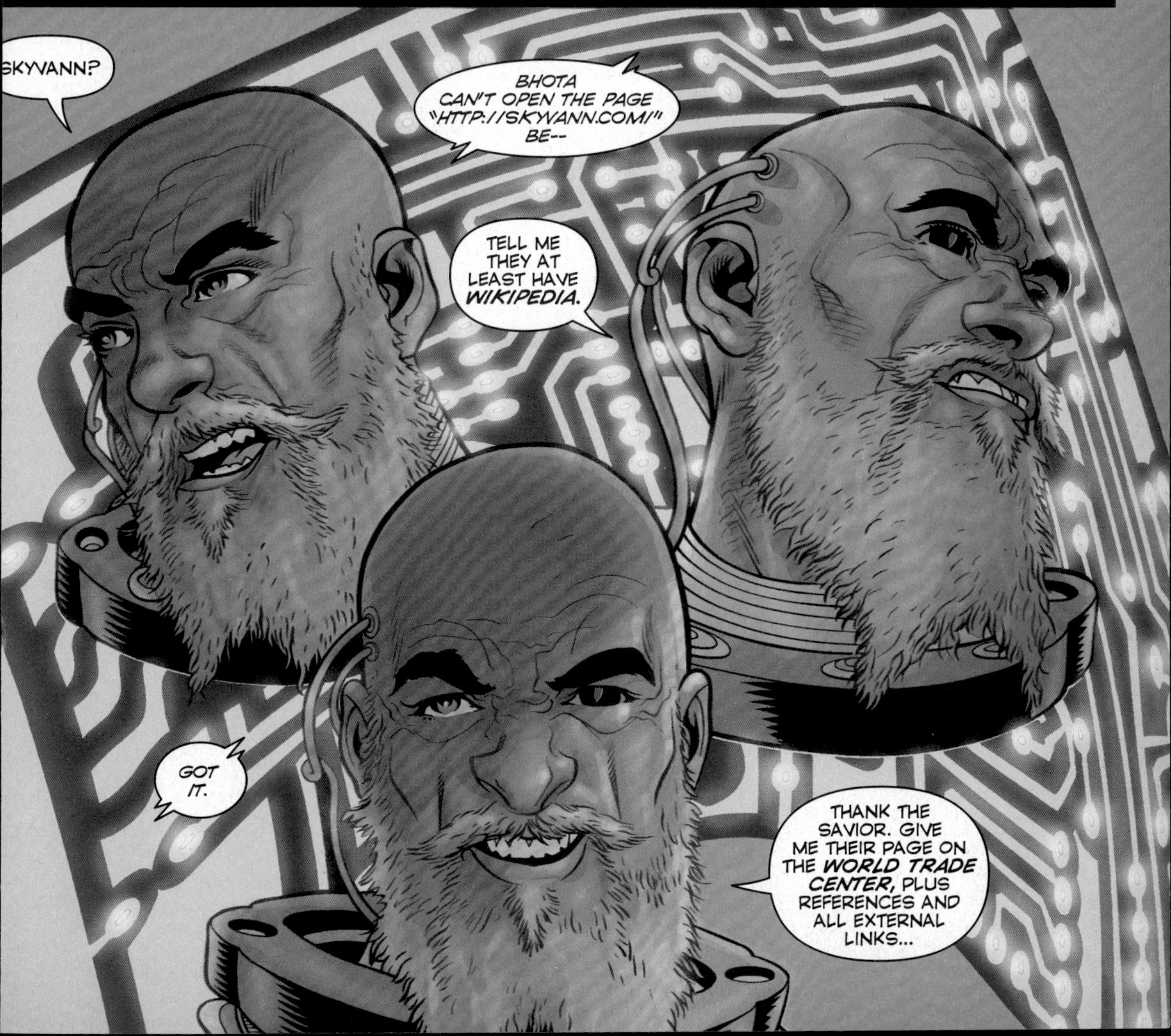
SKYVANN?
BHOTA CAN'T OPEN THE PAGE "HTTP://SKYVANN.COM/" BE--
TELL ME THEY AT LEAST HAVE ***WIKIPEDIA.***
GOT IT.
THANK THE SAVIOR. GIVE ME THEIR PAGE ON THE ***WORLD TRADE CENTER,*** PLUS REFERENCES AND ALL EXTERNAL LINKS...

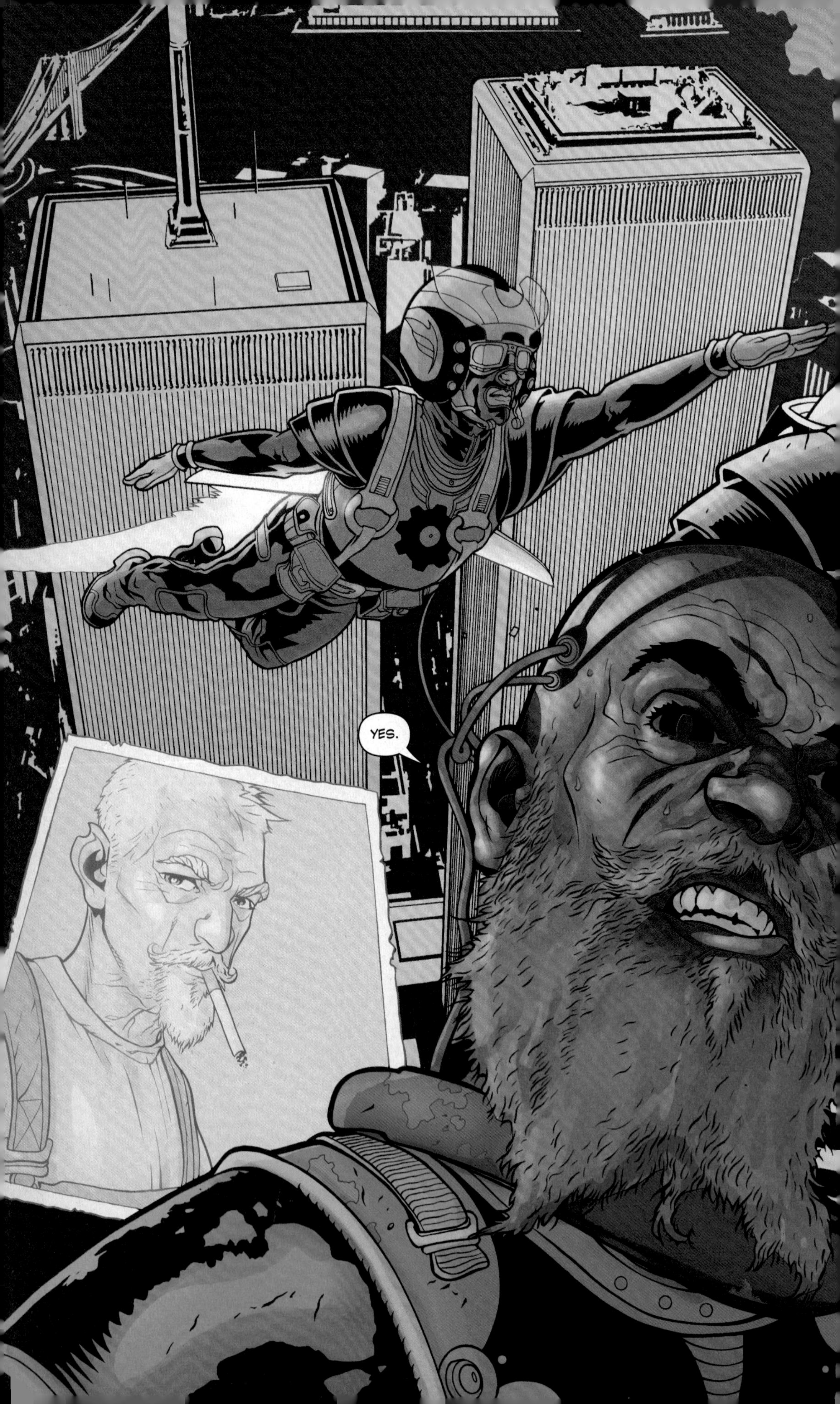
YES.

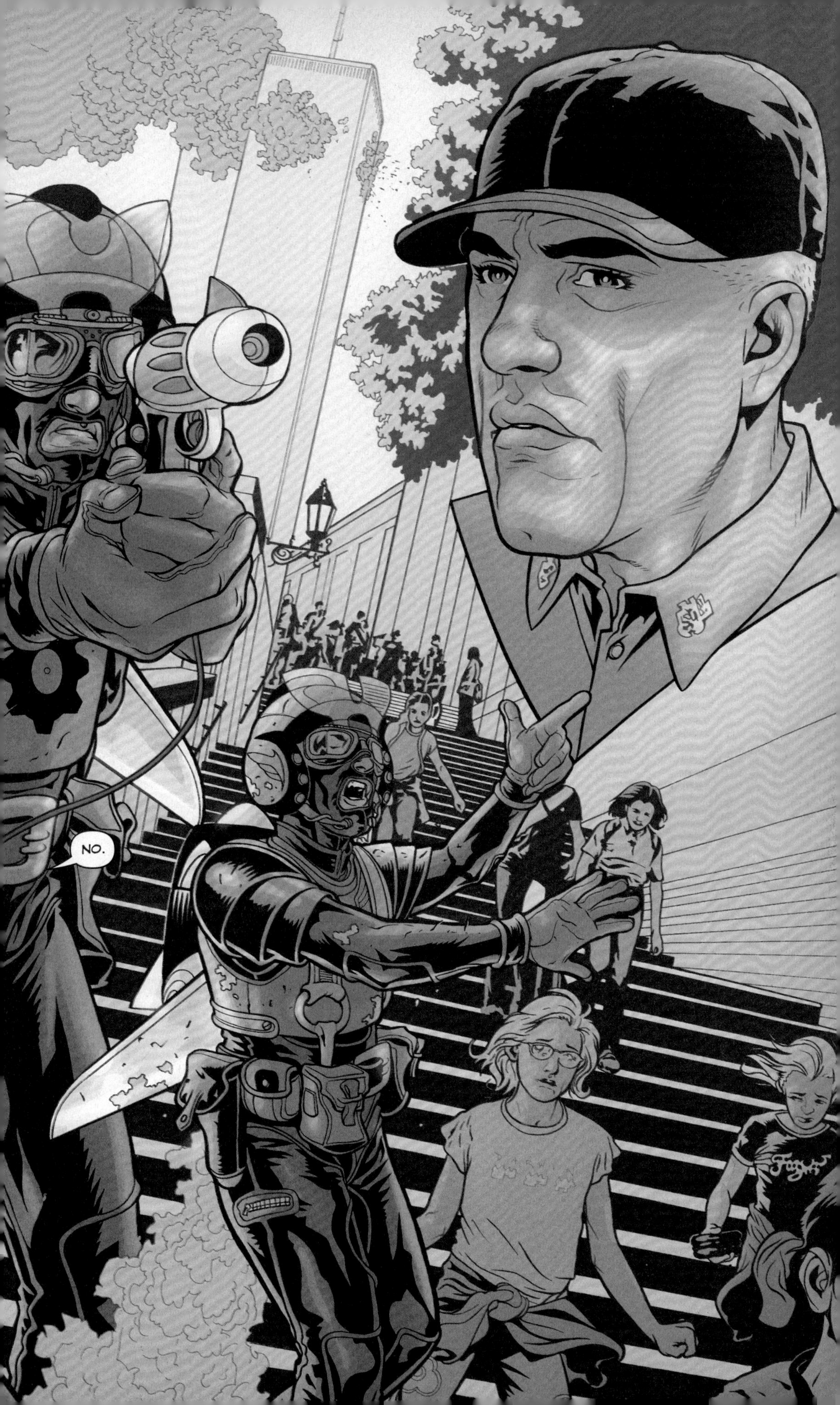
NO.

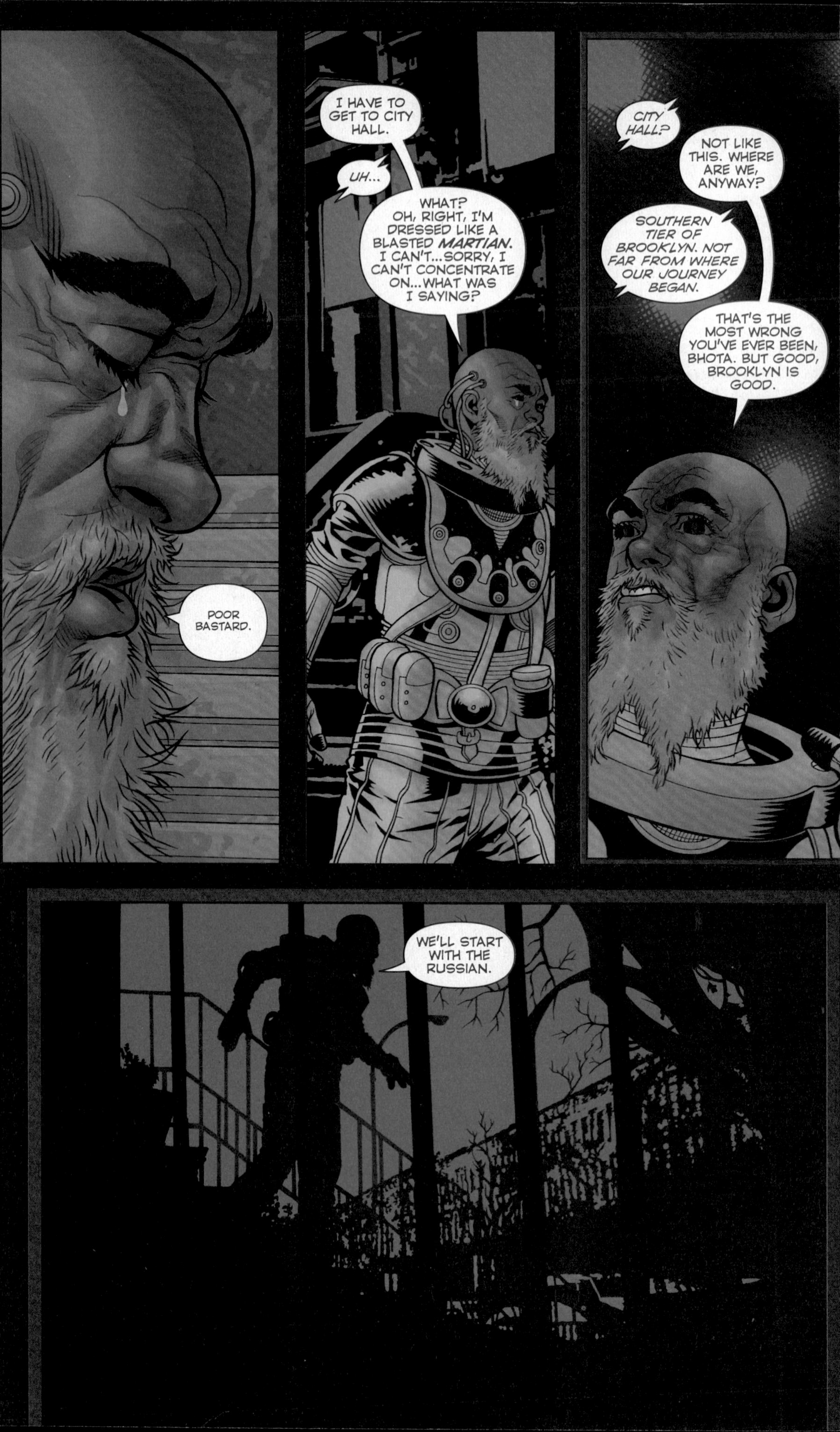
POOR BASTARD.
I HAVE TO GET TO CITY HALL.
UH...
WHAT? OH, RIGHT, I'M DRESSED LIKE A BLASTED MARTIAN. I CAN'T...SORRY, I CAN'T CONCENTRATE ON...WHAT WAS I SAYING?
CITY HALL?
NOT LIKE THIS. WHERE ARE WE, ANYWAY?
SOUTHERN TIER OF BROOKLYN. NOT FAR FROM WHERE OUR JOURNEY BEGAN.
THAT'S THE MOST WRONG YOU'VE EVER BEEN, BHOTA. BUT GOOD, BROOKLYN IS GOOD.
WE'LL START WITH THE RUSSIAN.

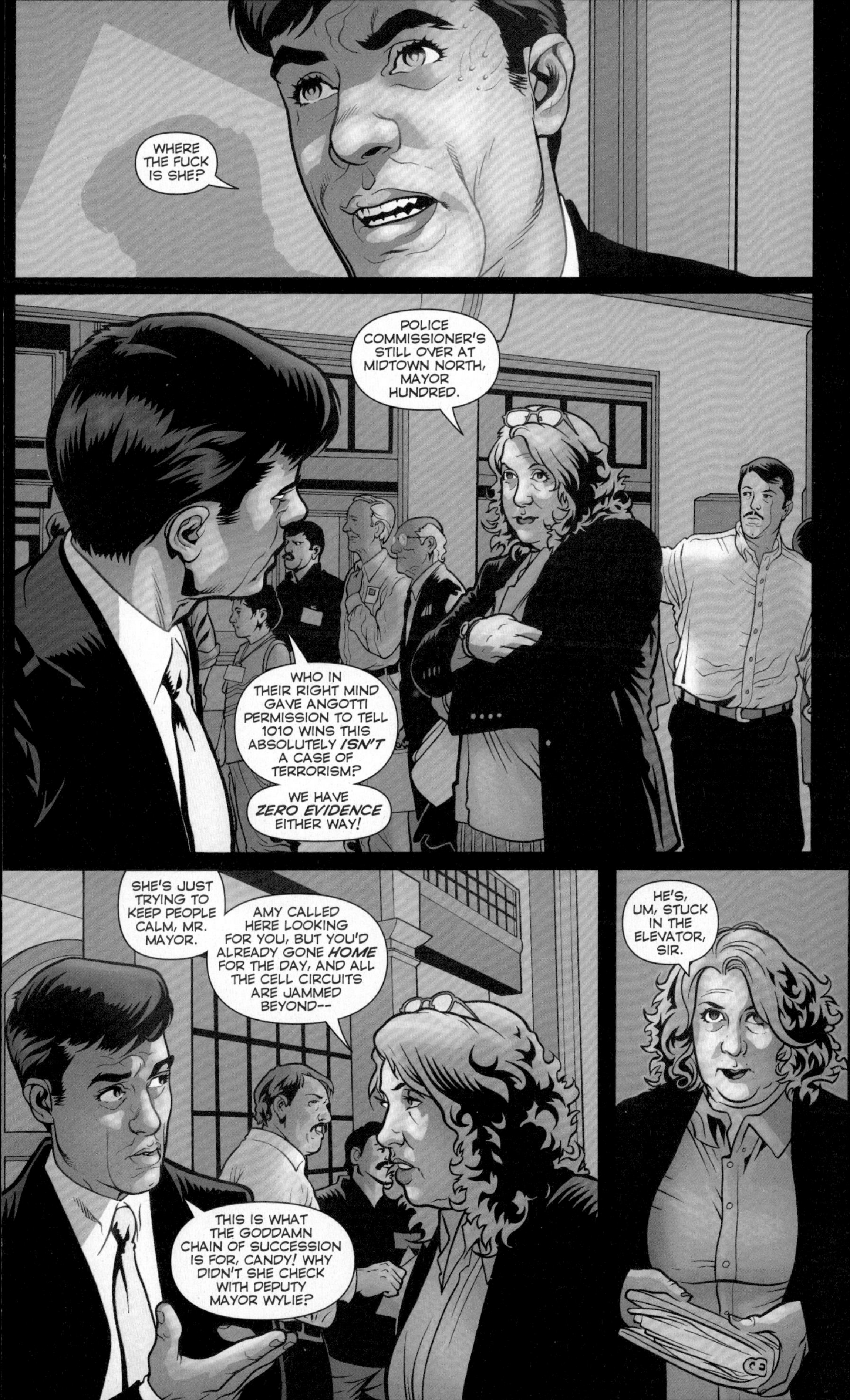
WHERE THE FUCK IS SHE?
POLICE COMMISSIONER'S STILL OVER AT MIDTOWN NORTH, MAYOR HUNDRED.
WHO IN THEIR RIGHT MIND GAVE ANGOTTI PERMISSION TO TELL 1010 WINS THIS ABSOLUTELY ISN'T A CASE OF TERRORISM?
WE HAVE ZERO EVIDENCE EITHER WAY!
SHE'S JUST TRYING TO KEEP PEOPLE CALM, MR. MAYOR.
AMY CALLED HERE LOOKING FOR YOU, BUT YOU'D ALREADY GONE HOME FOR THE DAY, AND ALL THE CELL CIRCUITS ARE JAMMED BEYOND--
THIS IS WHAT THE GODDAMN CHAIN OF SUCCESSION IS FOR, CANDY! WHY DIDN'T SHE CHECK WITH DEPUTY MAYOR WYLIE?
HE'S, UM, STUCK IN THE ELEVATOR, SIR.

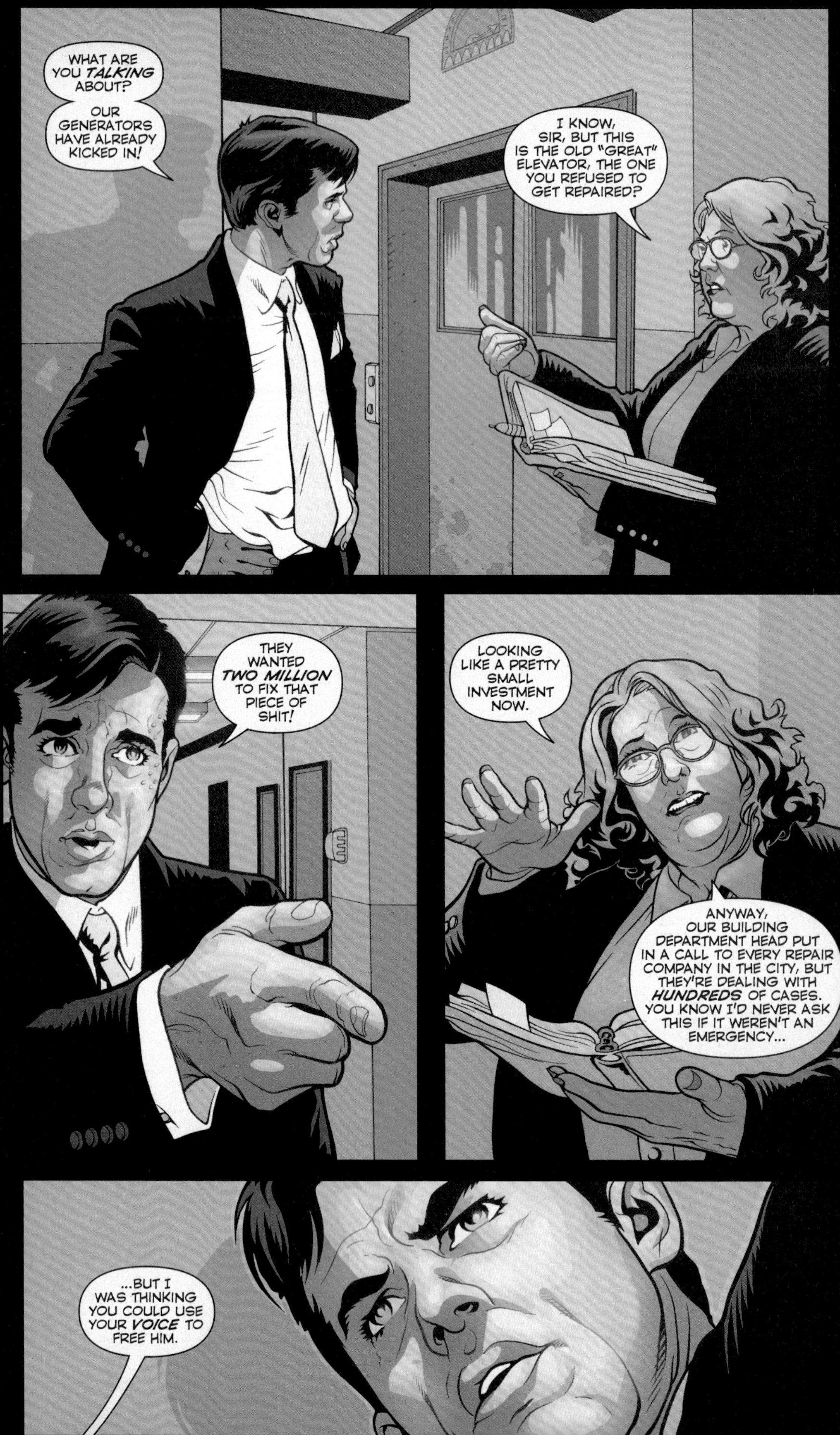

WHAT ARE YOU TALKING ABOUT?
OUR GENERATORS HAVE ALREADY KICKED IN!
I KNOW, SIR, BUT THIS IS THE OLD "GREAT" ELEVATOR, THE ONE YOU REFUSED TO GET REPAIRED?
THEY WANTED TWO MILLION TO FIX THAT PIECE OF SHIT!
LOOKING LIKE A PRETTY SMALL INVESTMENT NOW.
ANYWAY, OUR BUILDING DEPARTMENT HEAD PUT IN A CALL TO EVERY REPAIR COMPANY IN THE CITY, BUT THEY'RE DEALING WITH HUNDREDS OF CASES. YOU KNOW I'D NEVER ASK THIS IF IT WEREN'T AN EMERGENCY...
...BUT I WAS THINKING YOU COULD USE YOUR VOICE TO FREE HIM.

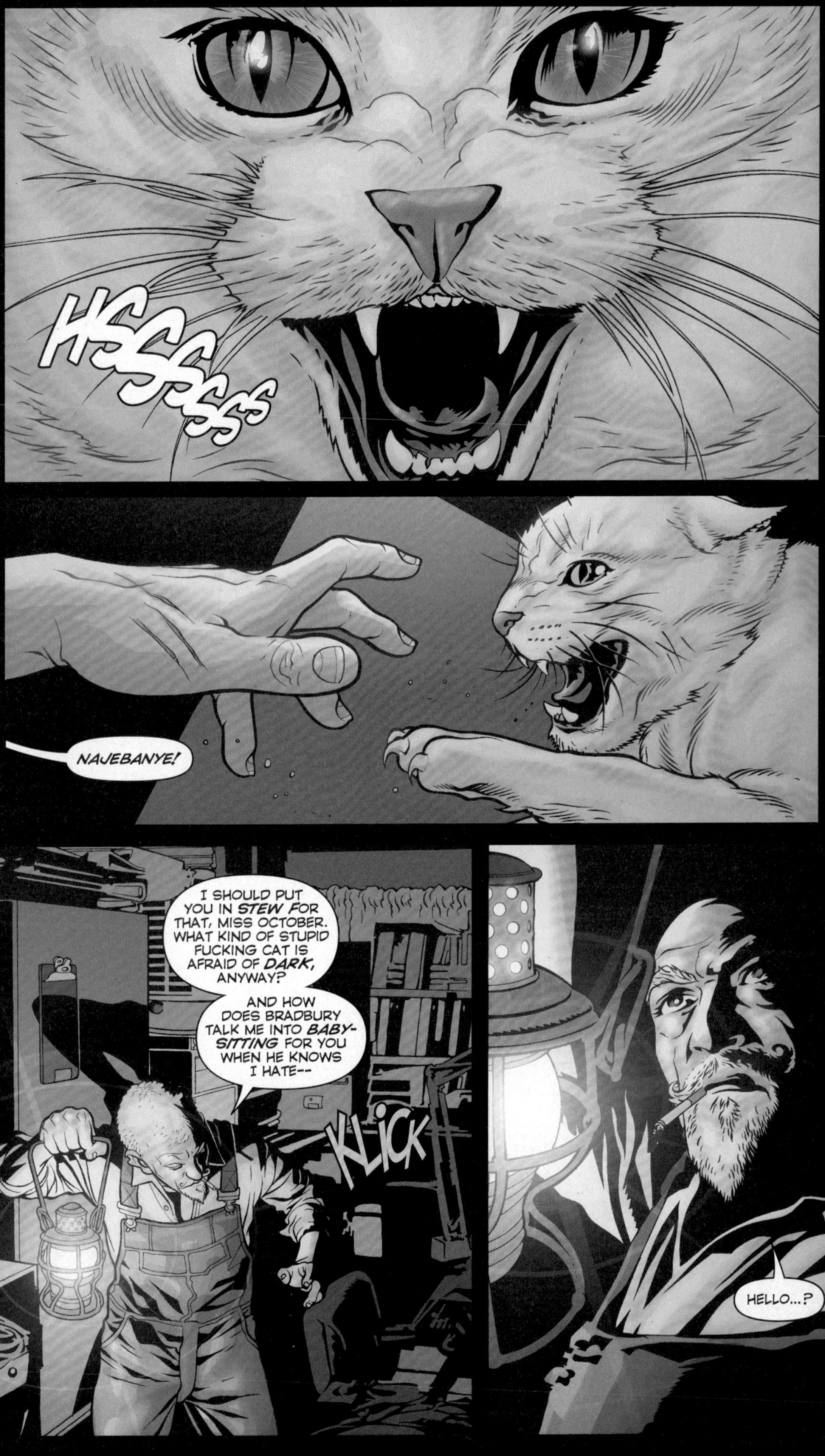
HSSSSSS
NAJEBANYE!
I SHOULD PUT YOU IN STEW FOR THAT, MISS OCTOBER. WHAT KIND OF STUPID FUCKING CAT IS AFRAID OF DARK, ANYWAY?
AND HOW DOES BRADBURY TALK ME INTO BABY-SITTING FOR YOU WHEN HE KNOWS I HATE--
KLICK
HELLO...?

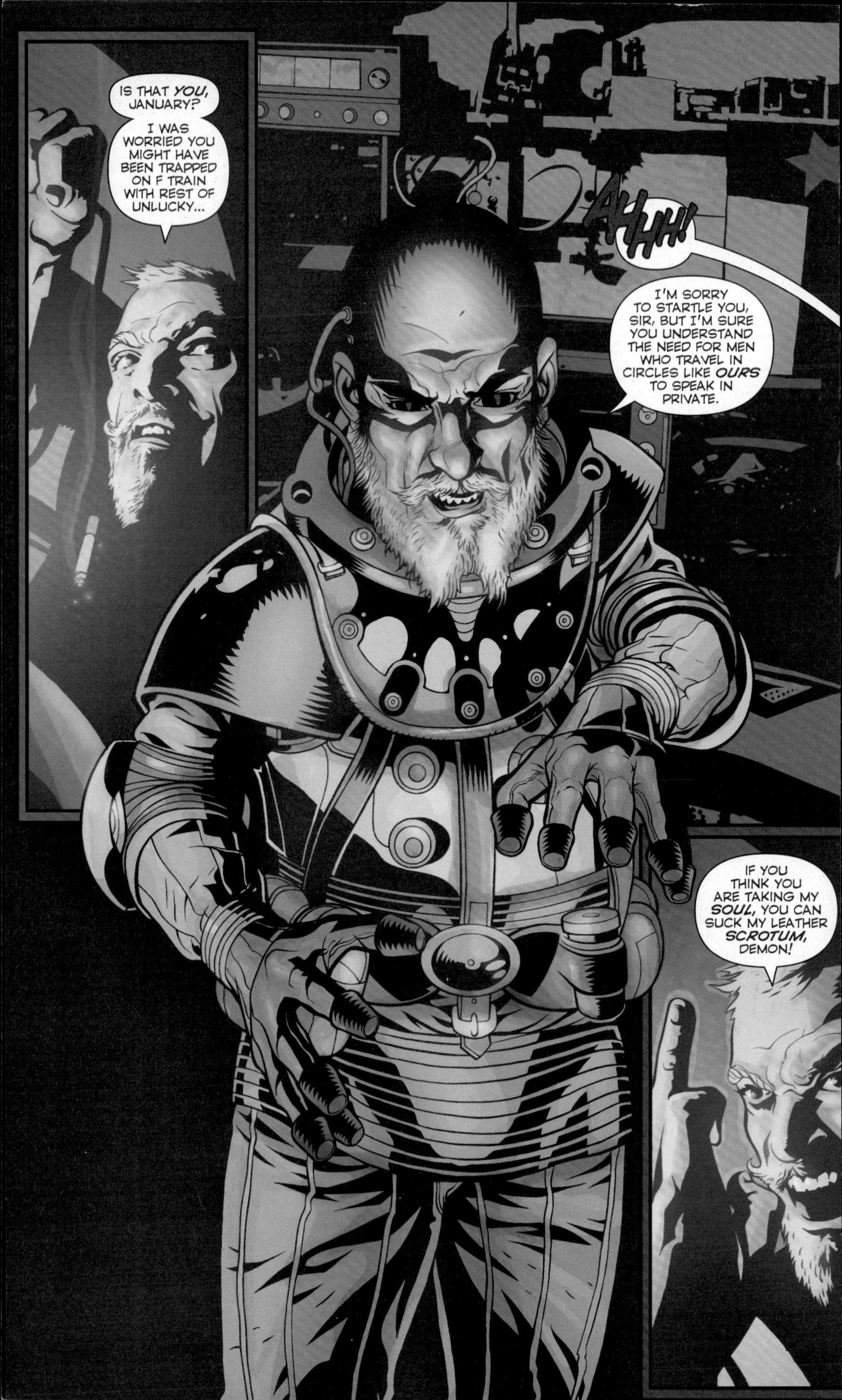
IS THAT YOU, JANUARY?
I WAS WORRIED YOU MIGHT HAVE BEEN TRAPPED ON F TRAIN WITH REST OF UNLUCKY...
AHHH!
I'M SORRY TO STARTLE YOU, SIR, BUT I'M SURE YOU UNDERSTAND THE NEED FOR MEN WHO TRAVEL IN CIRCLES LIKE OURS TO SPEAK IN PRIVATE.
IF YOU THINK YOU ARE TAKING MY SOUL, YOU CAN SUCK MY LEATHER SCROTUM, DEMON!

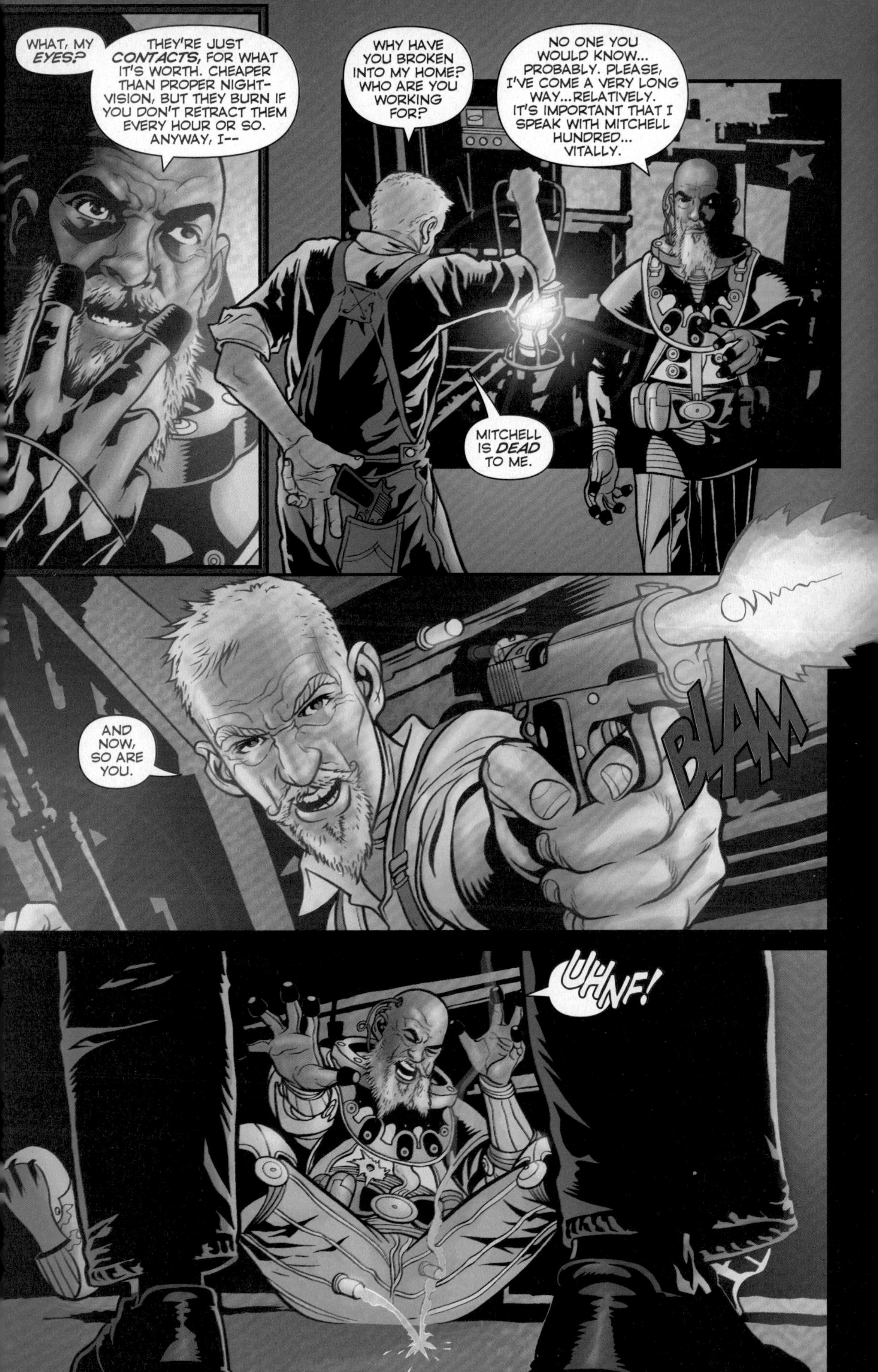

WHAT, MY *EYES?*
THEY'RE JUST *CONTACTS,* FOR WHAT IT'S WORTH. CHEAPER THAN PROPER NIGHT-VISION, BUT THEY BURN IF YOU DON'T RETRACT THEM EVERY HOUR OR SO. ANYWAY, I--
WHY HAVE YOU BROKEN INTO MY HOME? WHO ARE YOU WORKING FOR?
NO ONE YOU WOULD KNOW... PROBABLY. PLEASE, I'VE COME A VERY LONG WAY...RELATIVELY. IT'S IMPORTANT THAT I SPEAK WITH MITCHELL HUNDRED... VITALLY.
MITCHELL IS *DEAD* TO ME.
AND NOW, SO ARE YOU.
BLAM
UHNF!

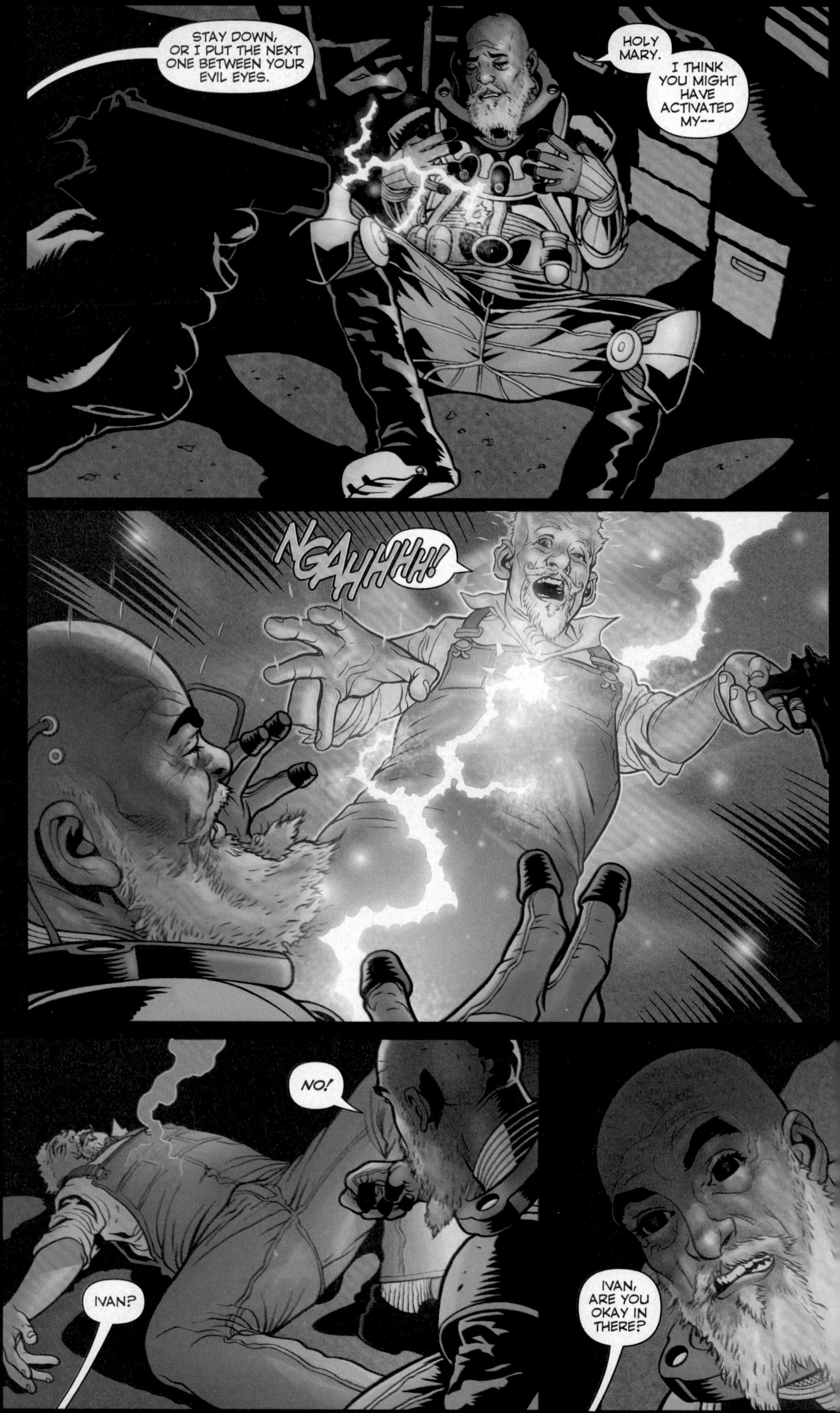

STAY DOWN, OR I PUT THE NEXT ONE BETWEEN YOUR EVIL EYES.
HOLY MARY.
I THINK YOU MIGHT HAVE ACTIVATED MY--
NGAHHHH!
NO!
IVAN?
IVAN, ARE YOU OKAY IN THERE?

I ALWAYS KNEW THIS PLACE WOULD BE THE DEATH OF ME.

JUST HANG TIGHT, DAVE. I'D USE MY "ABILITIES," BUT, UH...

...IT WOULDN'T BE FAIR TO OUR CONSTITUENTS IN THE SAME SITUATION. I UNDERSTAND COMPLETELY, SIR.

SCOOT AND I WILL BE FINE.

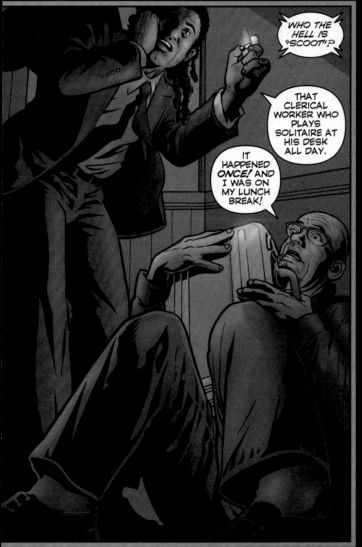

WHO THE HELL IS "SCOOT"?

THAT CLERICAL WORKER WHO PLAYS SOLITAIRE AT HIS DESK ALL DAY.

IT HAPPENED ONCE! AND I WAS ON MY LUNCH BREAK!

WELL, MAYBE YOU'VE MADE A LOVE CONNECTION.

YOU KNOW WHAT HAPPENED NINE MONTHS AFTER THE LAST BLACKOUT.

ACTUALLY, THE BIRTH RATE WENT DOWN THAT YEAR, SIR.

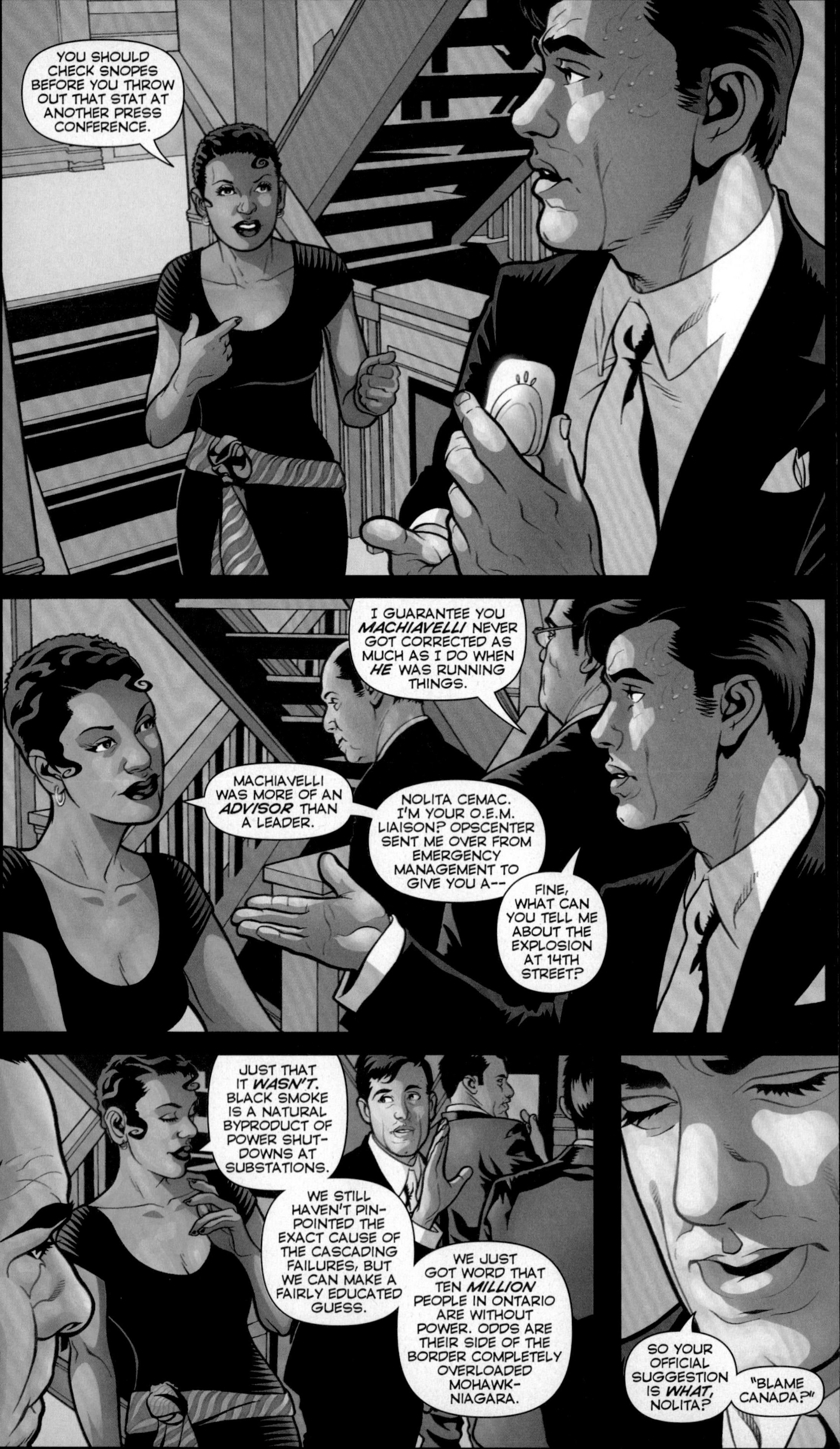
YOU SHOULD CHECK SNOPES BEFORE YOU THROW OUT THAT STAT AT ANOTHER PRESS CONFERENCE.
I GUARANTEE YOU MACHIAVELLI NEVER GOT CORRECTED AS MUCH AS I DO WHEN HE WAS RUNNING THINGS.
MACHIAVELLI WAS MORE OF AN ADVISOR THAN A LEADER.
NOLITA CEMAC. I'M YOUR O.E.M. LIAISON? OPSCENTER SENT ME OVER FROM EMERGENCY MANAGEMENT TO GIVE YOU A--
FINE, WHAT CAN YOU TELL ME ABOUT THE EXPLOSION AT 14TH STREET?
JUST THAT IT WASN'T. BLACK SMOKE IS A NATURAL BYPRODUCT OF POWER SHUT-DOWNS AT SUBSTATIONS.
WE STILL HAVEN'T PIN-POINTED THE EXACT CAUSE OF THE CASCADING FAILURES, BUT WE CAN MAKE A FAIRLY EDUCATED GUESS.
WE JUST GOT WORD THAT TEN MILLION PEOPLE IN ONTARIO ARE WITHOUT POWER. ODDS ARE THEIR SIDE OF THE BORDER COMPLETELY OVERLOADED MOHAWK-NIAGARA.
SO YOUR OFFICIAL SUGGESTION IS WHAT, NOLITA?
"BLAME CANADA?"

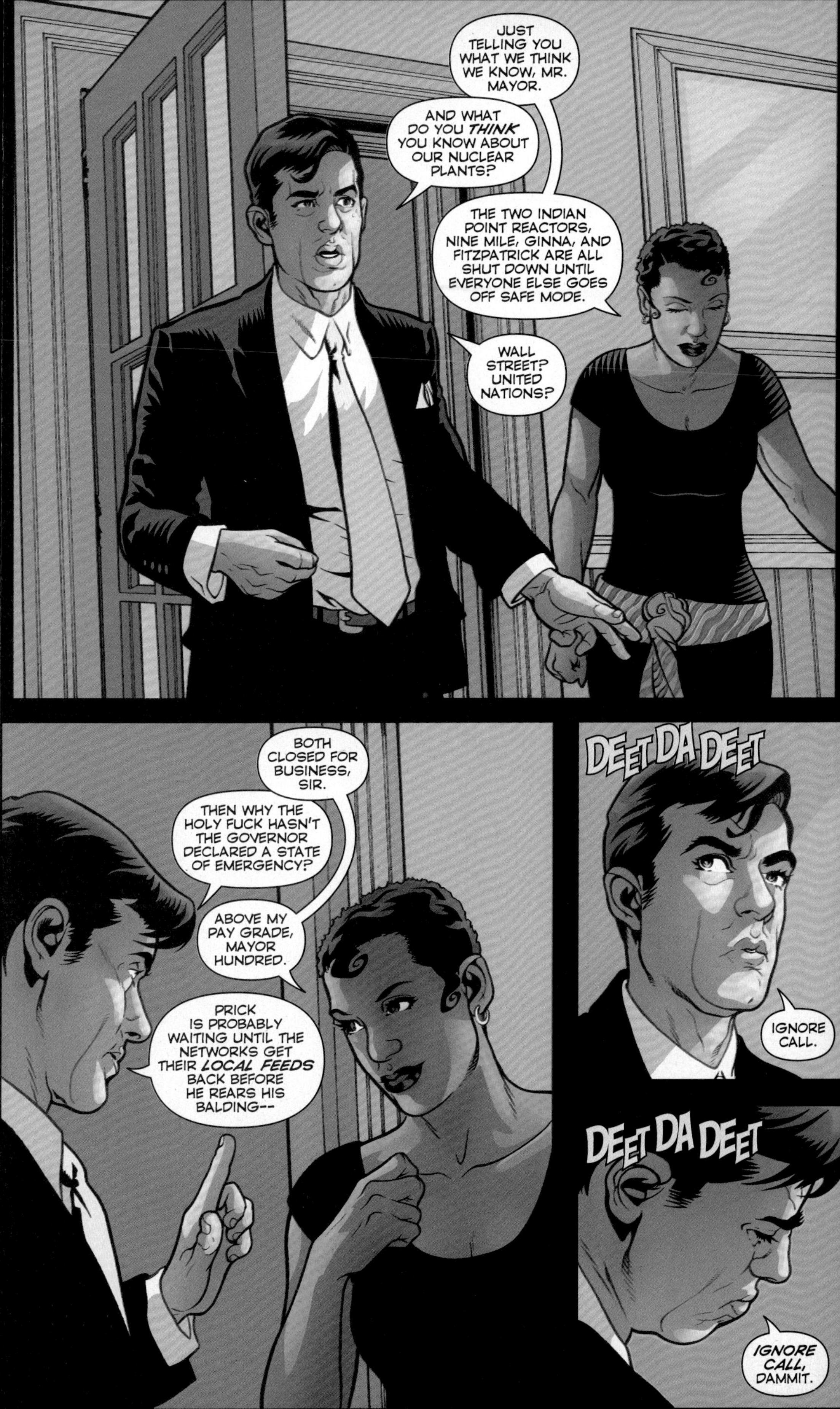

JUST TELLING YOU WHAT WE THINK WE KNOW, MR. MAYOR.
AND WHAT DO YOU *THINK* YOU KNOW ABOUT OUR NUCLEAR PLANTS?
THE TWO INDIAN POINT REACTORS, NINE MILE, GINNA, AND FITZPATRICK ARE ALL SHUT DOWN UNTIL EVERYONE ELSE GOES OFF SAFE MODE.
WALL STREET? UNITED NATIONS?
BOTH CLOSED FOR BUSINESS, SIR.
THEN WHY THE HOLY FUCK HASN'T THE GOVERNOR DECLARED A STATE OF EMERGENCY?
ABOVE MY PAY GRADE, MAYOR HUNDRED.
PRICK IS PROBABLY WAITING UNTIL THE NETWORKS GET THEIR *LOCAL FEEDS* BACK BEFORE HE REARS HIS BALDING--
DEET DA DEET
IGNORE CALL.
DEET DA DEET
IGNORE CALL, DAMMIT.

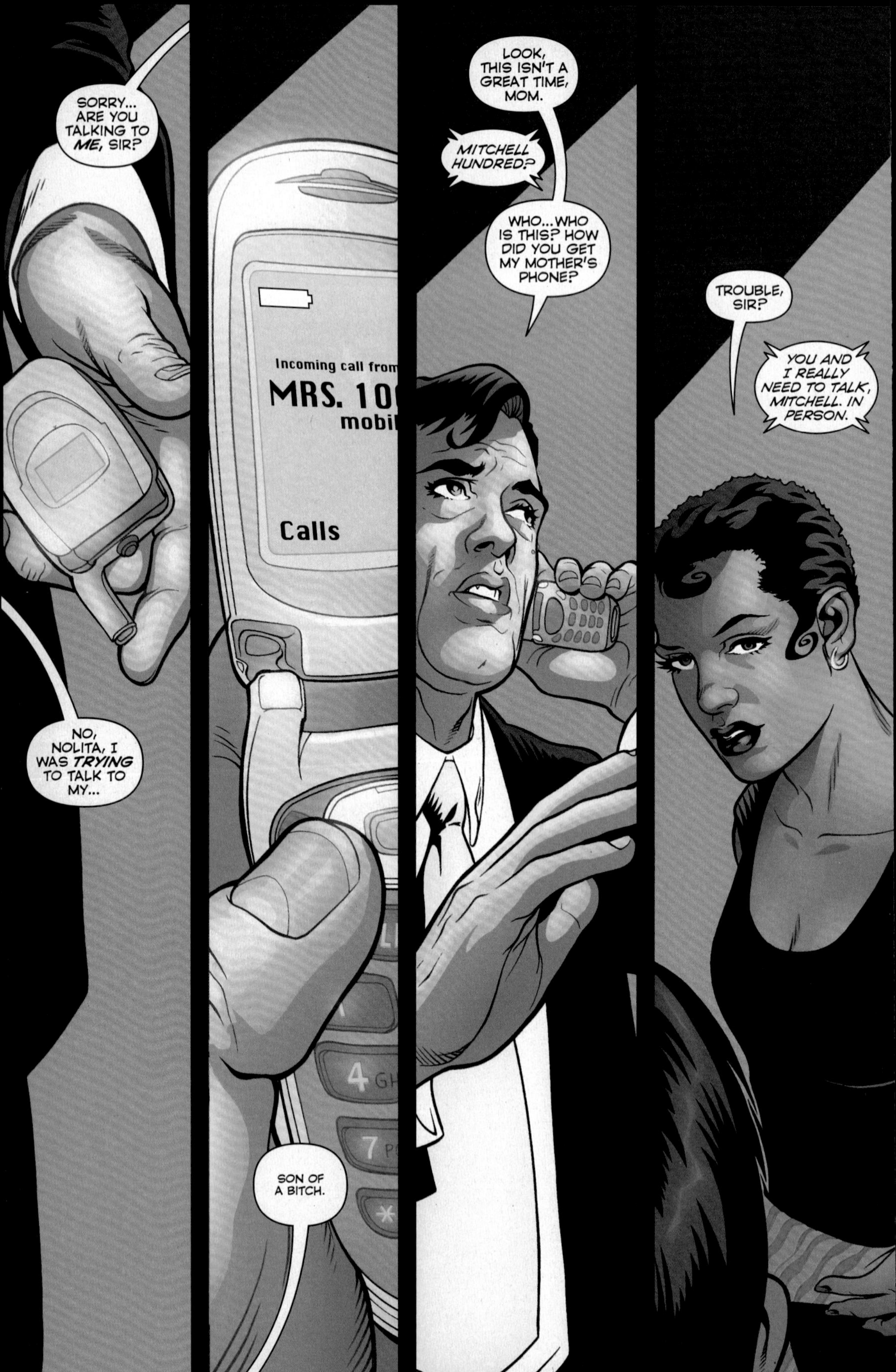
SORRY... ARE YOU TALKING TO ME, SIR?
NO, NOLITA, I WAS TRYING TO TALK TO MY...
Incoming call from
MRS. 10
mobil
Calls
SON OF A BITCH.
LOOK, THIS ISN'T A GREAT TIME, MOM.
MITCHELL HUNDRED?
WHO...WHO IS THIS? HOW DID YOU GET MY MOTHER'S PHONE?
TROUBLE, SIR?
YOU AND I REALLY NEED TO TALK, MITCHELL. IN PERSON.

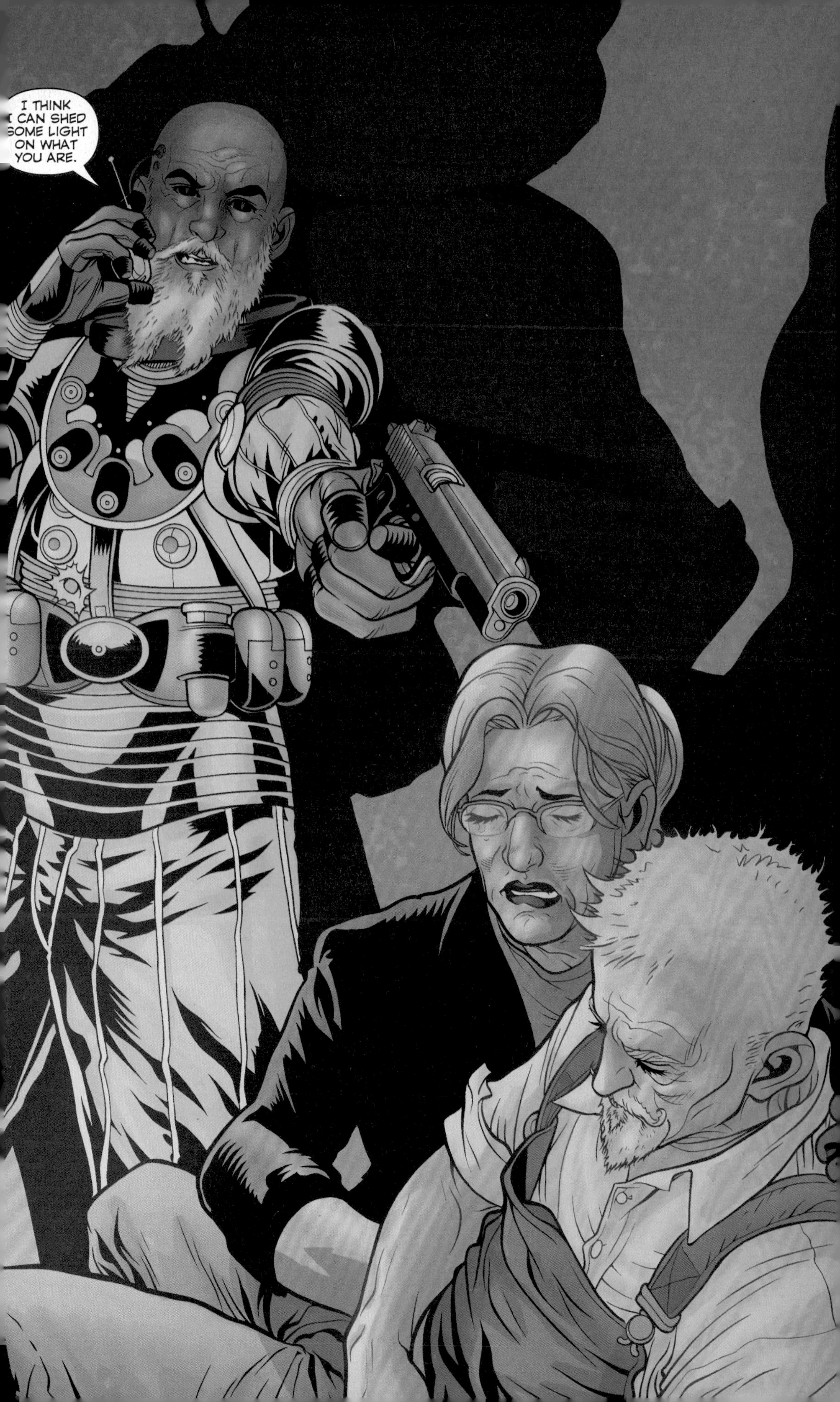
I THINK I CAN SHED SOME LIGHT ON WHAT YOU ARE.

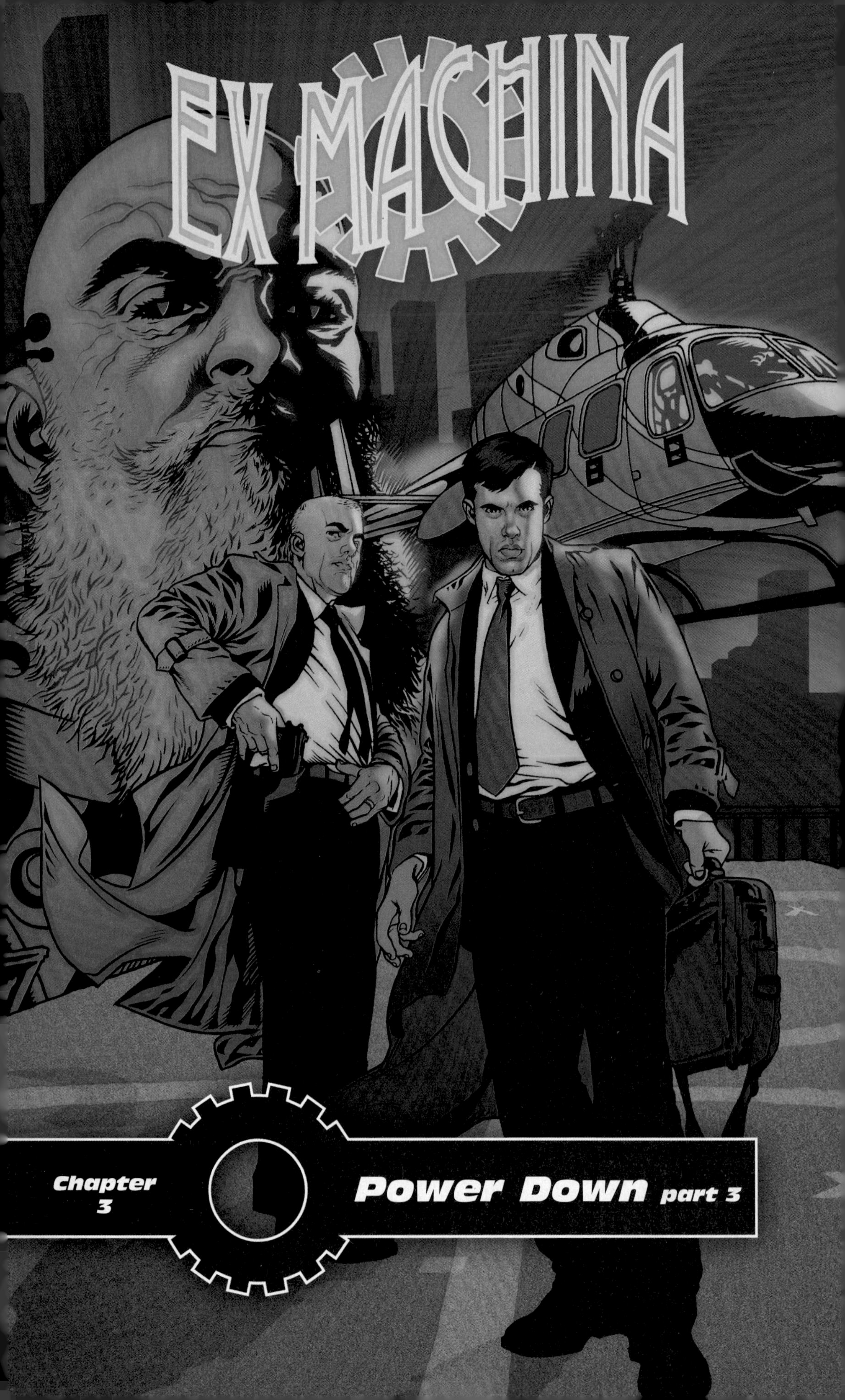
EX MACHINA
Chapter 3
Power Down part 3

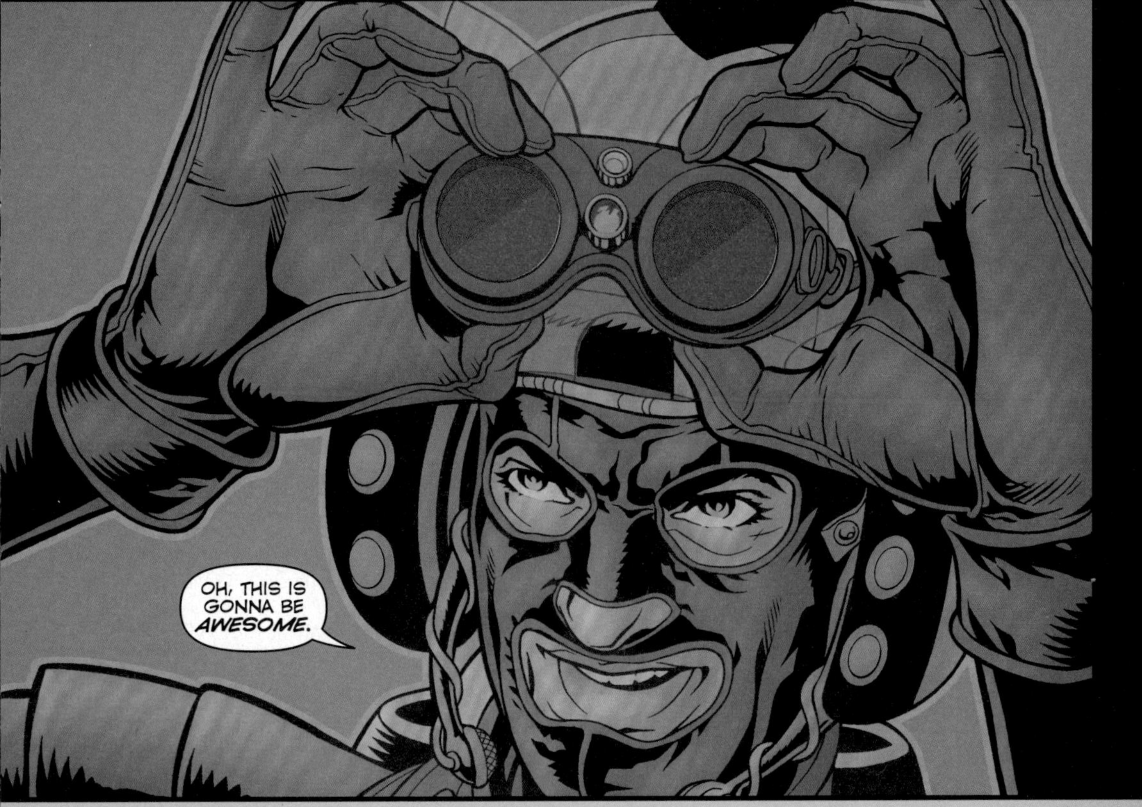
OH, THIS IS GONNA BE *AWESOME*.

SATURDAY, MARCH 11, 2000

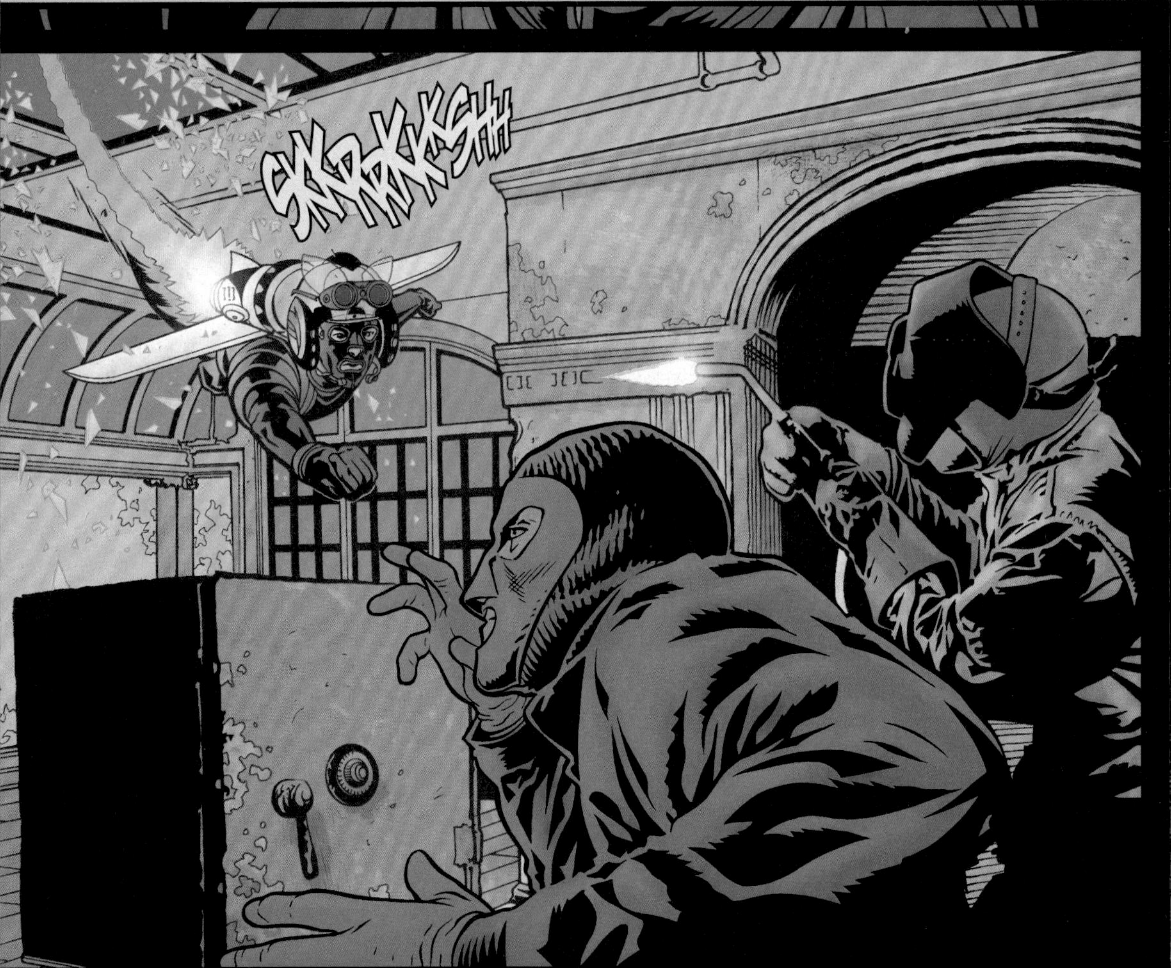
SKRRKKSHH

ONN!

SON OF A BASTARD!

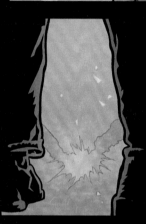

UHNF!

YOU KNOW OUR ORDERS. NO MERCY.

TRIGGER LOCK!

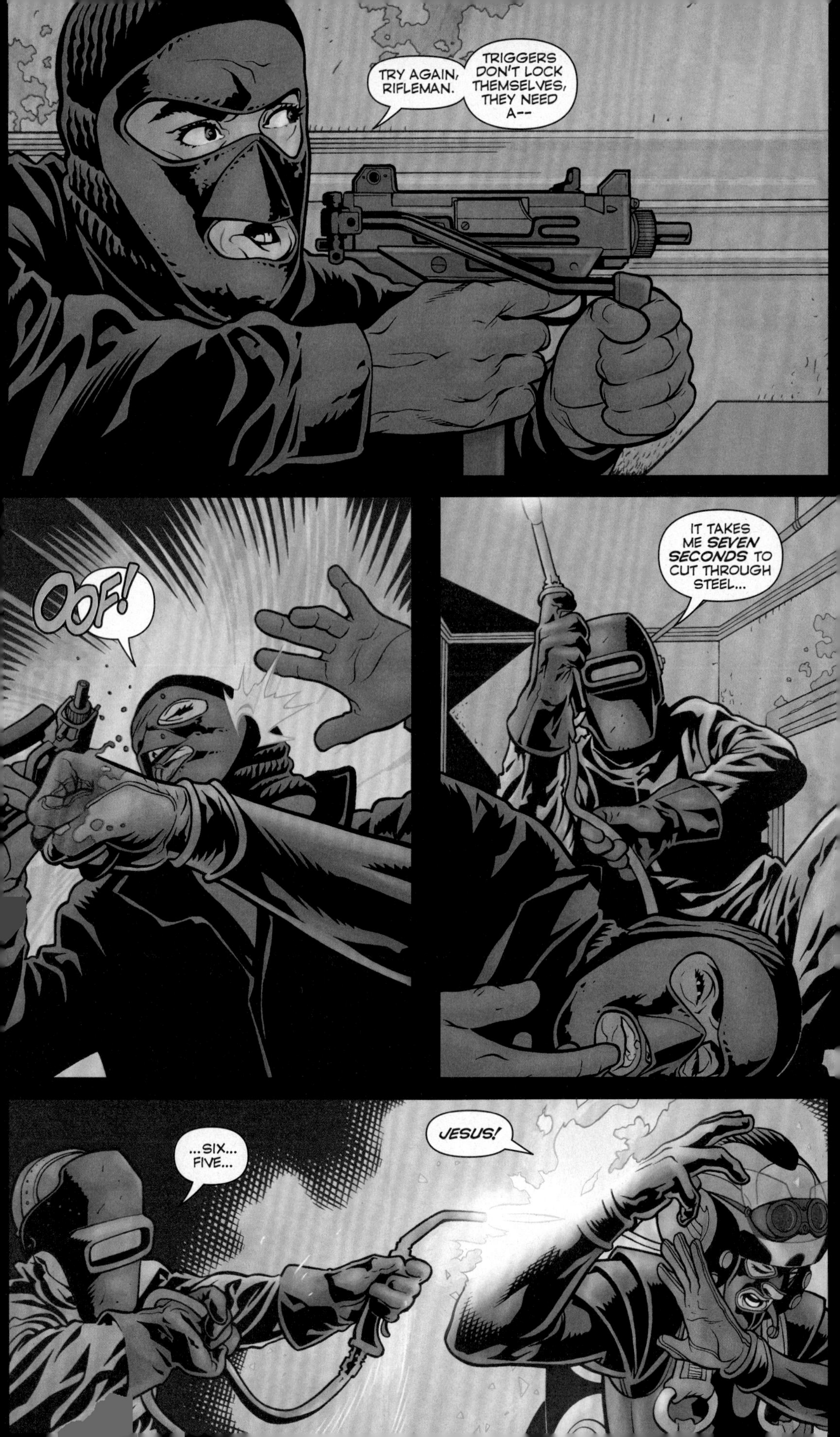
TRY AGAIN, RIFLEMAN.
TRIGGERS DON'T LOCK THEMSELVES, THEY NEED A--
OOF!
IT TAKES ME SEVEN SECONDS TO CUT THROUGH STEEL...
...SIX... FIVE...
JESUS!

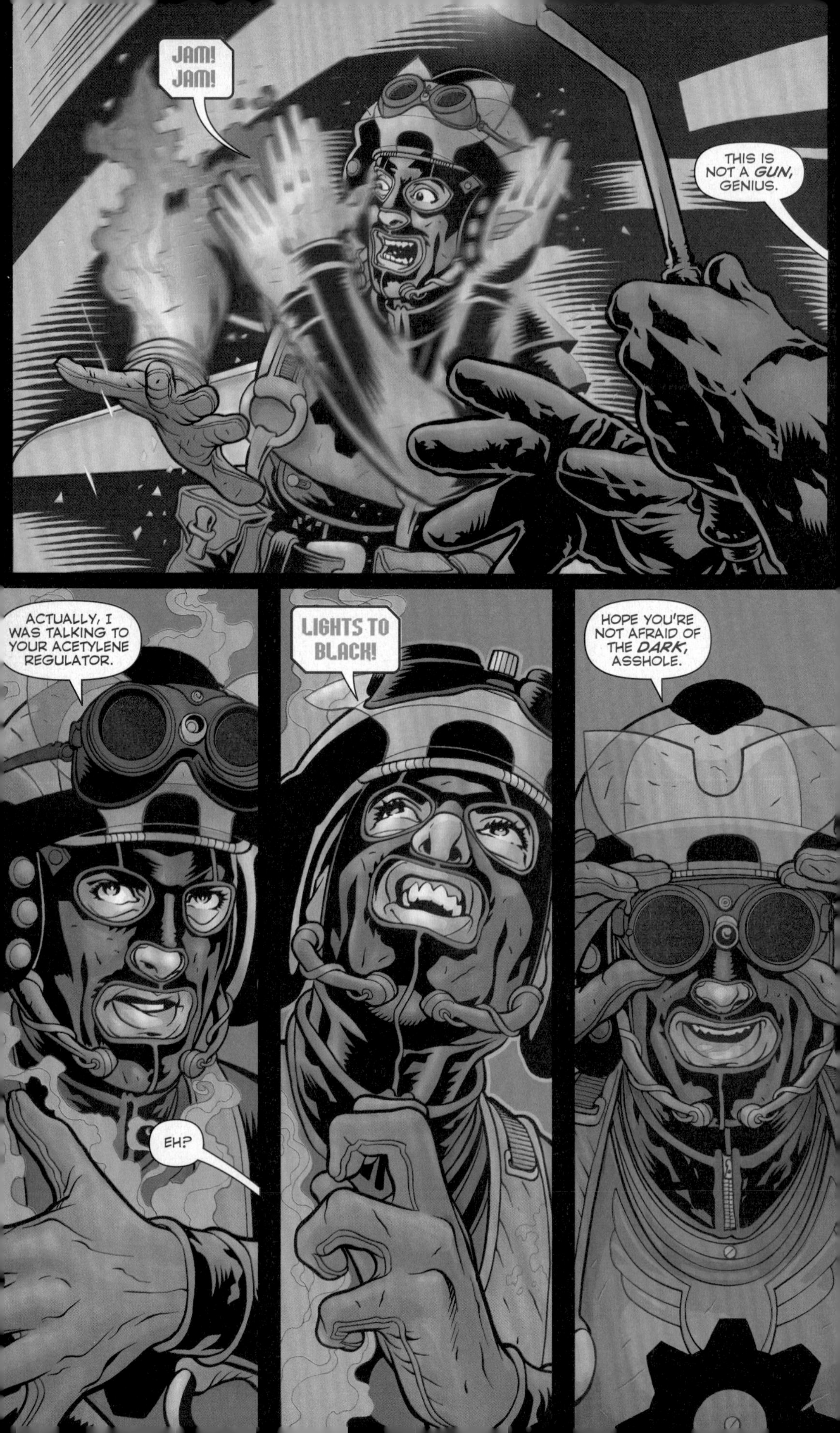
JAM! JAM!
THIS IS NOT A GUN, GENIUS.
ACTUALLY, I WAS TALKING TO YOUR ACETYLENE REGULATOR.
EH?
LIGHTS TO BLACK!
HOPE YOU'RE NOT AFRAID OF THE DARK, ASSHOLE.

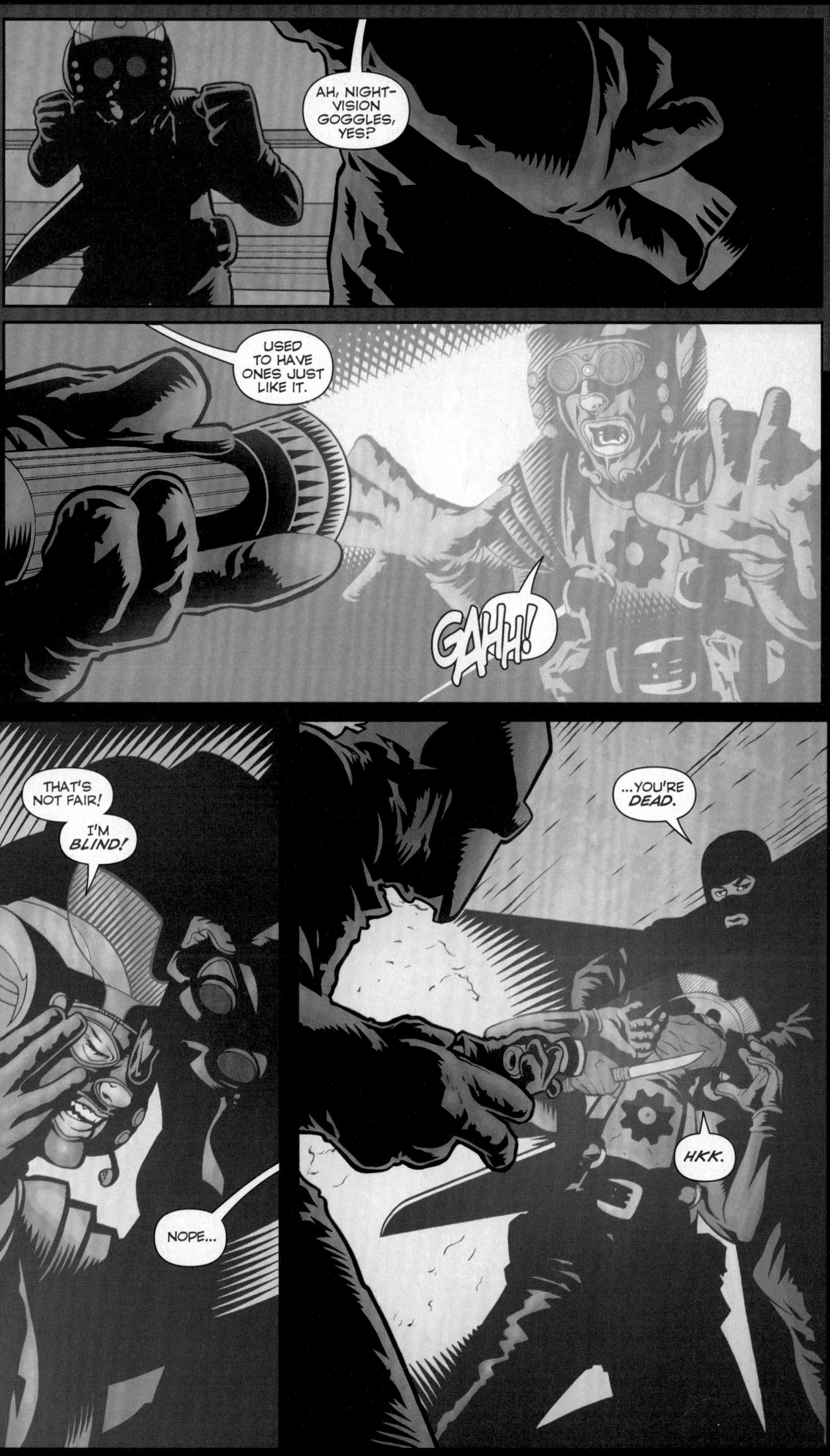
AH, NIGHT-VISION GOGGLES, YES?
USED TO HAVE ONES JUST LIKE IT.
GAHH!
THAT'S NOT FAIR!
I'M *BLIND!*
NOPE...
...YOU'RE *DEAD.*
HKK.

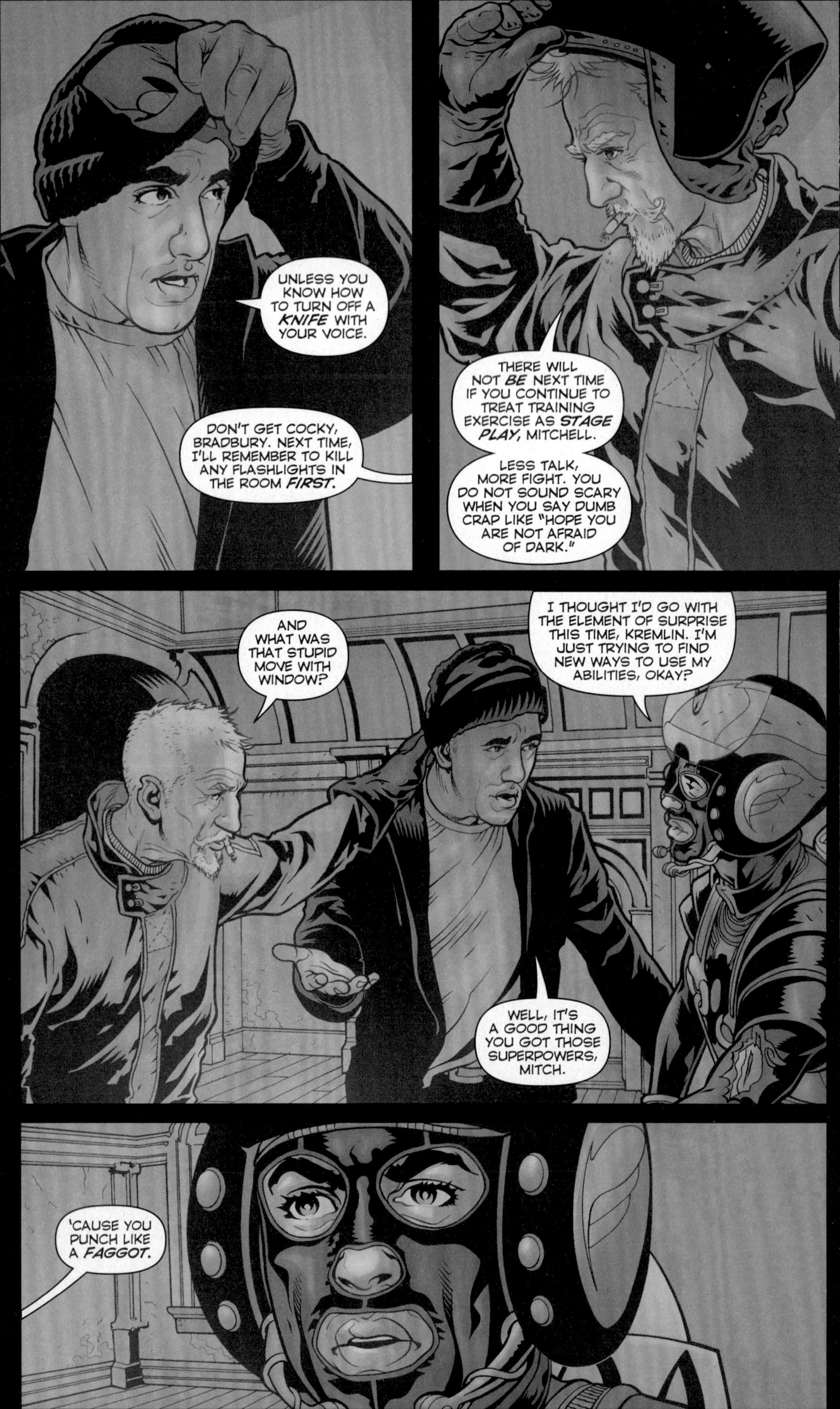
UNLESS YOU KNOW HOW TO TURN OFF A KNIFE WITH YOUR VOICE.
DON'T GET COCKY, BRADBURY. NEXT TIME, I'LL REMEMBER TO KILL ANY FLASHLIGHTS IN THE ROOM FIRST.
THERE WILL NOT BE NEXT TIME IF YOU CONTINUE TO TREAT TRAINING EXERCISE AS STAGE PLAY, MITCHELL.
LESS TALK, MORE FIGHT. YOU DO NOT SOUND SCARY WHEN YOU SAY DUMB CRAP LIKE "HOPE YOU ARE NOT AFRAID OF DARK."
AND WHAT WAS THAT STUPID MOVE WITH WINDOW?
I THOUGHT I'D GO WITH THE ELEMENT OF SURPRISE THIS TIME, KREMLIN. I'M JUST TRYING TO FIND NEW WAYS TO USE MY ABILITIES, OKAY?
WELL, IT'S A GOOD THING YOU GOT THOSE SUPERPOWERS, MITCH.
'CAUSE YOU PUNCH LIKE A FAGGOT.

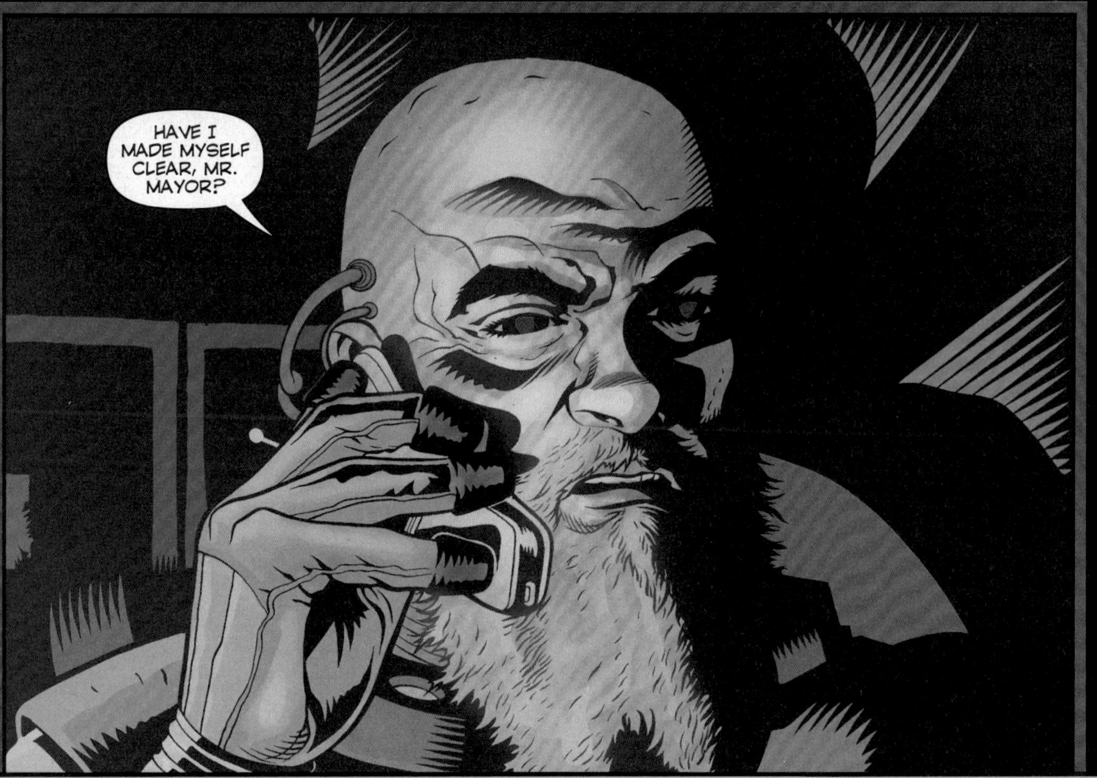
HAVE I MADE MYSELF CLEAR, MR. MAYOR?

THURSDAY, AUGUST 14, 2003

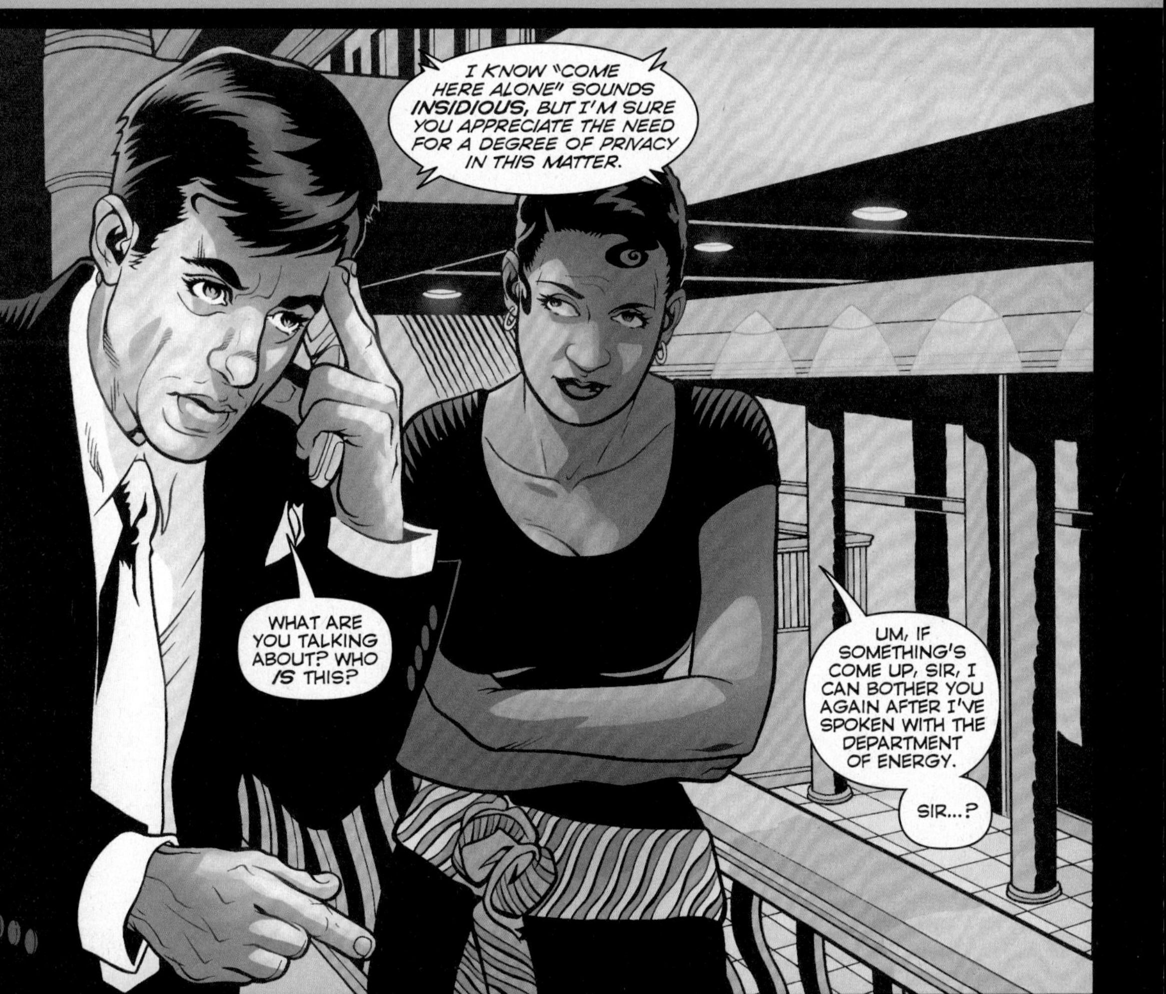
I KNOW "COME HERE ALONE" SOUNDS *INSIDIOUS*, BUT I'M SURE YOU APPRECIATE THE NEED FOR A DEGREE OF PRIVACY IN THIS MATTER.
WHAT ARE YOU TALKING ABOUT? WHO *IS* THIS?
UM, IF SOMETHING'S COME UP, SIR, I CAN BOTHER YOU AGAIN AFTER I'VE SPOKEN WITH THE DEPARTMENT OF ENERGY.
SIR...?

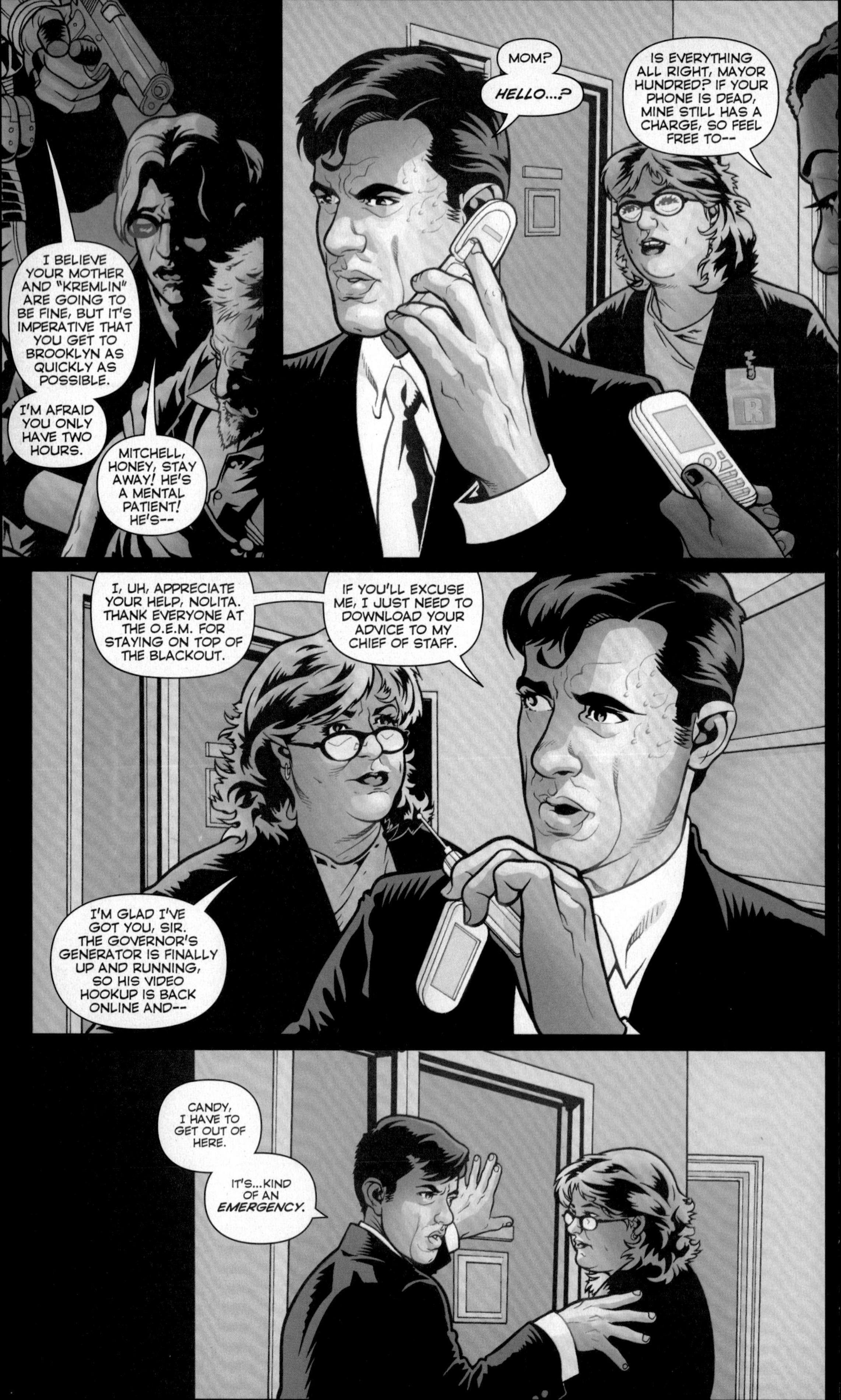
I BELIEVE YOUR MOTHER AND "KREMLIN" ARE GOING TO BE FINE, BUT IT'S IMPERATIVE THAT YOU GET TO BROOKLYN AS QUICKLY AS POSSIBLE.
I'M AFRAID YOU ONLY HAVE TWO HOURS.
MITCHELL, HONEY, STAY AWAY! HE'S A MENTAL PATIENT! HE'S--
MOM? HELLO...?
IS EVERYTHING ALL RIGHT, MAYOR HUNDRED? IF YOUR PHONE IS DEAD, MINE STILL HAS A CHARGE, SO FEEL FREE TO--
I, UH, APPRECIATE YOUR HELP, NOLITA. THANK EVERYONE AT THE O.E.M. FOR STAYING ON TOP OF THE BLACKOUT.
IF YOU'LL EXCUSE ME, I JUST NEED TO DOWNLOAD YOUR ADVICE TO MY CHIEF OF STAFF.
I'M GLAD I'VE GOT YOU, SIR. THE GOVERNOR'S GENERATOR IS FINALLY UP AND RUNNING, SO HIS VIDEO HOOKUP IS BACK ONLINE AND--
CANDY, I HAVE TO GET OUT OF HERE.
IT'S...KIND OF AN EMERGENCY.

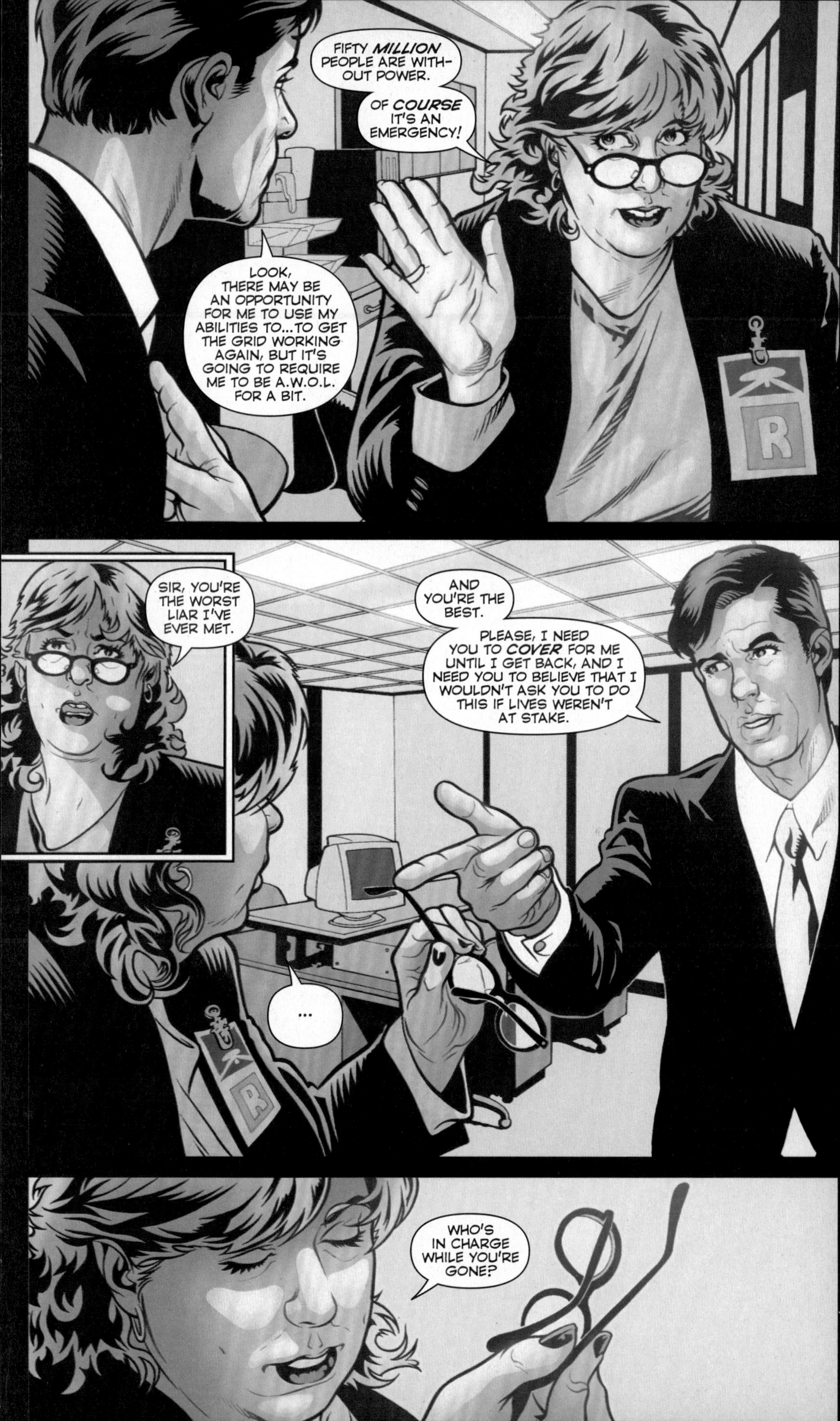
FIFTY *MILLION* PEOPLE ARE WITHOUT POWER.
OF *COURSE* IT'S AN EMERGENCY!
LOOK, THERE MAY BE AN OPPORTUNITY FOR ME TO USE MY ABILITIES TO...TO GET THE GRID WORKING AGAIN, BUT IT'S GOING TO REQUIRE ME TO BE A.W.O.L. FOR A BIT.
SIR, YOU'RE THE WORST LIAR I'VE EVER MET.
AND YOU'RE THE BEST.
PLEASE, I NEED YOU TO *COVER* FOR ME UNTIL I GET BACK, AND I NEED YOU TO BELIEVE THAT I WOULDN'T ASK YOU TO DO THIS IF LIVES WEREN'T AT STAKE.
...
WHO'S IN CHARGE WHILE YOU'RE GONE?

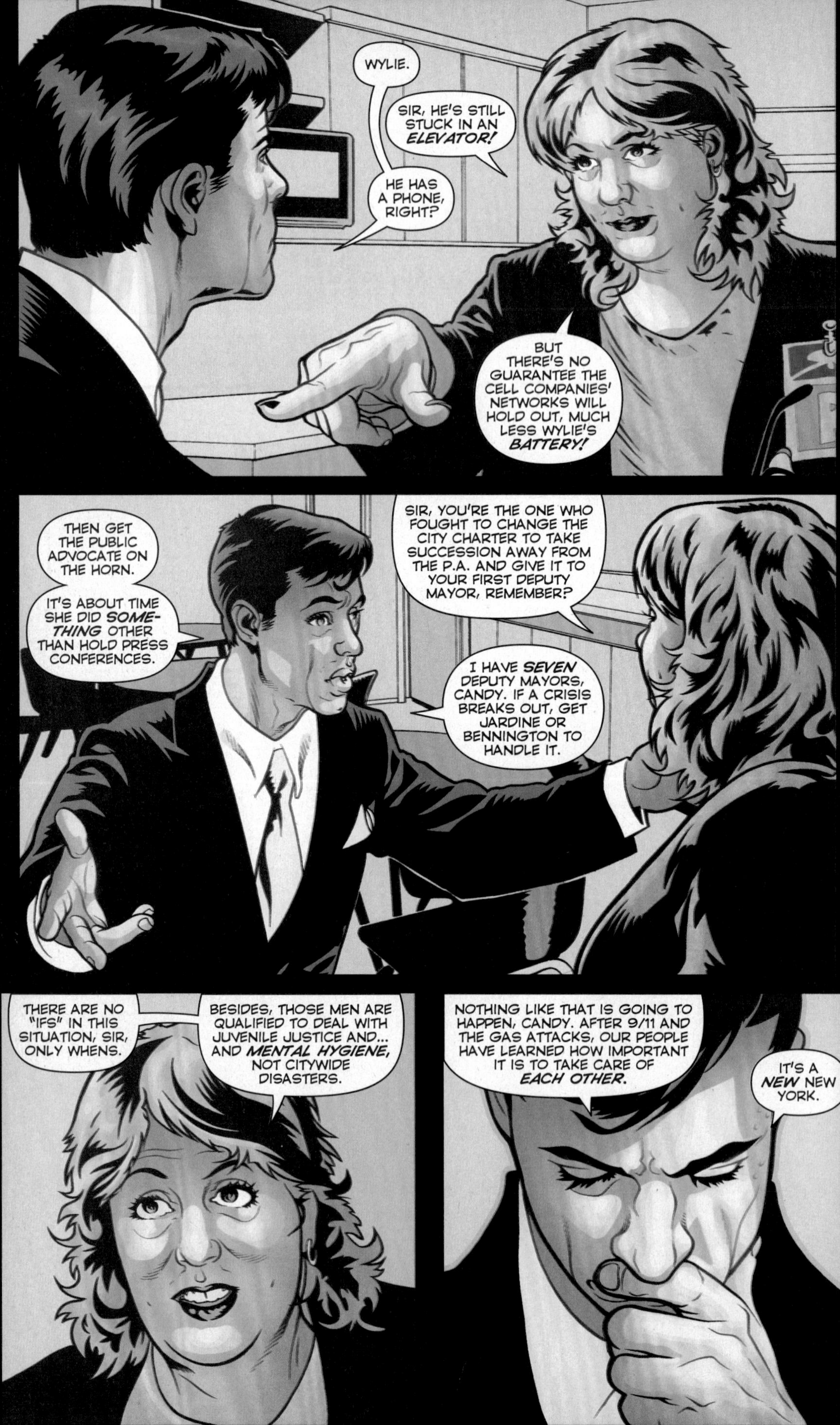
WYLIE.
SIR, HE'S STILL STUCK IN AN *ELEVATOR!*
HE HAS A PHONE, RIGHT?
BUT THERE'S NO GUARANTEE THE CELL COMPANIES' NETWORKS WILL HOLD OUT, MUCH LESS WYLIE'S *BATTERY!*
THEN GET THE PUBLIC ADVOCATE ON THE HORN.
IT'S ABOUT TIME SHE DID *SOMETHING* OTHER THAN HOLD PRESS CONFERENCES.
SIR, YOU'RE THE ONE WHO FOUGHT TO CHANGE THE CITY CHARTER TO TAKE SUCCESSION AWAY FROM THE P.A. AND GIVE IT TO YOUR FIRST DEPUTY MAYOR, REMEMBER?
I HAVE *SEVEN* DEPUTY MAYORS, CANDY. IF A CRISIS BREAKS OUT, GET JARDINE OR BENNINGTON TO HANDLE IT.
THERE ARE NO "IFS" IN THIS SITUATION, SIR, ONLY WHENS.
BESIDES, THOSE MEN ARE QUALIFIED TO DEAL WITH JUVENILE JUSTICE AND... AND *MENTAL HYGIENE,* NOT CITYWIDE DISASTERS.
NOTHING LIKE THAT IS GOING TO HAPPEN, CANDY. AFTER 9/11 AND THE GAS ATTACKS, OUR PEOPLE HAVE LEARNED HOW IMPORTANT IT IS TO TAKE CARE OF *EACH OTHER*.
IT'S A *NEW* NEW YORK.

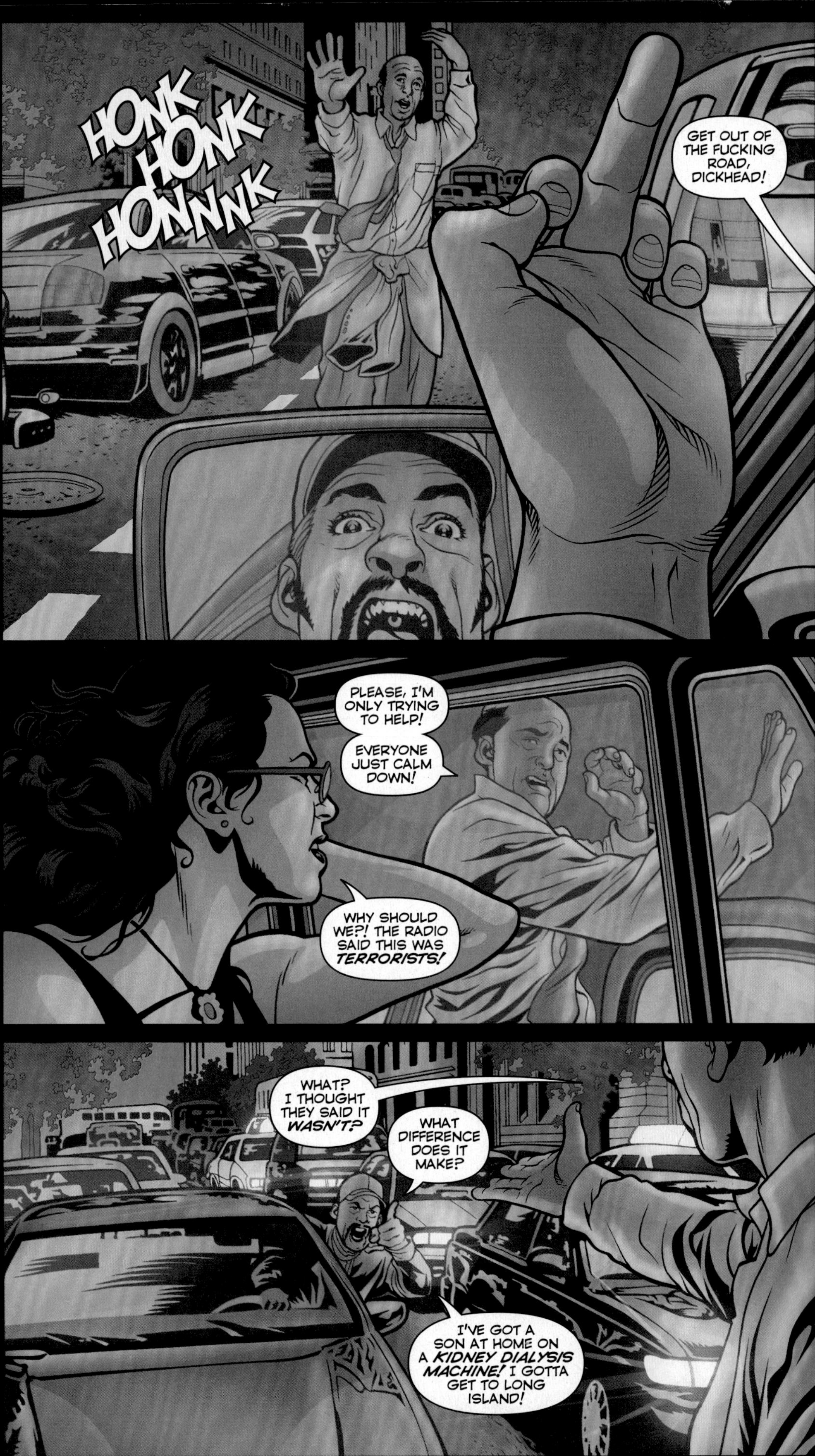
HONK HONK HONNNK
GET OUT OF THE FUCKING ROAD, DICKHEAD!
PLEASE, I'M ONLY TRYING TO HELP!
EVERYONE JUST CALM DOWN!
WHY SHOULD WE?! THE RADIO SAID THIS WAS TERRORISTS!
WHAT? I THOUGHT THEY SAID IT WASN'T?
WHAT DIFFERENCE DOES IT MAKE?
I'VE GOT A SON AT HOME ON A KIDNEY DIALYSIS MACHINE! I GOTTA GET TO LONG ISLAND!

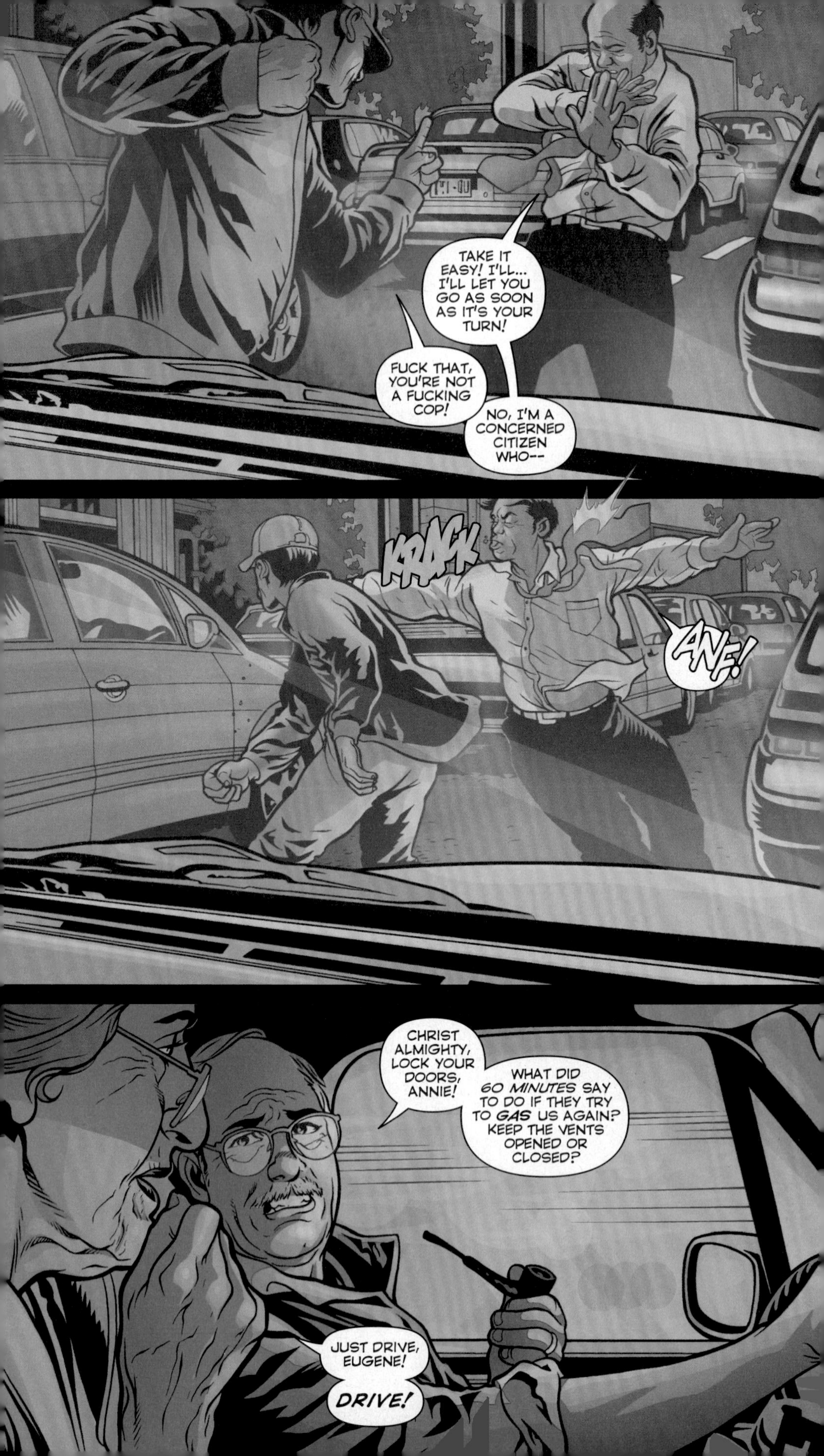
TAKE IT EASY! I'LL... I'LL LET YOU GO AS SOON AS IT'S YOUR TURN!
FUCK THAT, YOU'RE NOT A FUCKING COP!
NO, I'M A CONCERNED CITIZEN WHO--
KRACK
ANF!
CHRIST ALMIGHTY, LOCK YOUR DOORS, ANNIE!
WHAT DID *60 MINUTES* SAY TO DO IF THEY TRY TO *GAS* US AGAIN? KEEP THE VENTS OPENED OR CLOSED?
JUST DRIVE, EUGENE!
DRIVE!

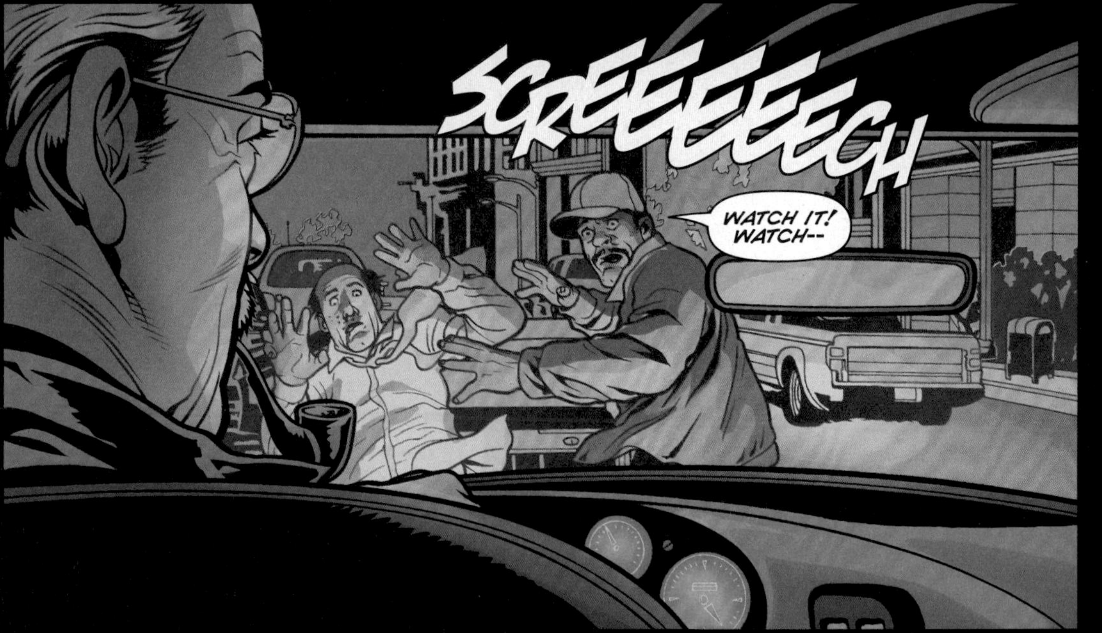
SCREEEEEECH
WATCH IT! WATCH--

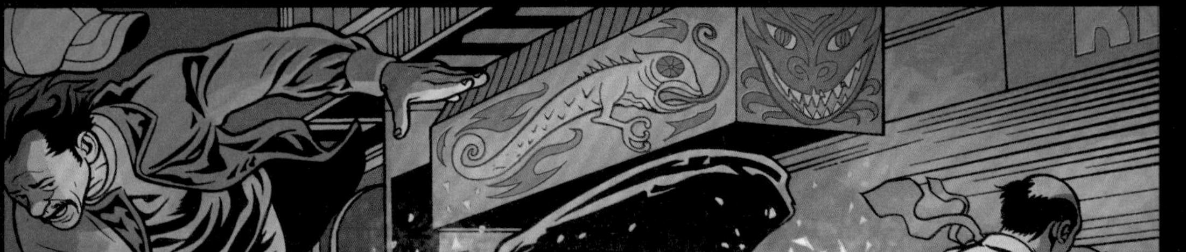

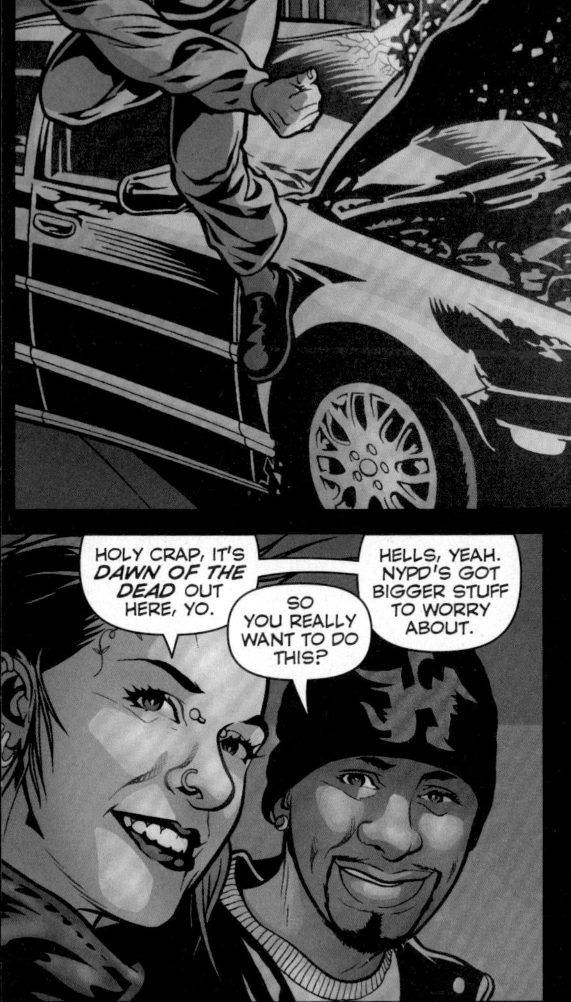
HOLY CRAP, IT'S *DAWN OF THE DEAD* OUT HERE, YO.
SO YOU REALLY WANT TO DO THIS?
HELLS, YEAH. NYPD'S GOT BIGGER STUFF TO WORRY ABOUT.

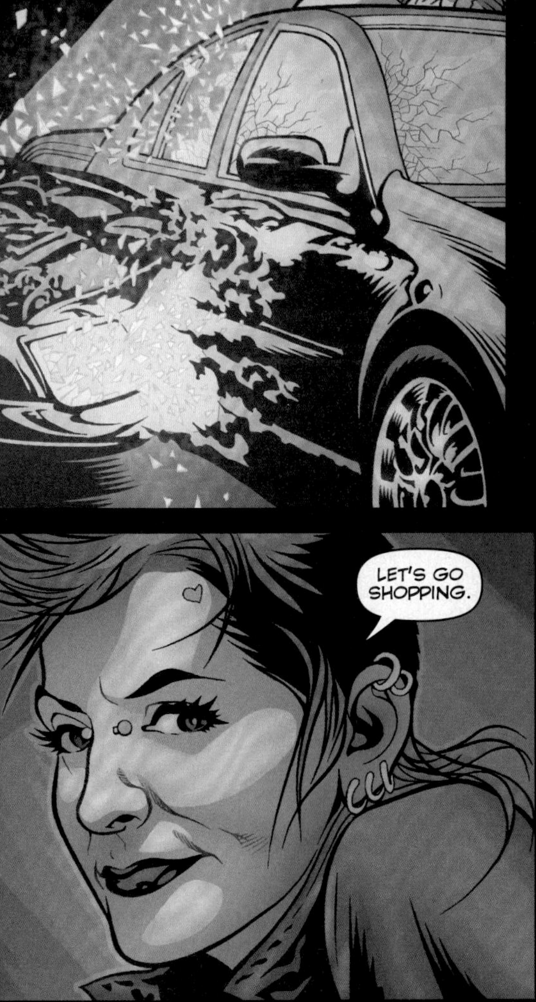
LET'S GO SHOPPING.

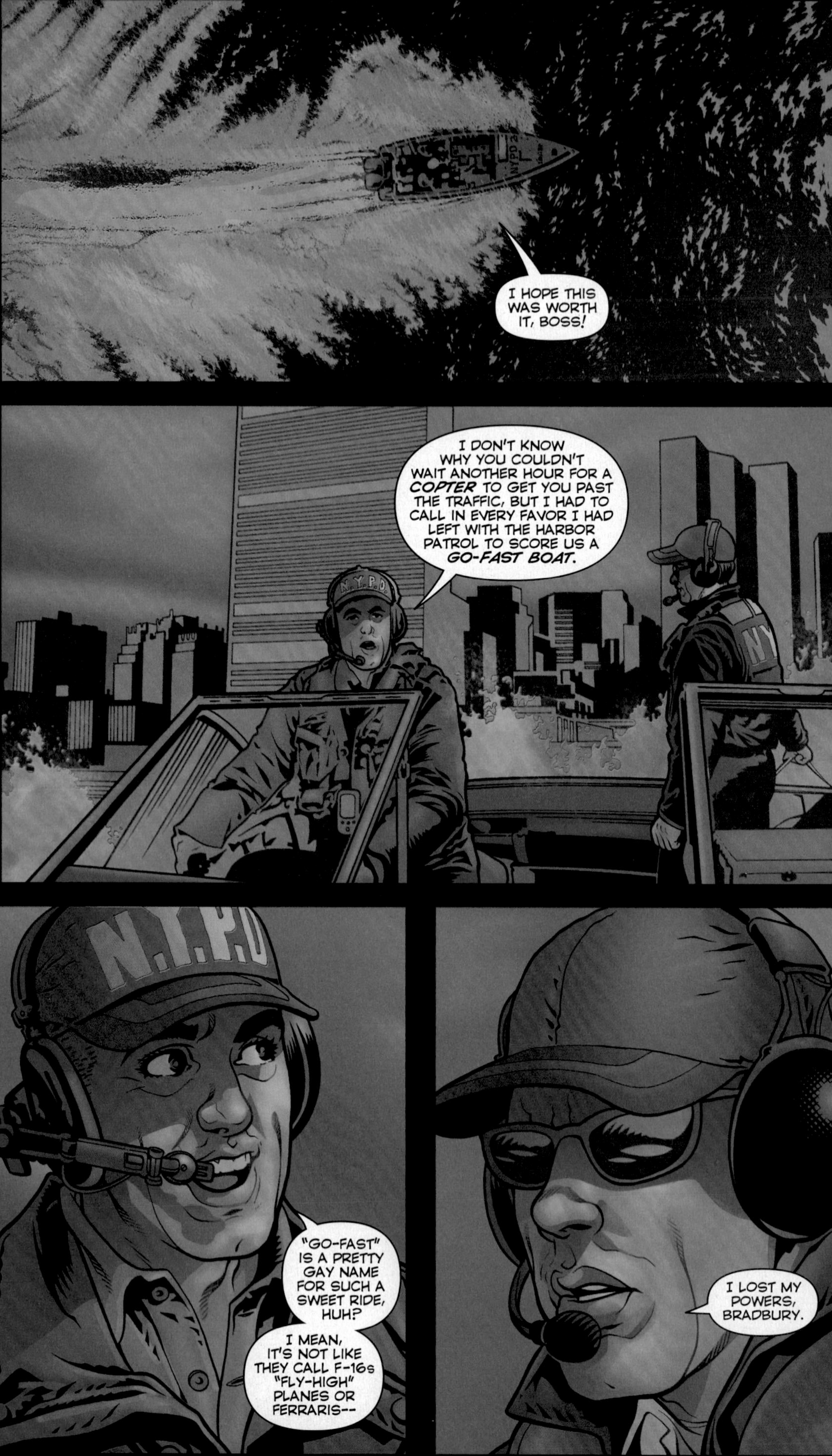
I HOPE THIS WAS WORTH IT, BOSS!
I DON'T KNOW WHY YOU COULDN'T WAIT ANOTHER HOUR FOR A *COPTER* TO GET YOU PAST THE TRAFFIC, BUT I HAD TO CALL IN EVERY FAVOR I HAD LEFT WITH THE HARBOR PATROL TO SCORE US A *GO-FAST BOAT*.
N.Y.P.D.
N.Y.P.D
"GO-FAST" IS A PRETTY GAY NAME FOR SUCH A SWEET RIDE, HUH?
I MEAN, IT'S NOT LIKE THEY CALL F-16s "FLY-HIGH" PLANES OR FERRARIS--
I LOST MY POWERS, BRADBURY.

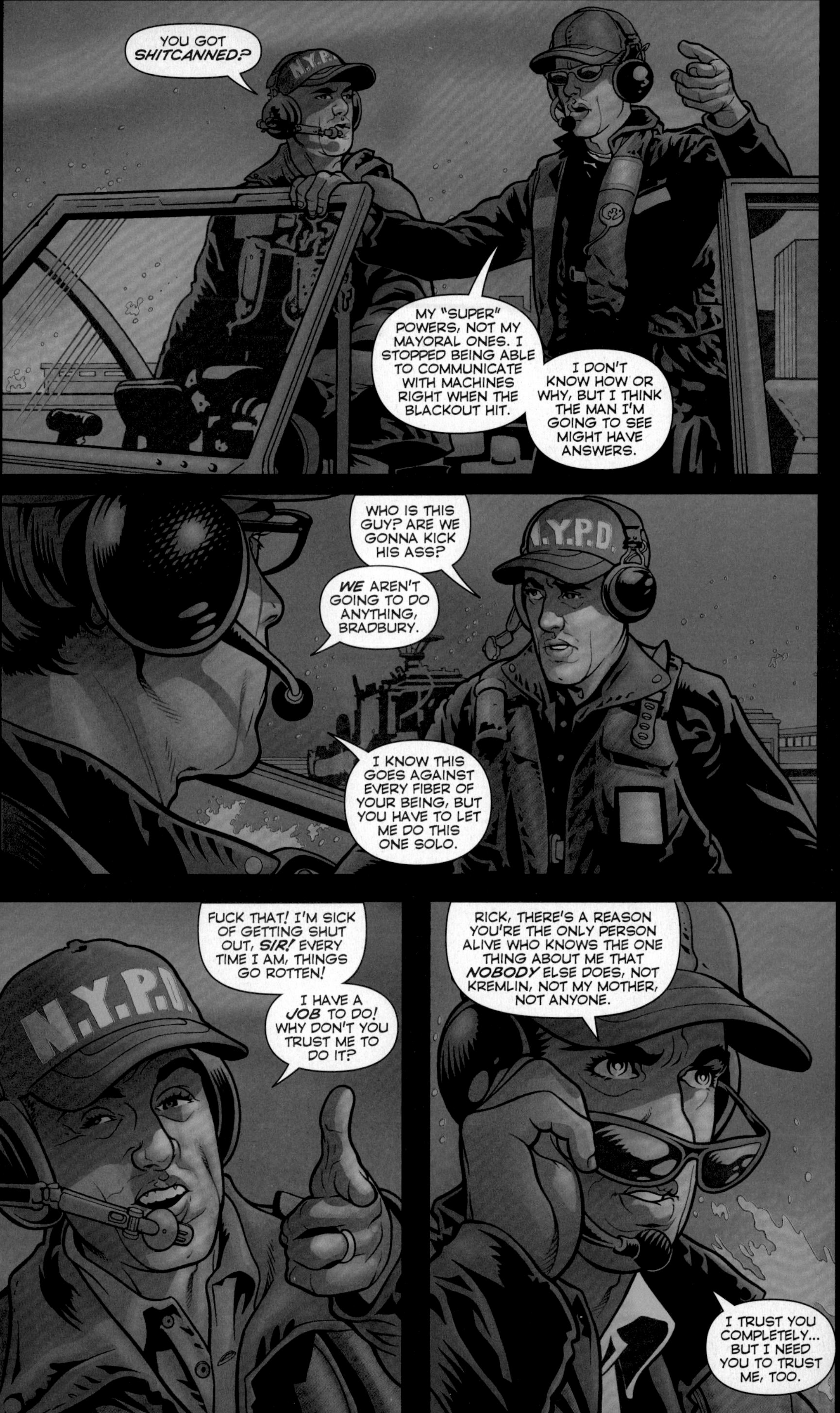
YOU GOT *SHITCANNED?*
MY "SUPER" POWERS, NOT MY MAYORAL ONES. I STOPPED BEING ABLE TO COMMUNICATE WITH MACHINES RIGHT WHEN THE BLACKOUT HIT.
I DON'T KNOW HOW OR WHY, BUT I THINK THE MAN I'M GOING TO SEE MIGHT HAVE ANSWERS.
WHO IS THIS GUY? ARE WE GONNA KICK HIS ASS?
WE AREN'T GOING TO DO ANYTHING, BRADBURY.
I KNOW THIS GOES AGAINST EVERY FIBER OF YOUR BEING, BUT YOU HAVE TO LET ME DO THIS ONE SOLO.
FUCK THAT! I'M SICK OF GETTING SHUT OUT, *SIR!* EVERY TIME I AM, THINGS GO ROTTEN!
I HAVE A *JOB* TO DO! WHY DON'T YOU TRUST ME TO DO IT?
RICK, THERE'S A REASON YOU'RE THE ONLY PERSON ALIVE WHO KNOWS THE ONE THING ABOUT ME THAT *NOBODY* ELSE DOES, NOT KREMLIN, NOT MY MOTHER, NOT ANYONE.
I TRUST YOU COMPLETELY... BUT I NEED YOU TO TRUST ME, TOO.

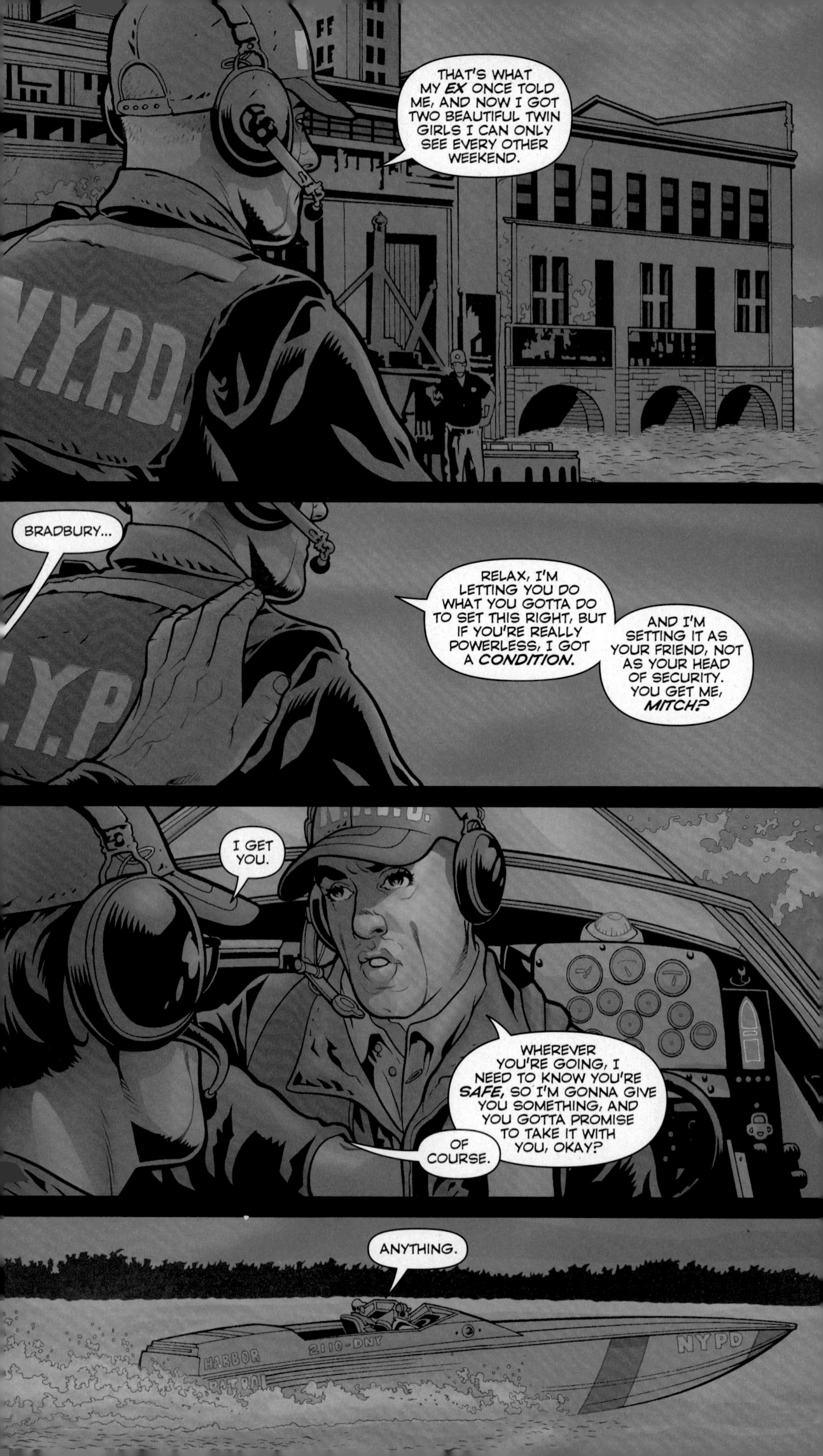
THAT'S WHAT MY EX ONCE TOLD ME, AND NOW I GOT TWO BEAUTIFUL TWIN GIRLS I CAN ONLY SEE EVERY OTHER WEEKEND.
N.Y.P.D.
BRADBURY...
RELAX, I'M LETTING YOU DO WHAT YOU GOTTA DO TO SET THIS RIGHT, BUT IF YOU'RE REALLY POWERLESS, I GOT A CONDITION.
AND I'M SETTING IT AS YOUR FRIEND, NOT AS YOUR HEAD OF SECURITY. YOU GET ME, MITCH?
I GET YOU.
WHEREVER YOU'RE GOING, I NEED TO KNOW YOU'RE SAFE, SO I'M GONNA GIVE YOU SOMETHING, AND YOU GOTTA PROMISE TO TAKE IT WITH YOU, OKAY?
OF COURSE.
ANYTHING.
2110-DNY
HARBOR PATROL
NYPD

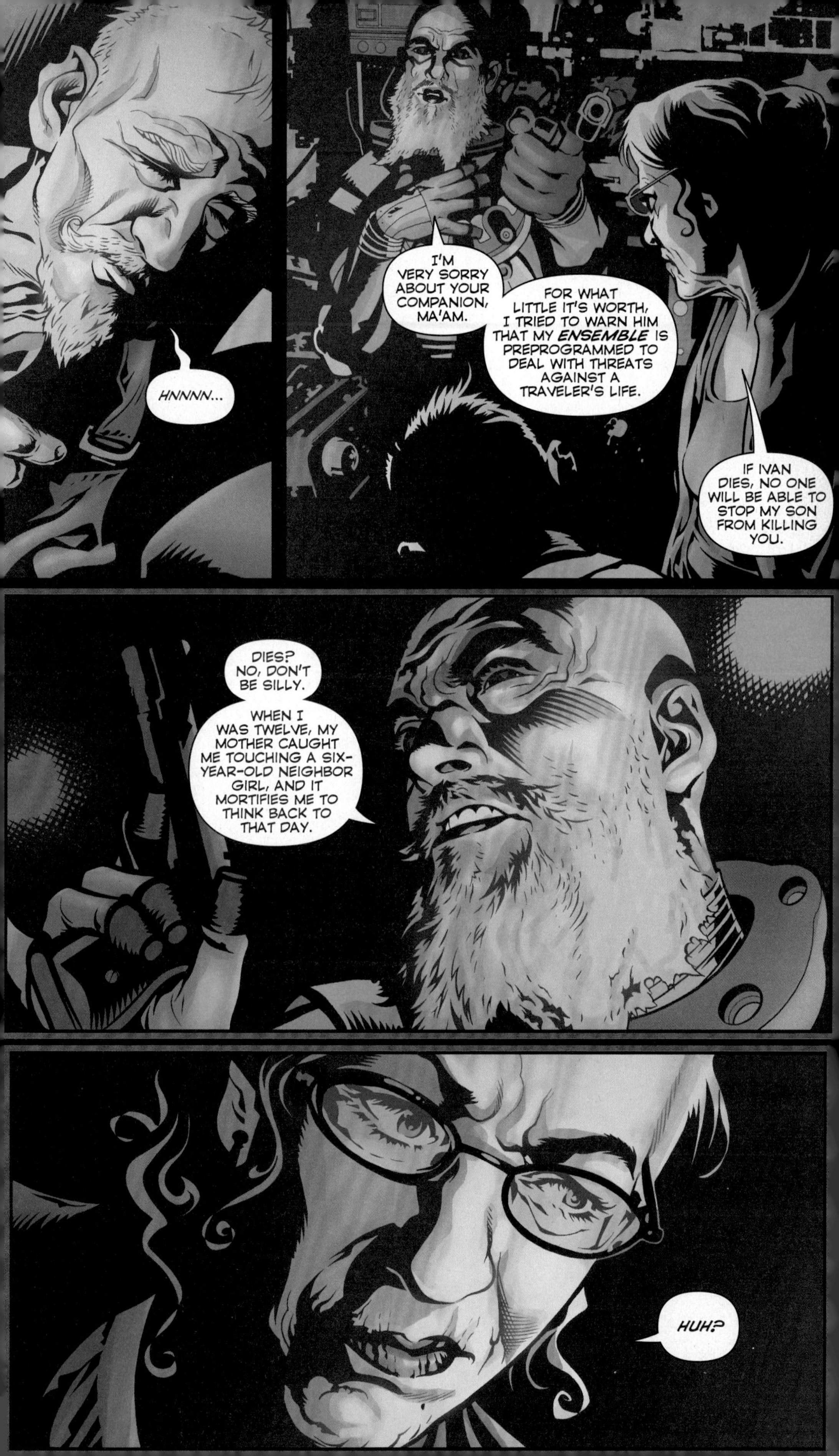
HNNNN...
I'M VERY SORRY ABOUT YOUR COMPANION, MA'AM.
FOR WHAT LITTLE IT'S WORTH, I TRIED TO WARN HIM THAT MY *ENSEMBLE* IS PREPROGRAMMED TO DEAL WITH THREATS AGAINST A TRAVELER'S LIFE.
IF IVAN DIES, NO ONE WILL BE ABLE TO STOP MY SON FROM KILLING YOU.
DIES? NO, DON'T BE SILLY.
WHEN I WAS TWELVE, MY MOTHER CAUGHT ME TOUCHING A SIX-YEAR-OLD NEIGHBOR GIRL, AND IT MORTIFIES ME TO THINK BACK TO THAT DAY.
HUH?

SORRY, DID I LOSE MY TRAIN OF THOUGHT? ALERT ME IF I DO THAT AGAIN, BHOTA.

EVERY OTHER SENTENCE FEELS LIKE I'M DRIFTING OFF TO SLEEP, YOU KNOW? IT'S... *CONFUSING* BEING HERE.

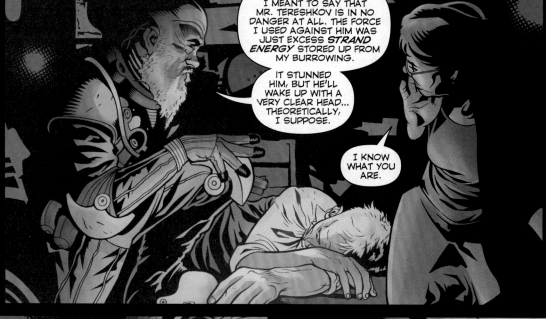

I MEANT TO SAY THAT MR. TERESHKOV IS IN NO DANGER AT ALL. THE FORCE I USED AGAINST HIM WAS JUST EXCESS *STRAND ENERGY* STORED UP FROM MY BURROWING.

IT STUNNED HIM, BUT HE'LL WAKE UP WITH A VERY CLEAR HEAD... THEORETICALLY, I SUPPOSE.

I KNOW WHAT YOU ARE.

YES, YES, "I'M INSANE," RIGHT?

IF THAT'S WHAT YOU NEED TO BELIEVE, BY ALL MEANS, PLEASE BE MY GUEST.

NO, YOU'RE FROM THE *FUTURE*.

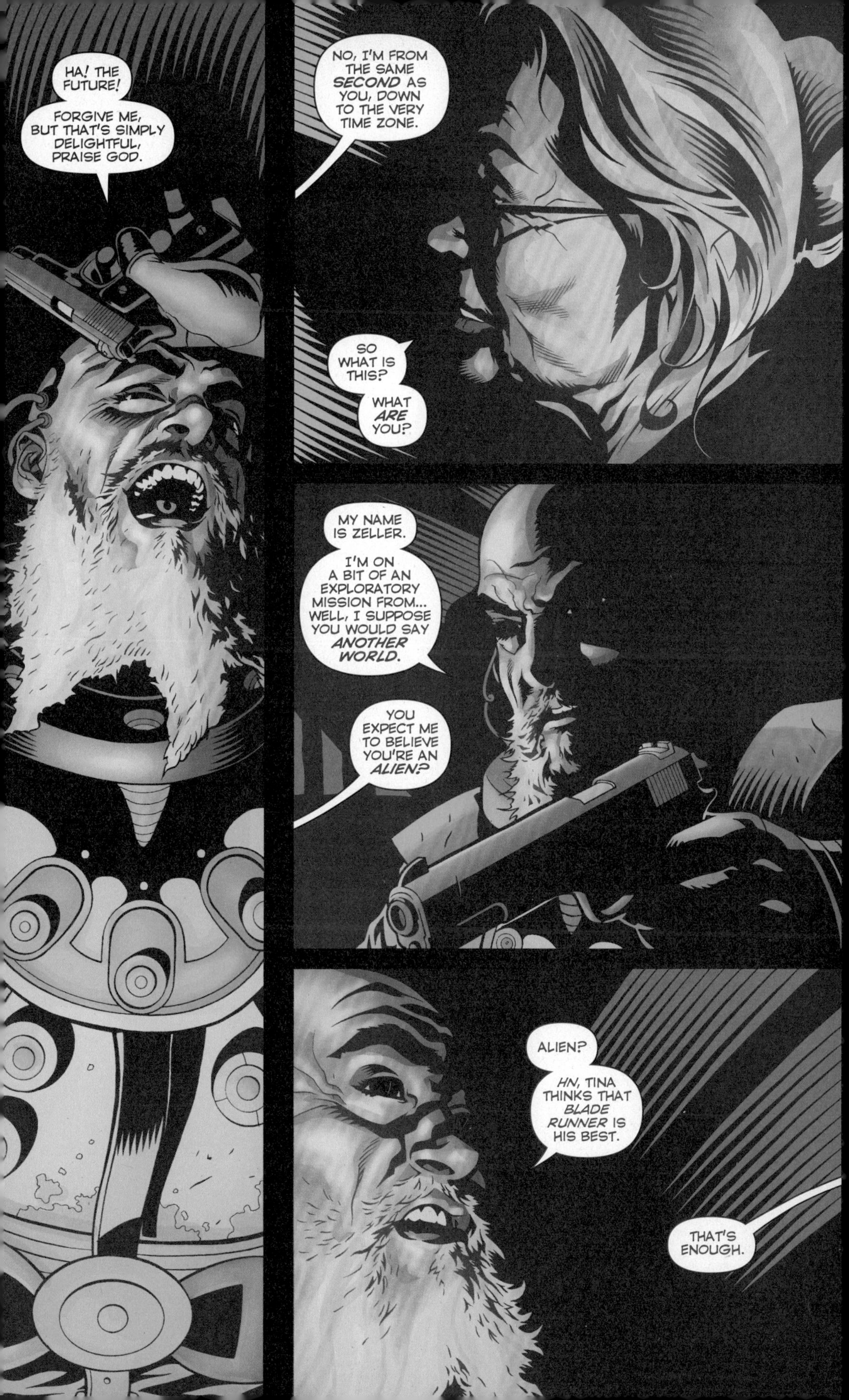
HA! THE FUTURE!
FORGIVE ME, BUT THAT'S SIMPLY DELIGHTFUL, PRAISE GOD.
NO, I'M FROM THE SAME SECOND AS YOU, DOWN TO THE VERY TIME ZONE.
SO WHAT IS THIS?
WHAT ARE YOU?
MY NAME IS ZELLER.
I'M ON A BIT OF AN EXPLORATORY MISSION FROM... WELL, I SUPPOSE YOU WOULD SAY ANOTHER WORLD.
YOU EXPECT ME TO BELIEVE YOU'RE AN ALIEN?
ALIEN?
HN, TINA THINKS THAT BLADE RUNNER IS HIS BEST.
THAT'S ENOUGH.

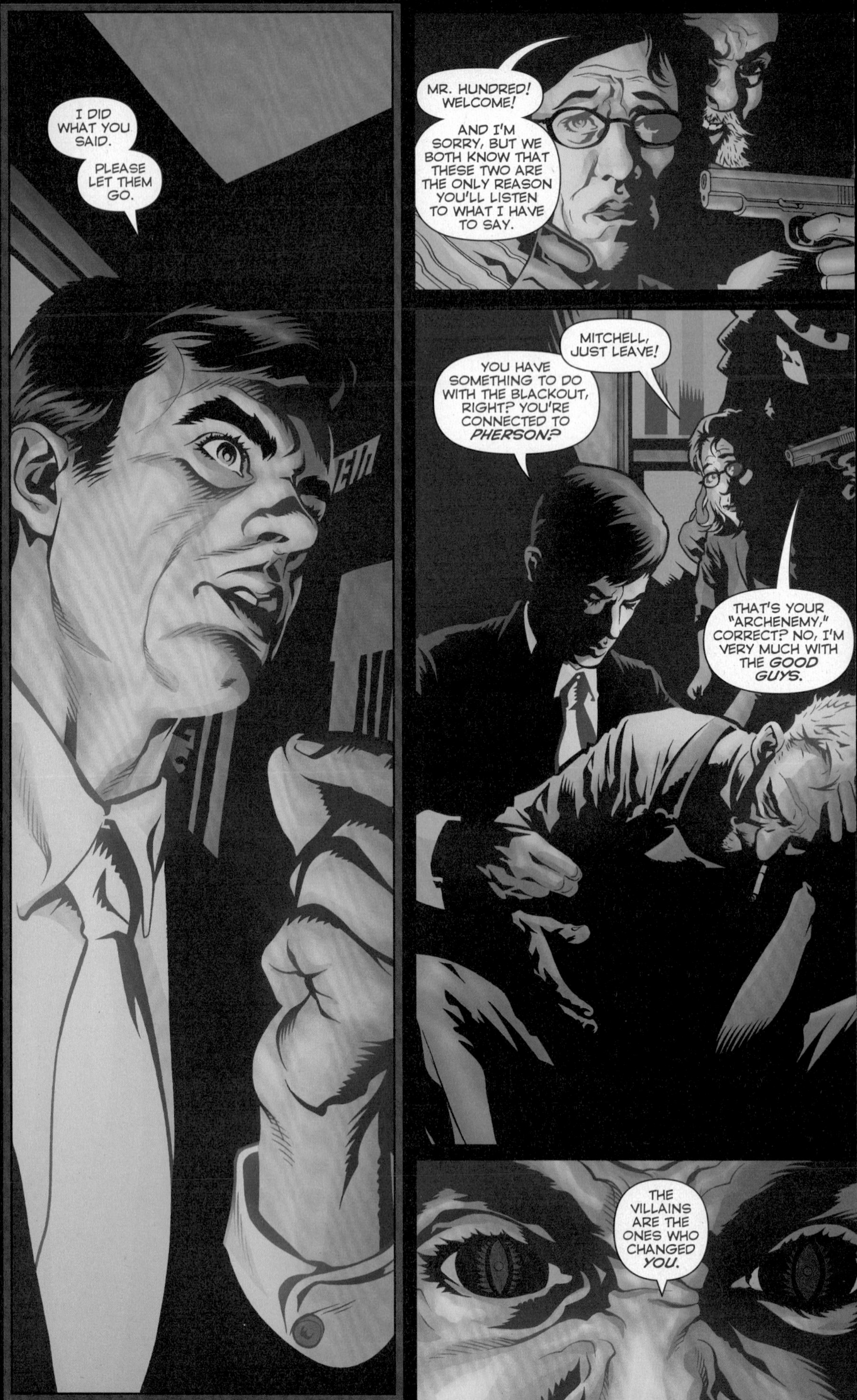
I DID WHAT YOU SAID.
PLEASE LET THEM GO.
MR. HUNDRED! WELCOME!
AND I'M SORRY, BUT WE BOTH KNOW THAT THESE TWO ARE THE ONLY REASON YOU'LL LISTEN TO WHAT I HAVE TO SAY.
MITCHELL, JUST LEAVE!
YOU HAVE SOMETHING TO DO WITH THE BLACKOUT, RIGHT? YOU'RE CONNECTED TO *PHERSON?*
THAT'S YOUR "ARCHENEMY," CORRECT? NO, I'M VERY MUCH WITH THE *GOOD GUYS.*
THE VILLAINS ARE THE ONES WHO CHANGED *YOU.*

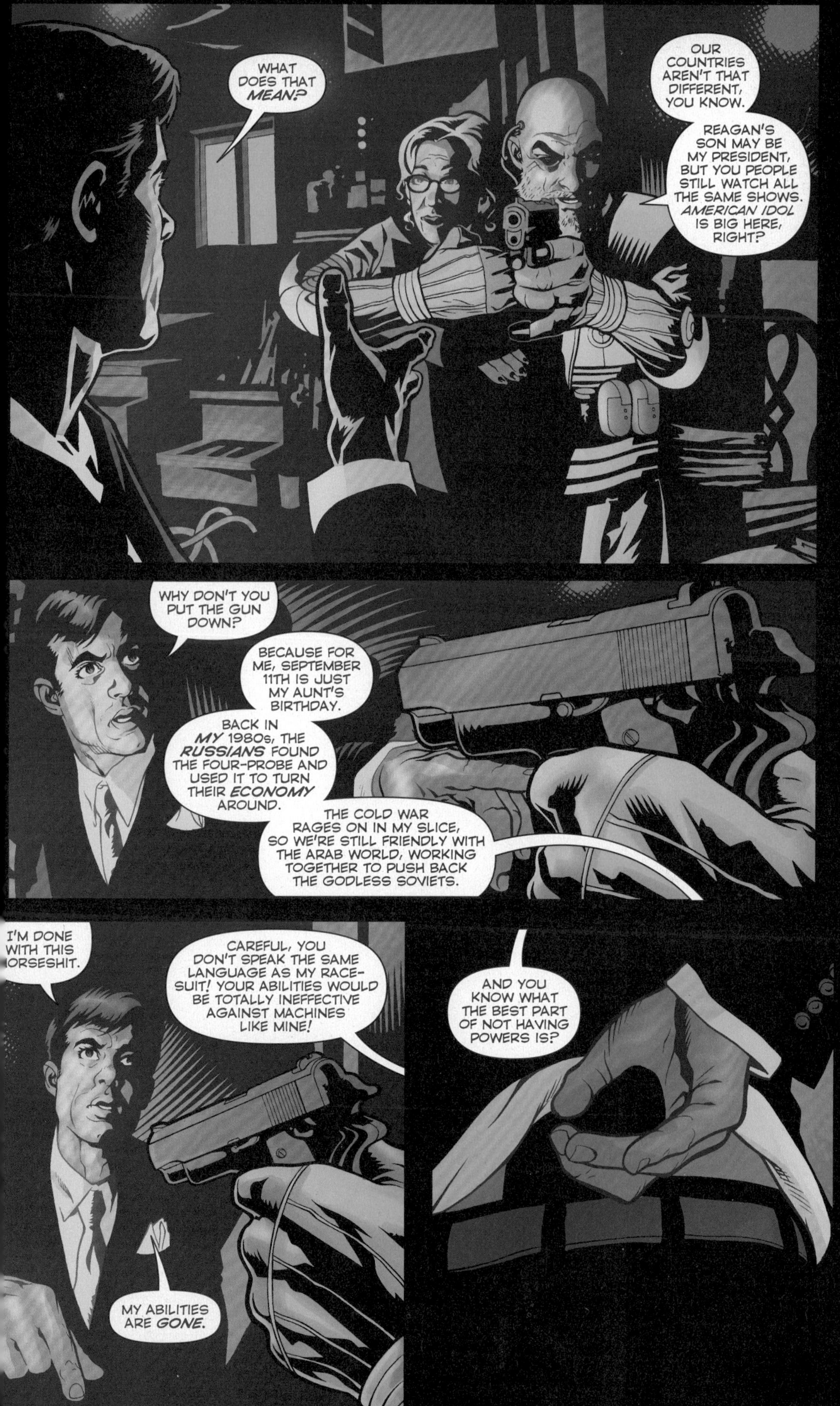
WHAT DOES THAT MEAN?
OUR COUNTRIES AREN'T THAT DIFFERENT, YOU KNOW.
REAGAN'S SON MAY BE MY PRESIDENT, BUT YOU PEOPLE STILL WATCH ALL THE SAME SHOWS. AMERICAN IDOL IS BIG HERE, RIGHT?
WHY DON'T YOU PUT THE GUN DOWN?
BECAUSE FOR ME, SEPTEMBER 11TH IS JUST MY AUNT'S BIRTHDAY.
BACK IN MY 1980s, THE RUSSIANS FOUND THE FOUR-PROBE AND USED IT TO TURN THEIR ECONOMY AROUND.
THE COLD WAR RAGES ON IN MY SLICE, SO WE'RE STILL FRIENDLY WITH THE ARAB WORLD, WORKING TOGETHER TO PUSH BACK THE GODLESS SOVIETS.
I'M DONE WITH THIS ORSESHIT.
CAREFUL, YOU DON'T SPEAK THE SAME LANGUAGE AS MY RACE-SUIT! YOUR ABILITIES WOULD BE TOTALLY INEFFECTIVE AGAINST MACHINES LIKE MINE!
MY ABILITIES ARE GONE.
AND YOU KNOW WHAT THE BEST PART OF NOT HAVING POWERS IS?

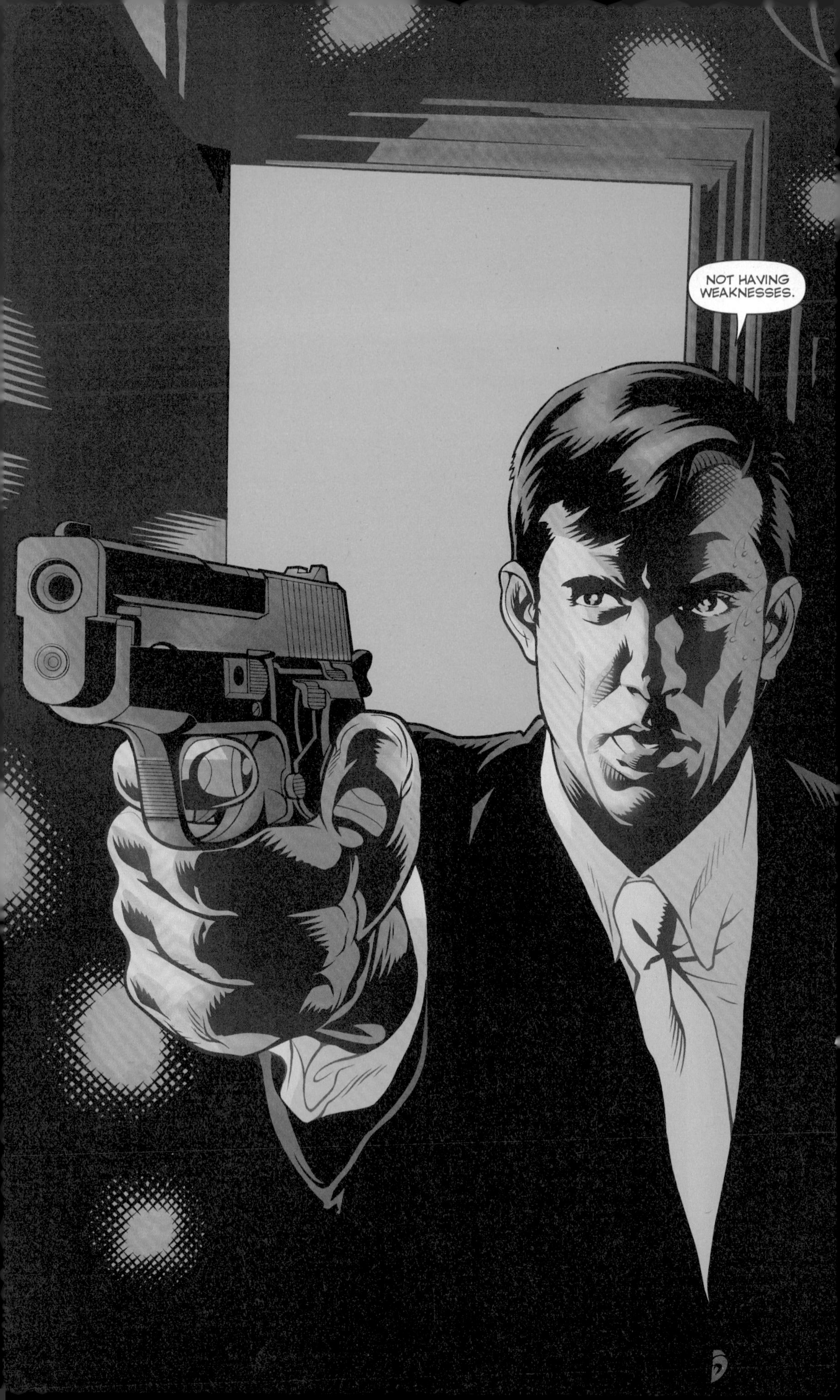
NOT HAVING WEAKNESSES.

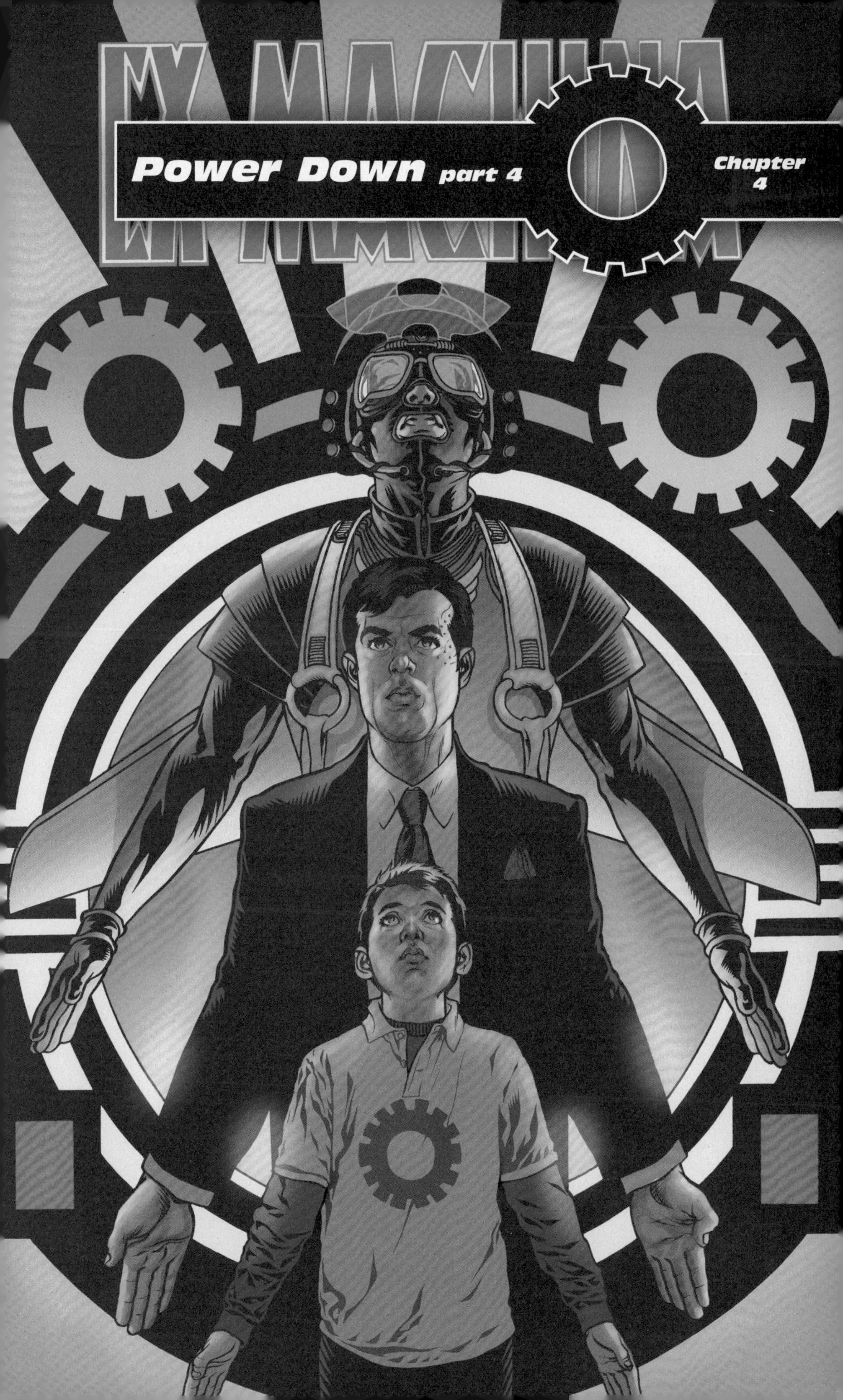
Power Down part 4
Chapter 4

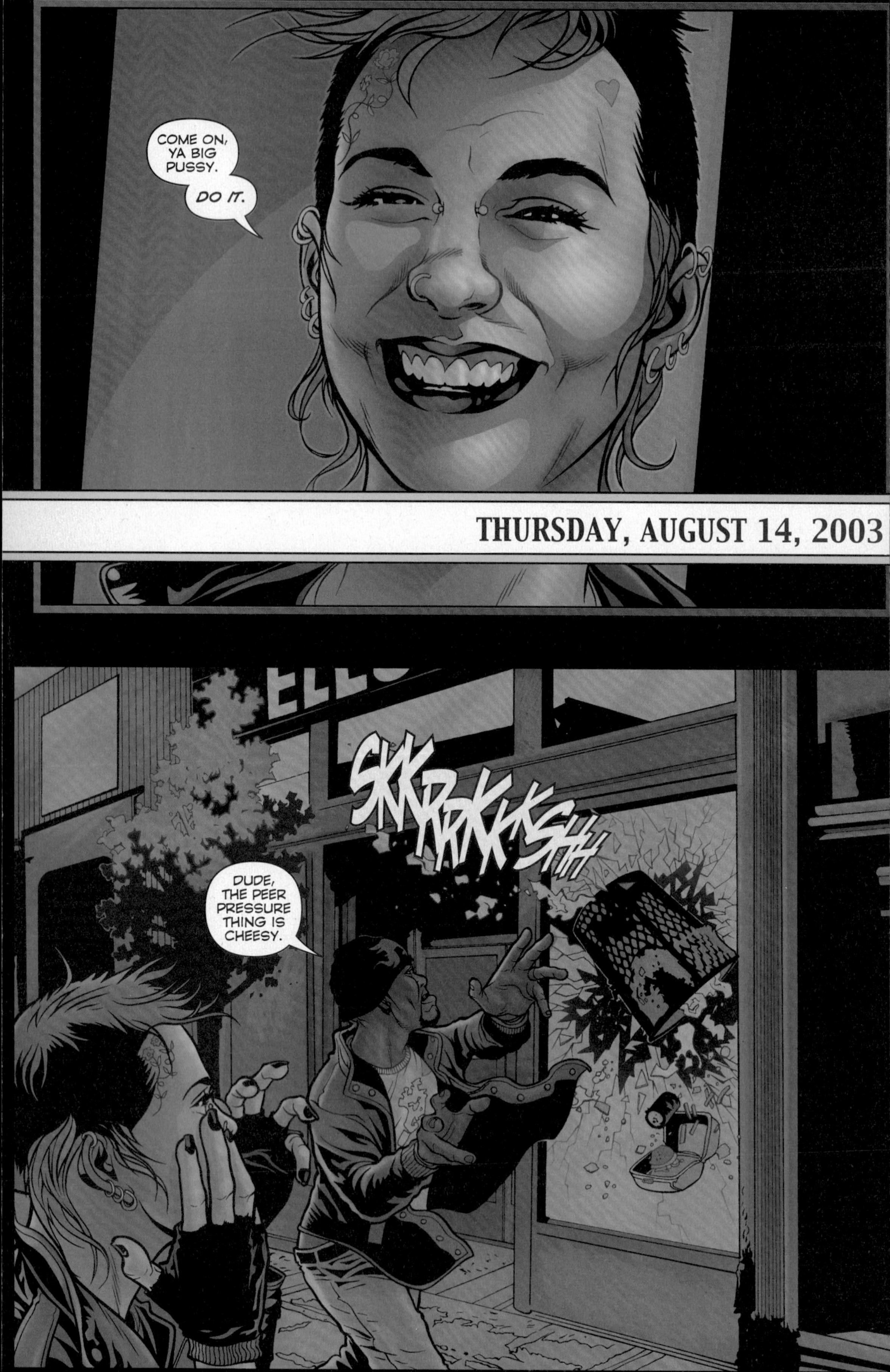
COME ON, YA BIG PUSSY.
DO IT.
THURSDAY, AUGUST 14, 2003
DUDE, THE PEER PRESSURE THING IS CHEESY.

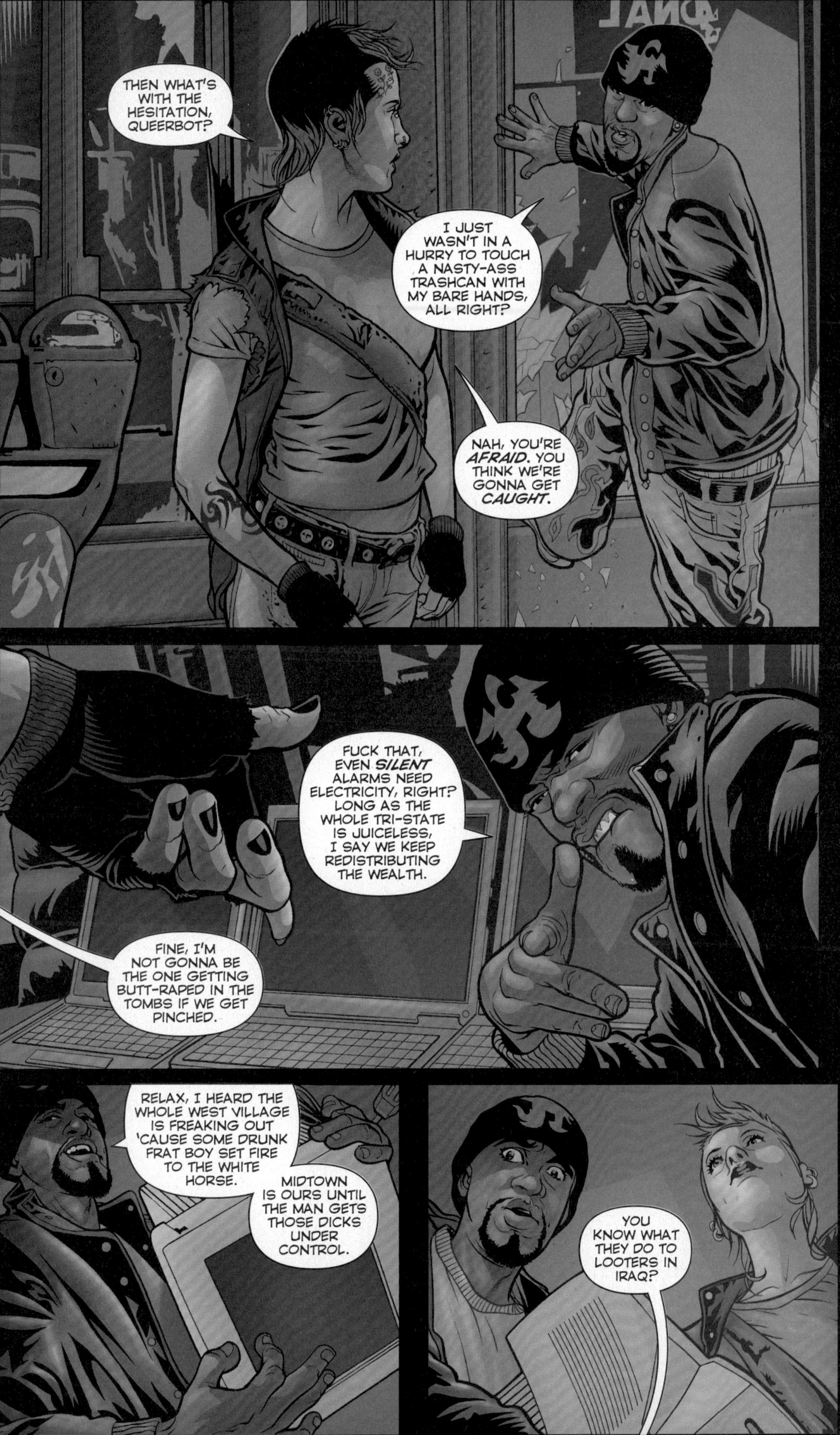
THEN WHAT'S WITH THE HESITATION, QUEERBOT?
I JUST WASN'T IN A HURRY TO TOUCH A NASTY-ASS TRASHCAN WITH MY BARE HANDS, ALL RIGHT?
NAH, YOU'RE *AFRAID*. YOU THINK WE'RE GONNA GET *CAUGHT*.
FUCK THAT, EVEN *SILENT* ALARMS NEED ELECTRICITY, RIGHT? LONG AS THE WHOLE TRI-STATE IS JUICELESS, I SAY WE KEEP REDISTRIBUTING THE WEALTH.
FINE, I'M NOT GONNA BE THE ONE GETTING BUTT-RAPED IN THE TOMBS IF WE GET PINCHED.
RELAX, I HEARD THE WHOLE WEST VILLAGE IS FREAKING OUT 'CAUSE SOME DRUNK FRAT BOY SET FIRE TO THE WHITE HORSE.
MIDTOWN IS OURS UNTIL THE MAN GETS THOSE DICKS UNDER CONTROL.
YOU KNOW WHAT THEY DO TO LOOTERS IN IRAQ?

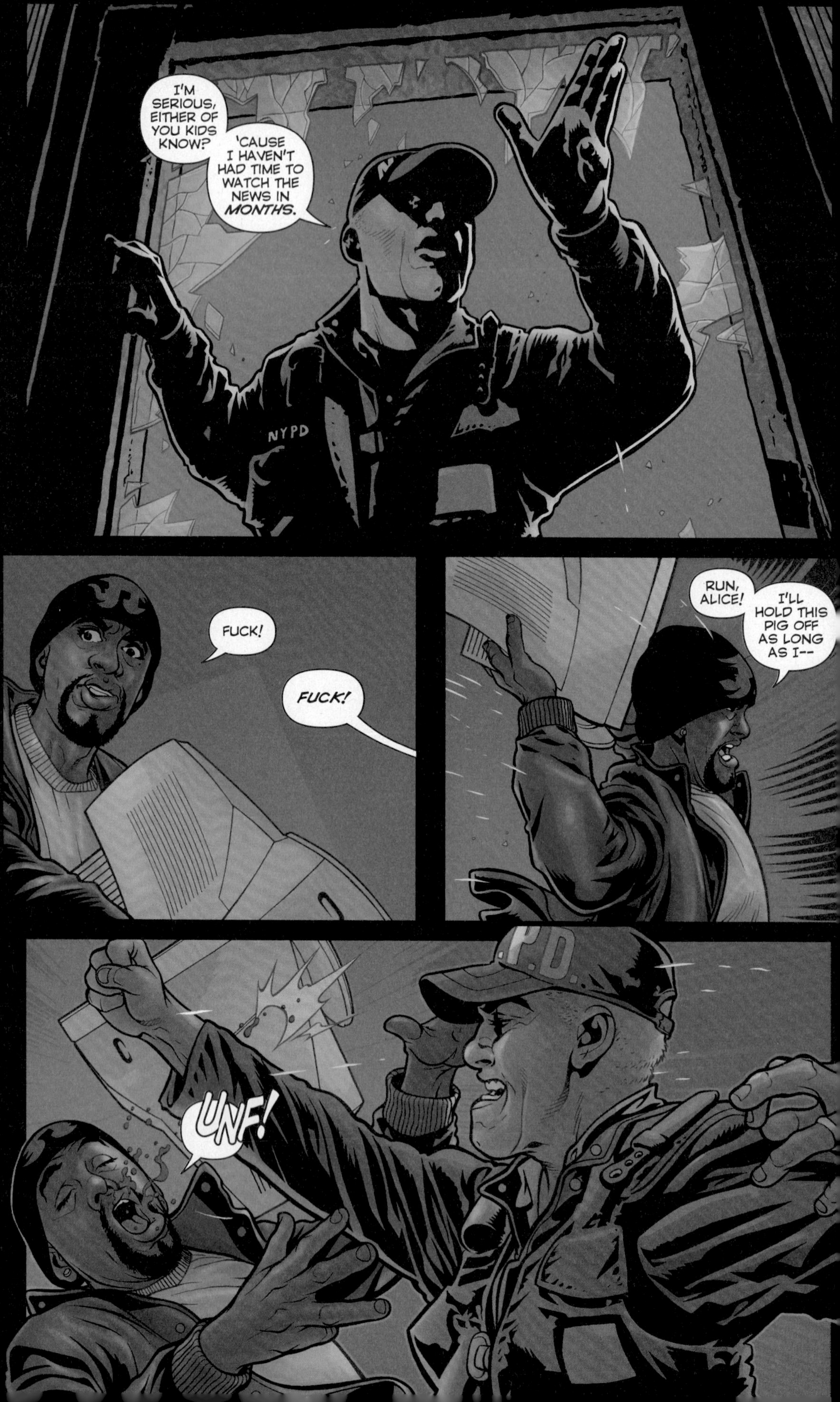
I'M SERIOUS, EITHER OF YOU KIDS KNOW?
'CAUSE I HAVEN'T HAD TIME TO WATCH THE NEWS IN *MONTHS*.
NYPD
FUCK!
FUCK!
RUN, ALICE!
I'LL HOLD THIS PIG OFF AS LONG AS I--
UNF!

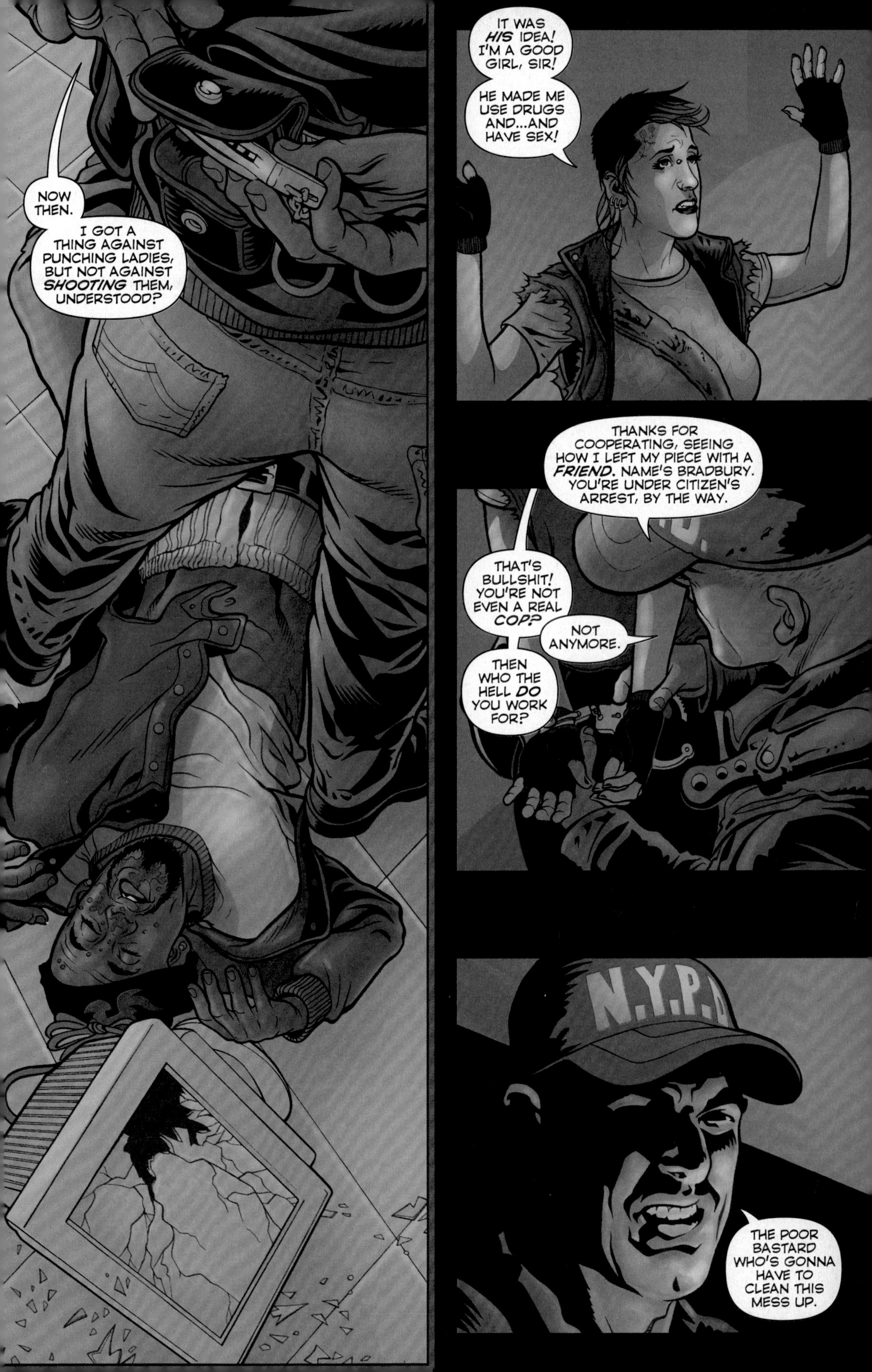
NOW THEN.
I GOT A THING AGAINST PUNCHING LADIES, BUT NOT AGAINST *SHOOTING* THEM, UNDERSTOOD?
IT WAS *HIS* IDEA! I'M A GOOD GIRL, SIR!
HE MADE ME USE DRUGS AND...AND HAVE SEX!
THANKS FOR COOPERATING, SEEING HOW I LEFT MY PIECE WITH A *FRIEND*. NAME'S BRADBURY. YOU'RE UNDER CITIZEN'S ARREST, BY THE WAY.
THAT'S BULLSHIT! YOU'RE NOT EVEN A REAL *COP?*
NOT ANYMORE.
THEN WHO THE HELL *DO* YOU WORK FOR?
N.Y.P.D.
THE POOR BASTARD WHO'S GONNA HAVE TO CLEAN THIS MESS UP.

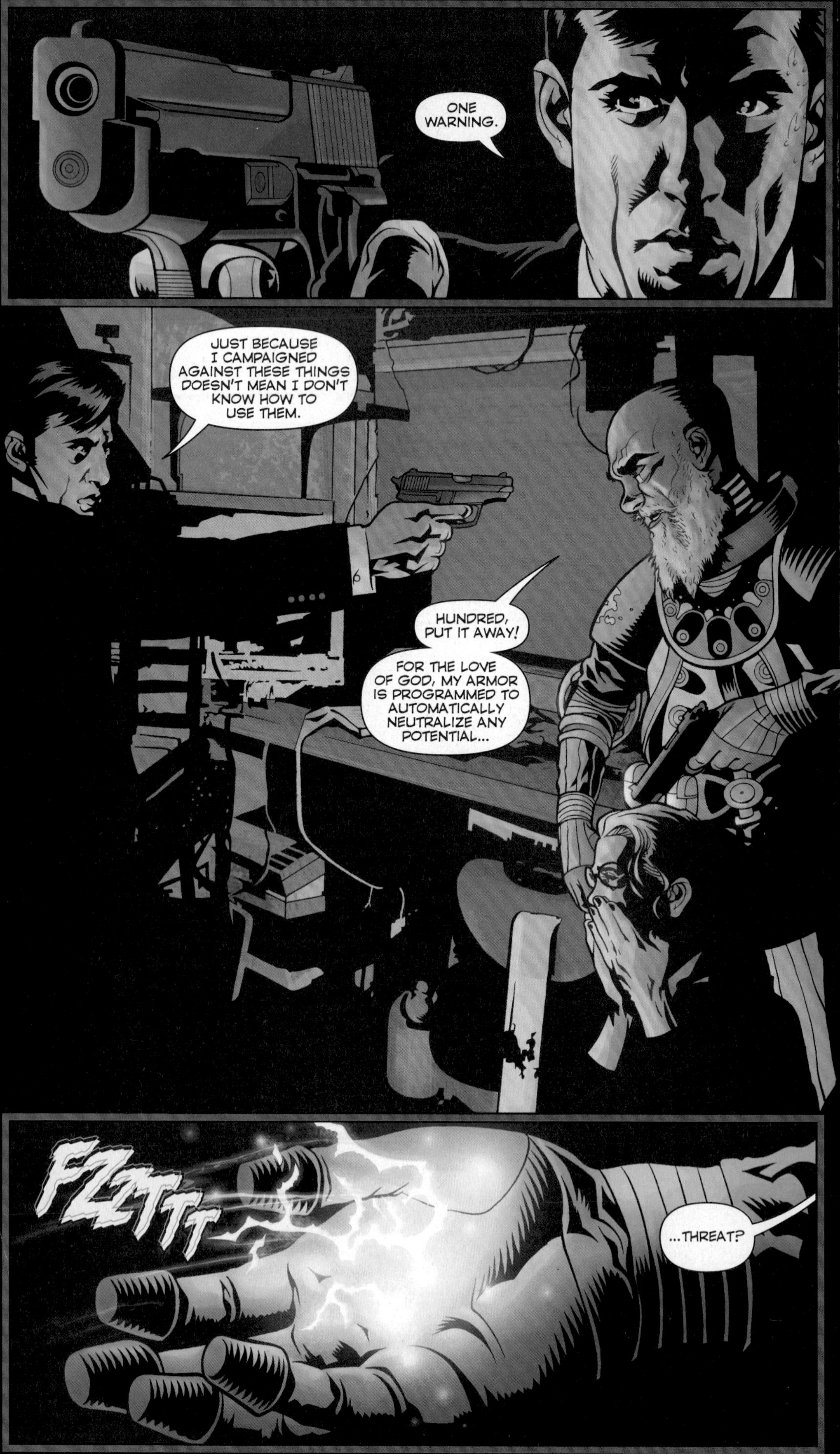
ONE WARNING.
JUST BECAUSE I CAMPAIGNED AGAINST THESE THINGS DOESN'T MEAN I DON'T KNOW HOW TO USE THEM.
HUNDRED, PUT IT AWAY!
FOR THE LOVE OF GOD, MY ARMOR IS PROGRAMMED TO AUTOMATICALLY NEUTRALIZE ANY POTENTIAL...
FZZTTT
...THREAT?

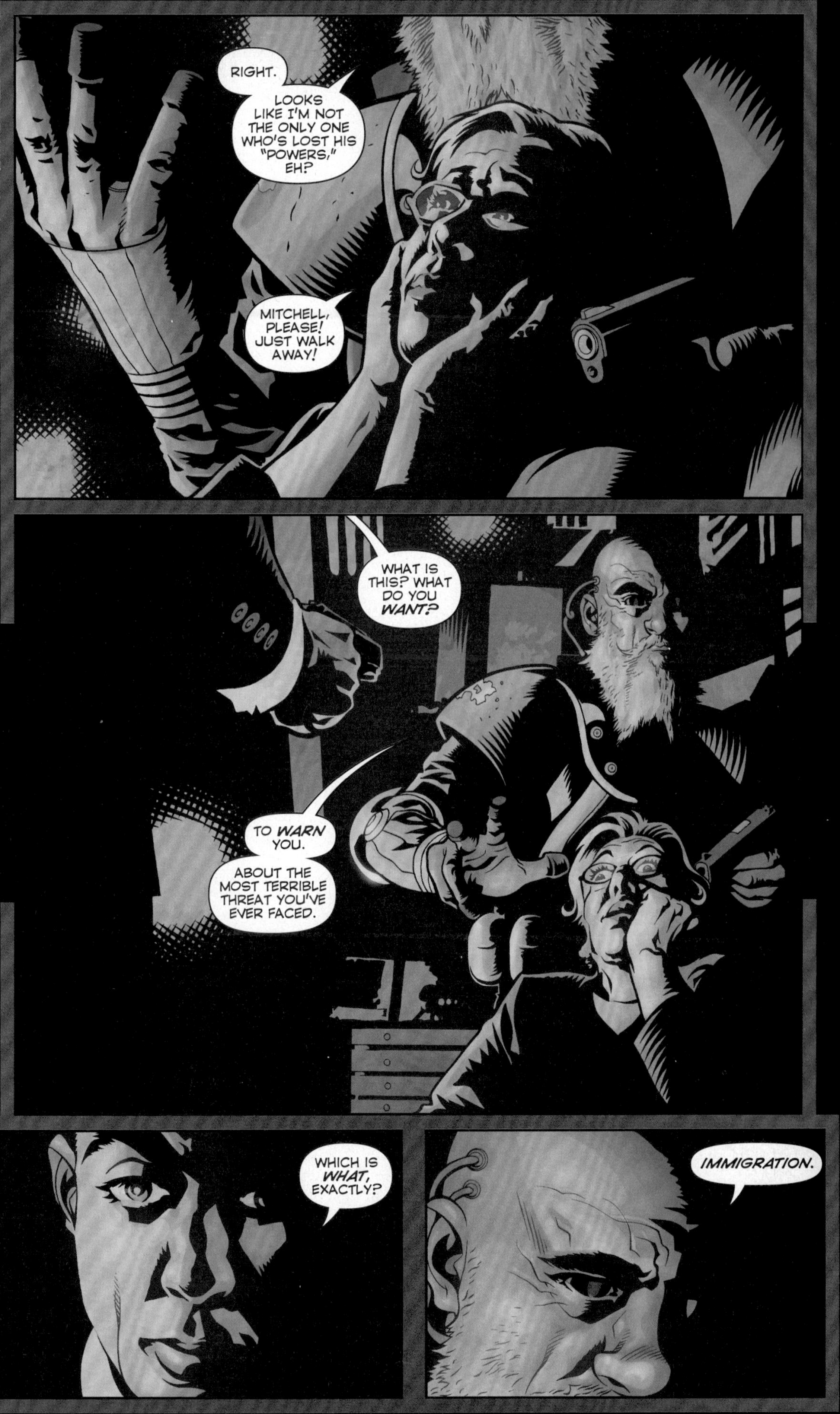
RIGHT.
LOOKS LIKE I'M NOT THE ONLY ONE WHO'S LOST HIS "POWERS," EH?
MITCHELL, PLEASE! JUST WALK AWAY!
WHAT IS THIS? WHAT DO YOU WANT?
TO WARN YOU.
ABOUT THE MOST TERRIBLE THREAT YOU'VE EVER FACED.
WHICH IS WHAT, EXACTLY?
IMMIGRATION.

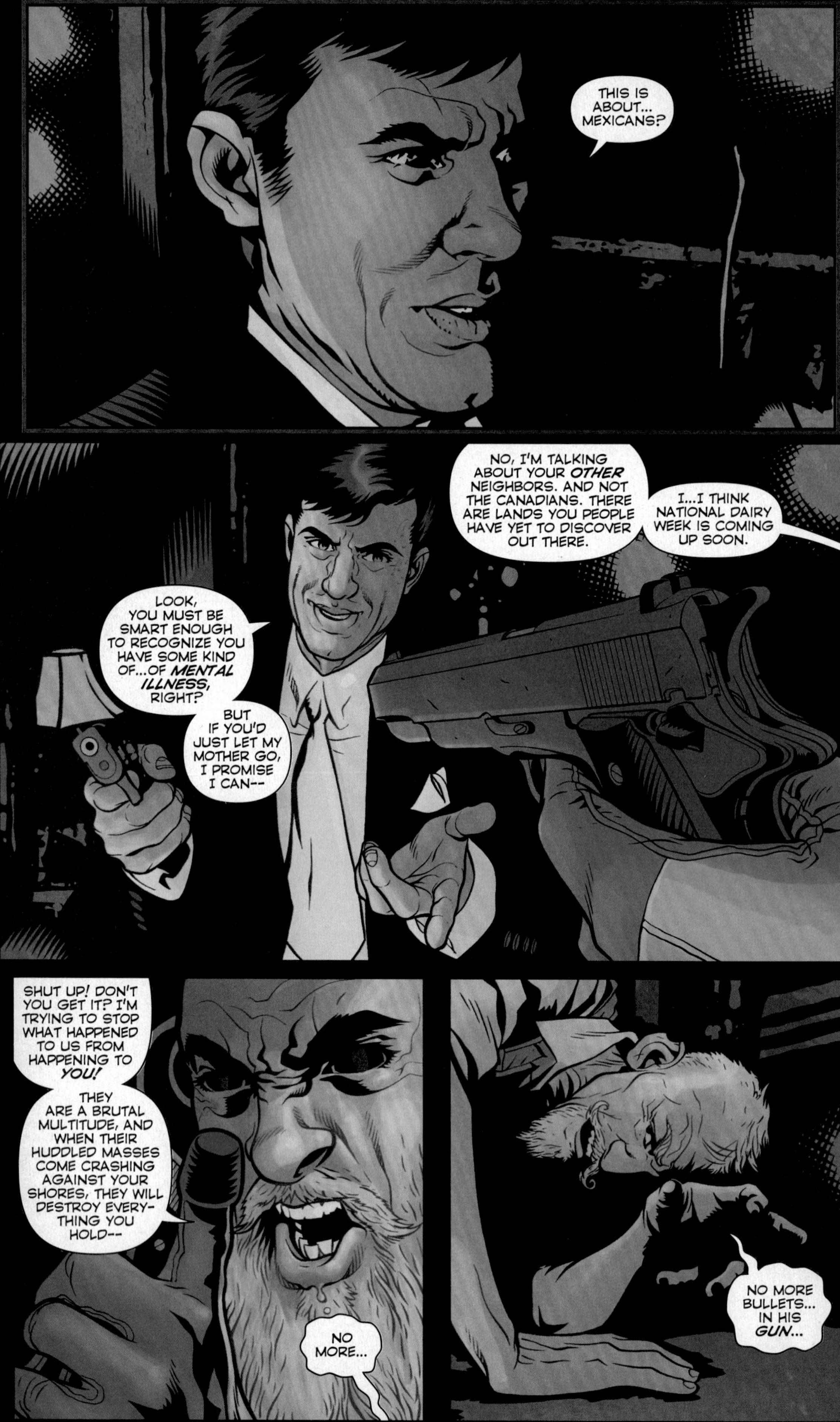
THIS IS ABOUT... MEXICANS?
NO, I'M TALKING ABOUT YOUR *OTHER* NEIGHBORS. AND NOT THE CANADIANS. THERE ARE LANDS YOU PEOPLE HAVE YET TO DISCOVER OUT THERE.
I...I THINK NATIONAL DAIRY WEEK IS COMING UP SOON.
LOOK, YOU MUST BE SMART ENOUGH TO RECOGNIZE YOU HAVE SOME KIND OF...OF *MENTAL ILLNESS,* RIGHT?
BUT IF YOU'D JUST LET MY MOTHER GO, I PROMISE I CAN--
SHUT UP! DON'T YOU GET IT? I'M TRYING TO STOP WHAT HAPPENED TO US FROM HAPPENING TO *YOU!*
THEY ARE A BRUTAL MULTITUDE, AND WHEN THEIR HUDDLED MASSES COME CRASHING AGAINST YOUR SHORES, THEY WILL DESTROY EVERY-THING YOU HOLD--
NO MORE...
NO MORE BULLETS... IN HIS *GUN...*

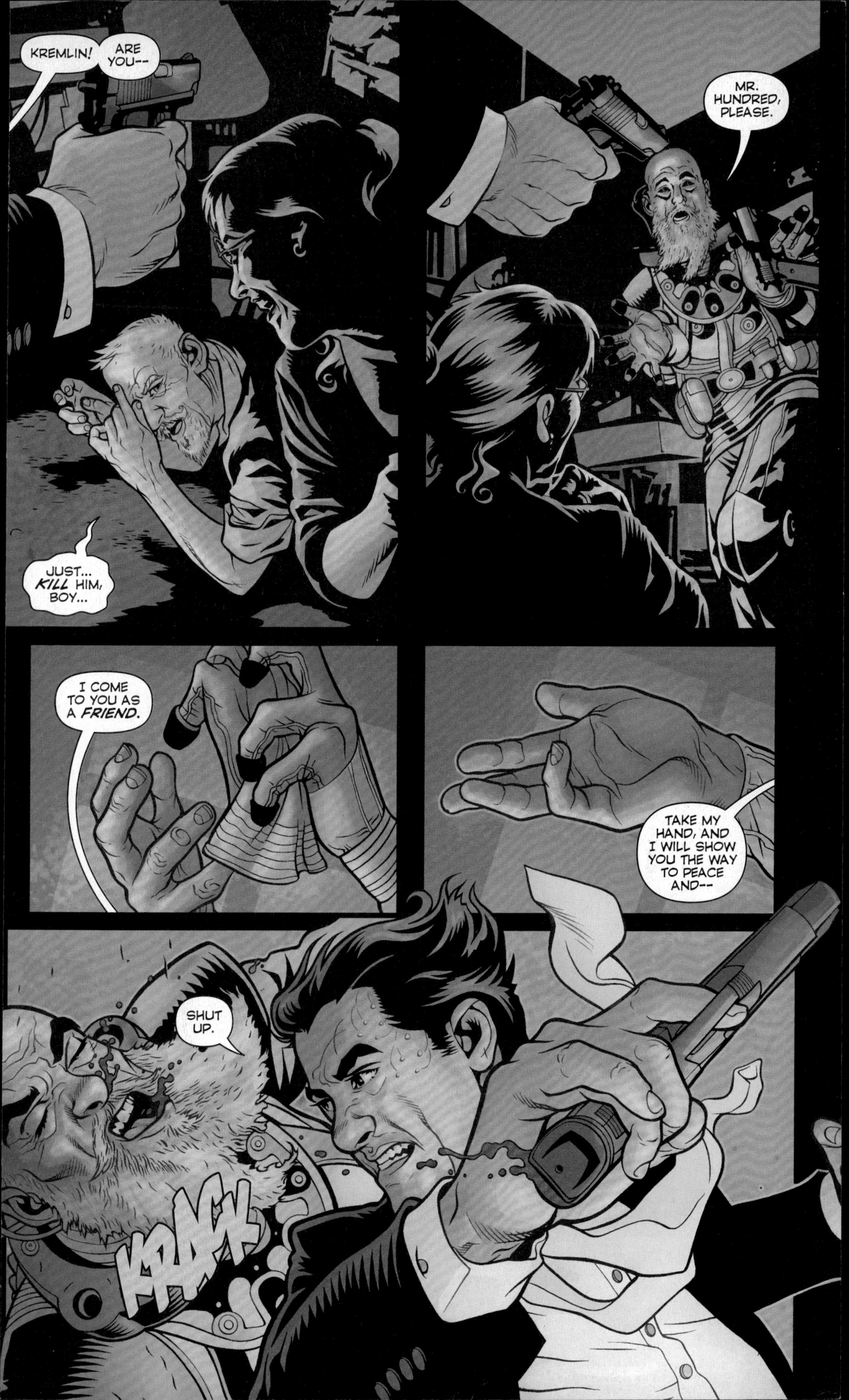
KREMLIN! ARE YOU--
JUST... *KILL* HIM, BOY...
MR. HUNDRED, PLEASE.
I COME TO YOU AS A *FRIEND*.
TAKE MY HAND, AND I WILL SHOW YOU THE WAY TO PEACE AND--
SHUT UP.
KRACK

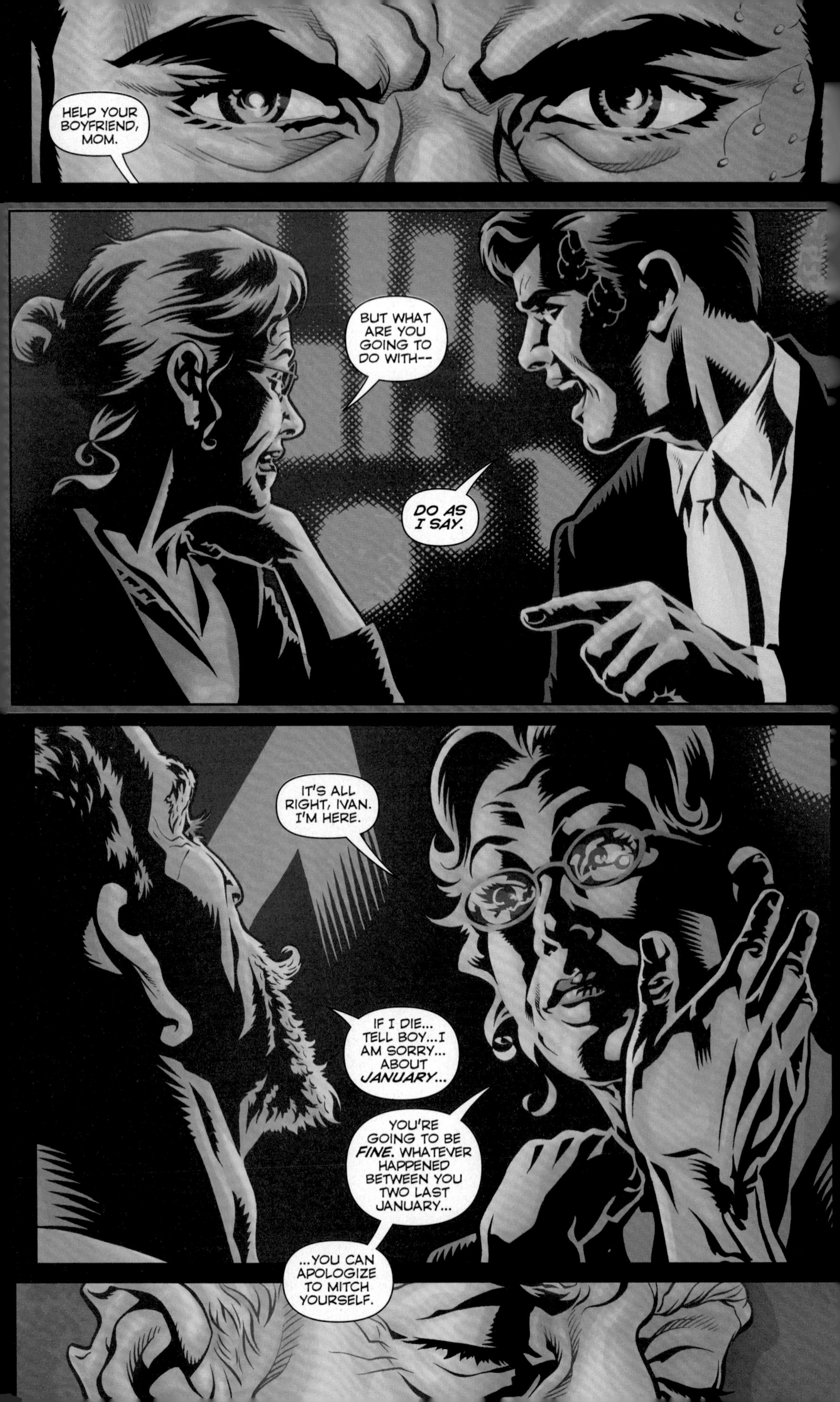

HELP YOUR BOYFRIEND, MOM.
BUT WHAT ARE YOU GOING TO DO WITH--
DO AS I SAY.
IT'S ALL RIGHT, IVAN. I'M HERE.
IF I DIE... TELL BOY...I AM SORRY... ABOUT JANUARY...
YOU'RE GOING TO BE FINE. WHATEVER HAPPENED BETWEEN YOU TWO LAST JANUARY...
...YOU CAN APOLOGIZE TO MITCH YOURSELF.

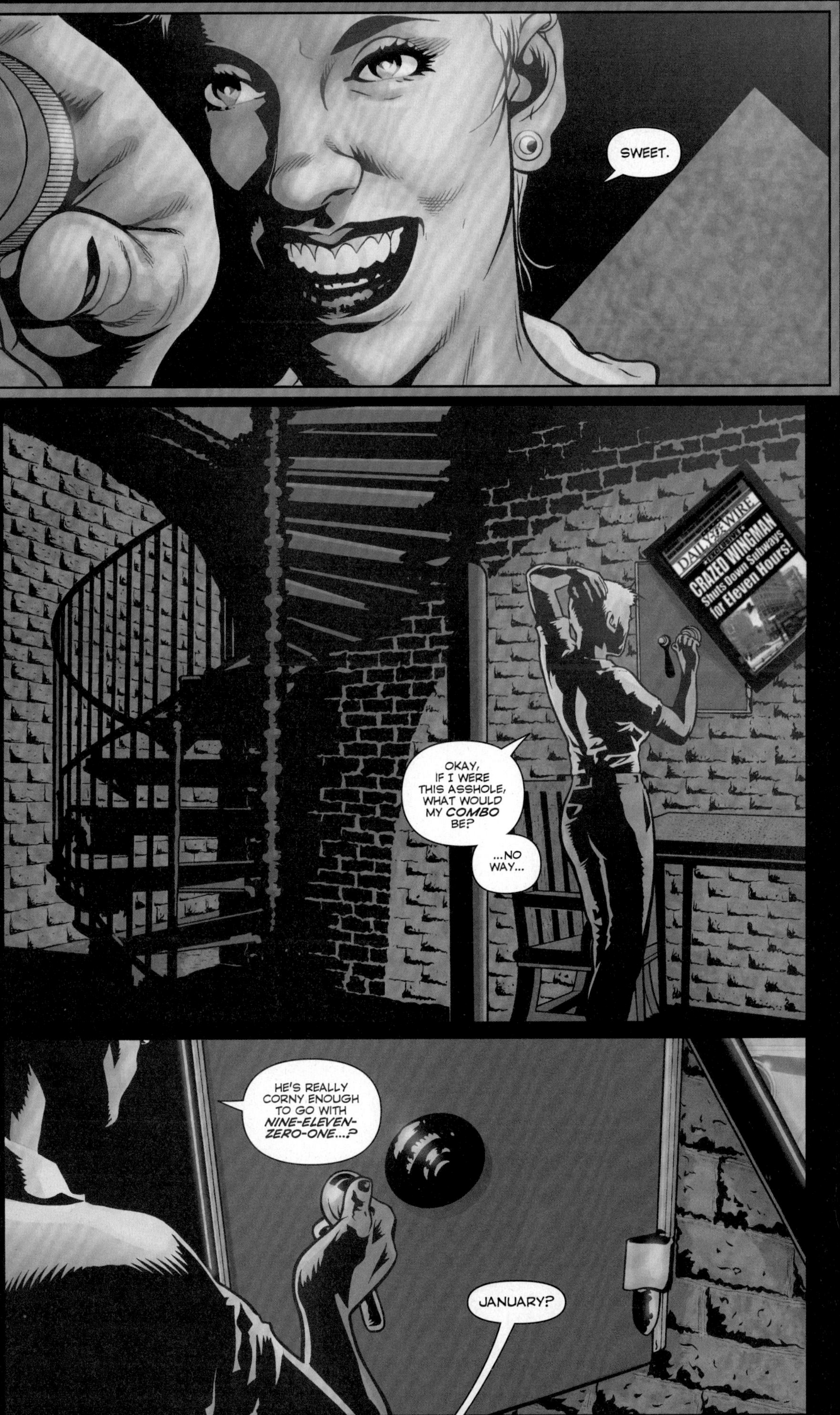
SWEET.
DAILY WIRE
CRAZED WINGMAN
Shuts Down Subways for Eleven Hours!
OKAY, IF I WERE THIS ASSHOLE, WHAT WOULD MY *COMBO* BE?
...NO WAY...
HE'S REALLY CORNY ENOUGH TO GO WITH *NINE-ELEVEN-ZERO-ONE...?*
JANUARY?

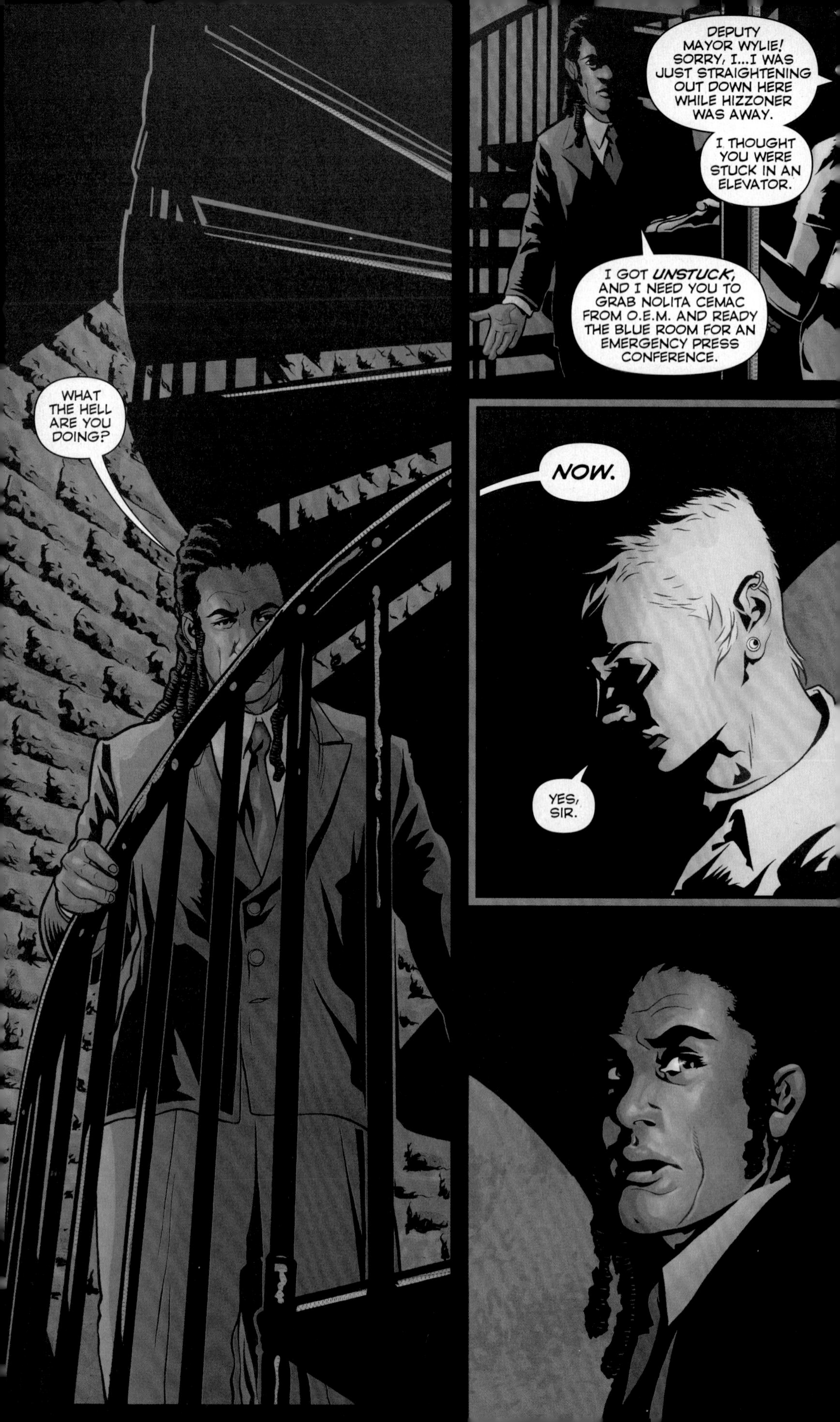
WHAT THE HELL ARE YOU DOING?
DEPUTY MAYOR WYLIE! SORRY, I...I WAS JUST STRAIGHTENING OUT DOWN HERE WHILE HIZZONER WAS AWAY.
I THOUGHT YOU WERE STUCK IN AN ELEVATOR.
I GOT UNSTUCK, AND I NEED YOU TO GRAB NOLITA CEMAC FROM O.E.M. AND READY THE BLUE ROOM FOR AN EMERGENCY PRESS CONFERENCE.
NOW.
YES, SIR.

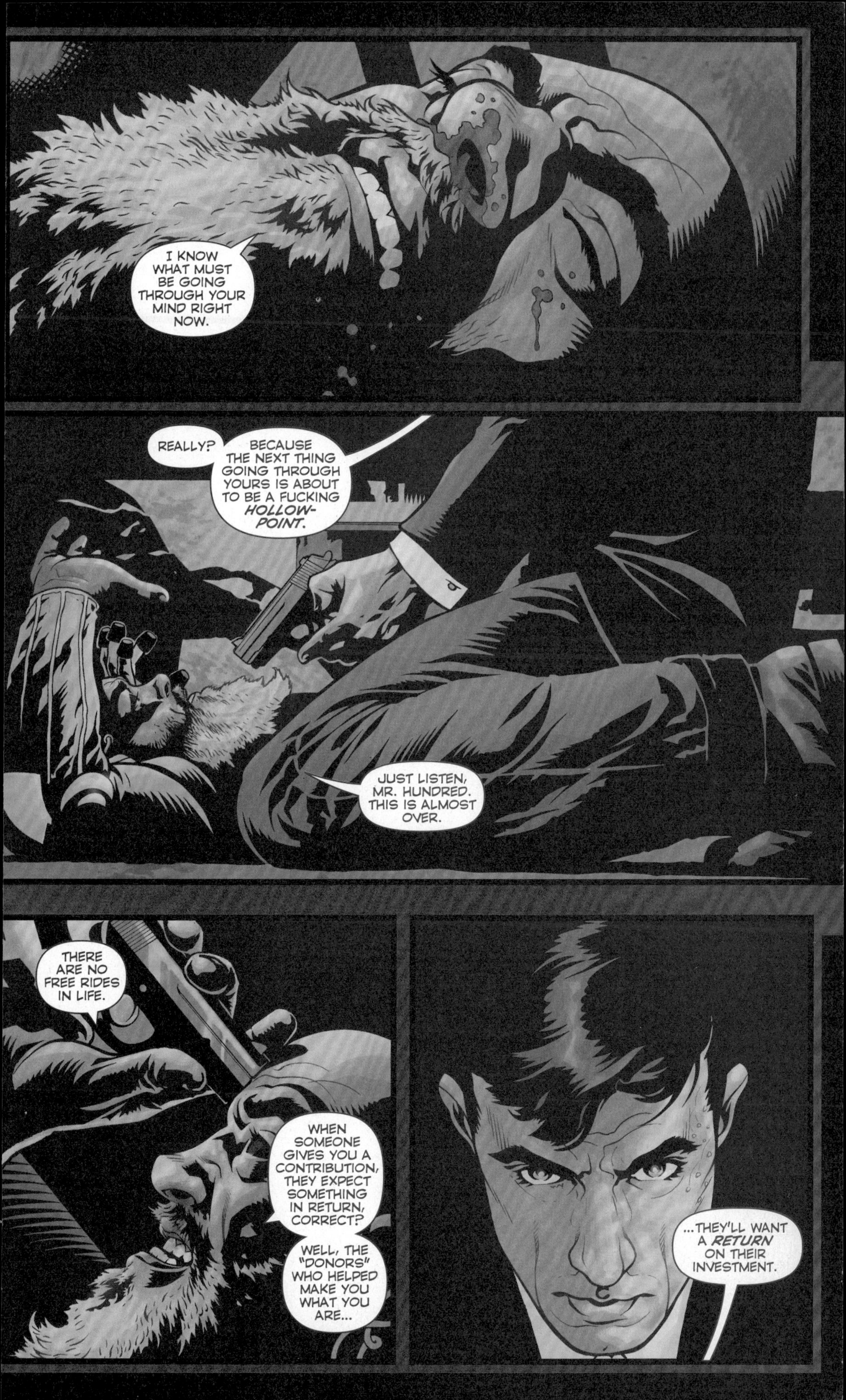

I KNOW WHAT MUST BE GOING THROUGH YOUR MIND RIGHT NOW.
REALLY?
BECAUSE THE NEXT THING GOING THROUGH YOURS IS ABOUT TO BE A FUCKING *HOLLOW-POINT*.
JUST LISTEN, MR. HUNDRED. THIS IS ALMOST OVER.
THERE ARE NO FREE RIDES IN LIFE.
WHEN SOMEONE GIVES YOU A CONTRIBUTION, THEY EXPECT SOMETHING IN RETURN, CORRECT?
WELL, THE "DONORS" WHO HELPED MAKE YOU WHAT YOU ARE...
...THEY'LL WANT A *RETURN* ON THEIR INVESTMENT.

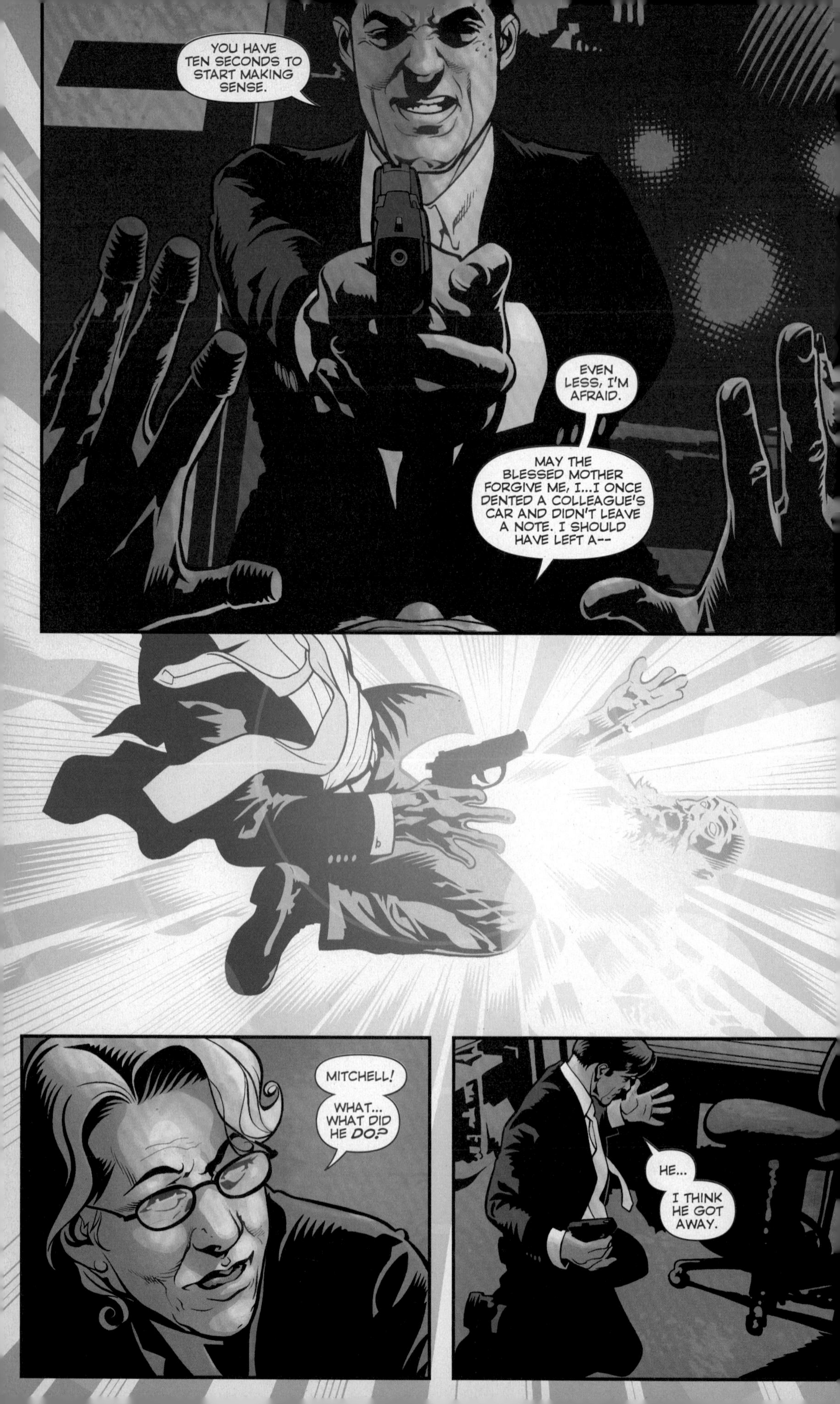
YOU HAVE TEN SECONDS TO START MAKING SENSE.
EVEN LESS, I'M AFRAID.
MAY THE BLESSED MOTHER FORGIVE ME, I...I ONCE DENTED A COLLEAGUE'S CAR AND DIDN'T LEAVE A NOTE. I SHOULD HAVE LEFT A--
MITCHELL!
WHAT... WHAT DID HE *DO*?
HE...
I THINK HE GOT AWAY.

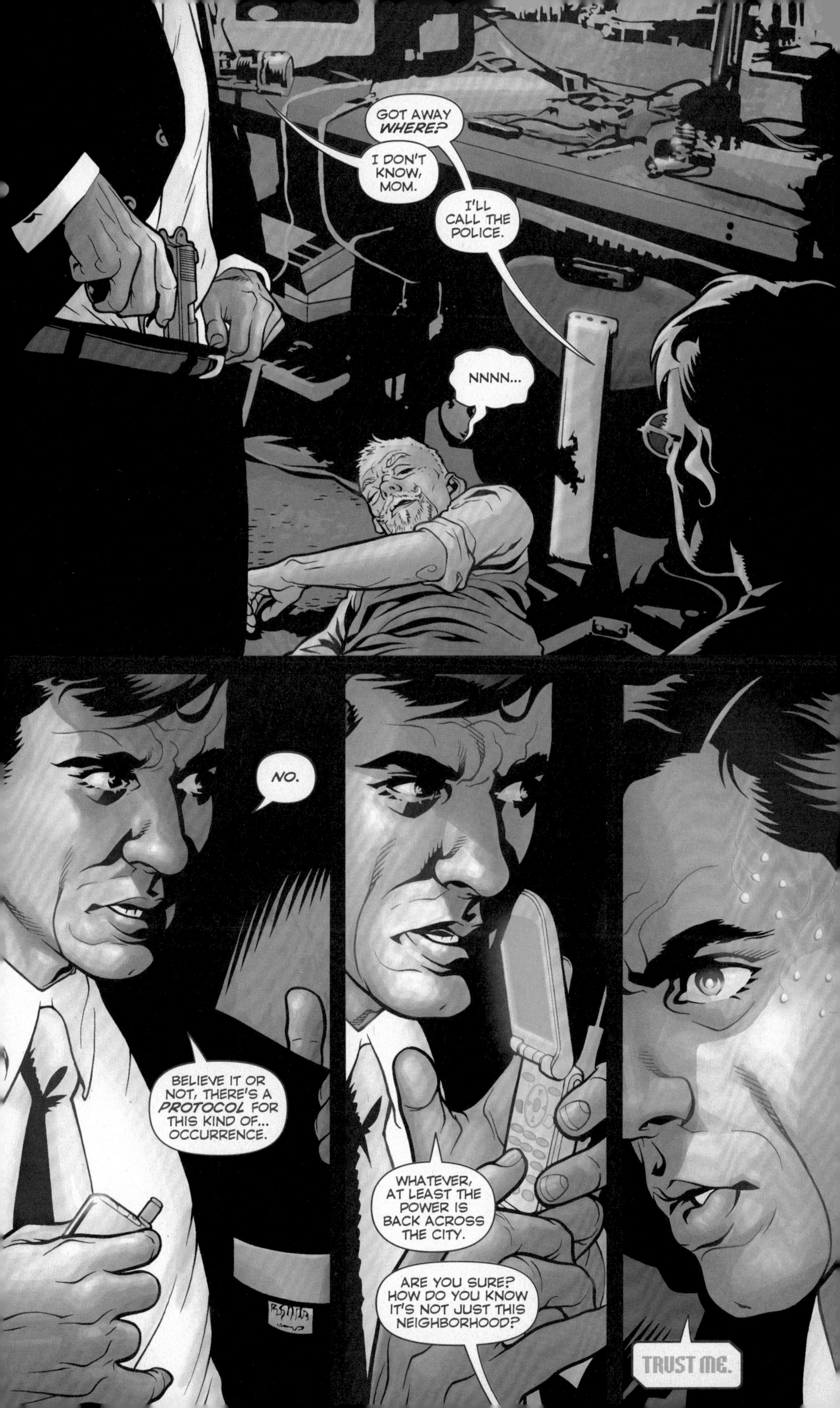
GOT AWAY *WHERE?*
I DON'T KNOW, MOM.
I'LL CALL THE POLICE.
NNNN...
NO.
BELIEVE IT OR NOT, THERE'S A *PROTOCOL* FOR THIS KIND OF... OCCURRENCE.
WHATEVER, AT LEAST THE POWER IS BACK ACROSS THE CITY.
ARE YOU SURE? HOW DO YOU KNOW IT'S NOT JUST THIS NEIGHBORHOOD?
TRUST ME.

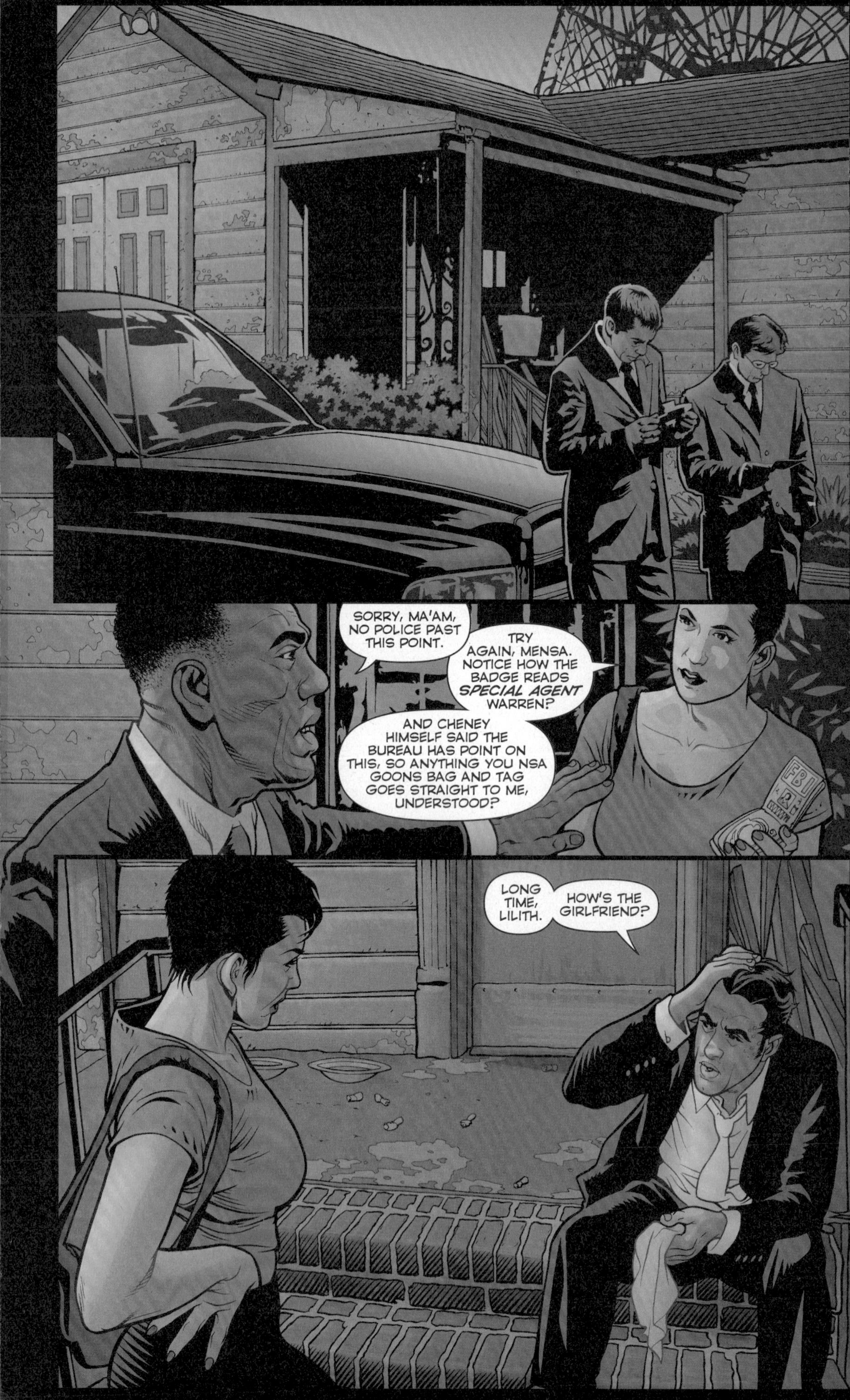
SORRY, MA'AM, NO POLICE PAST THIS POINT.
TRY AGAIN, MENSA. NOTICE HOW THE BADGE READS *SPECIAL AGENT* WARREN?
AND CHENEY HIMSELF SAID THE BUREAU HAS POINT ON THIS, SO ANYTHING YOU NSA GOONS BAG AND TAG GOES STRAIGHT TO ME, UNDERSTOOD?
FBI
LONG TIME, LILITH.
HOW'S THE GIRLFRIEND?

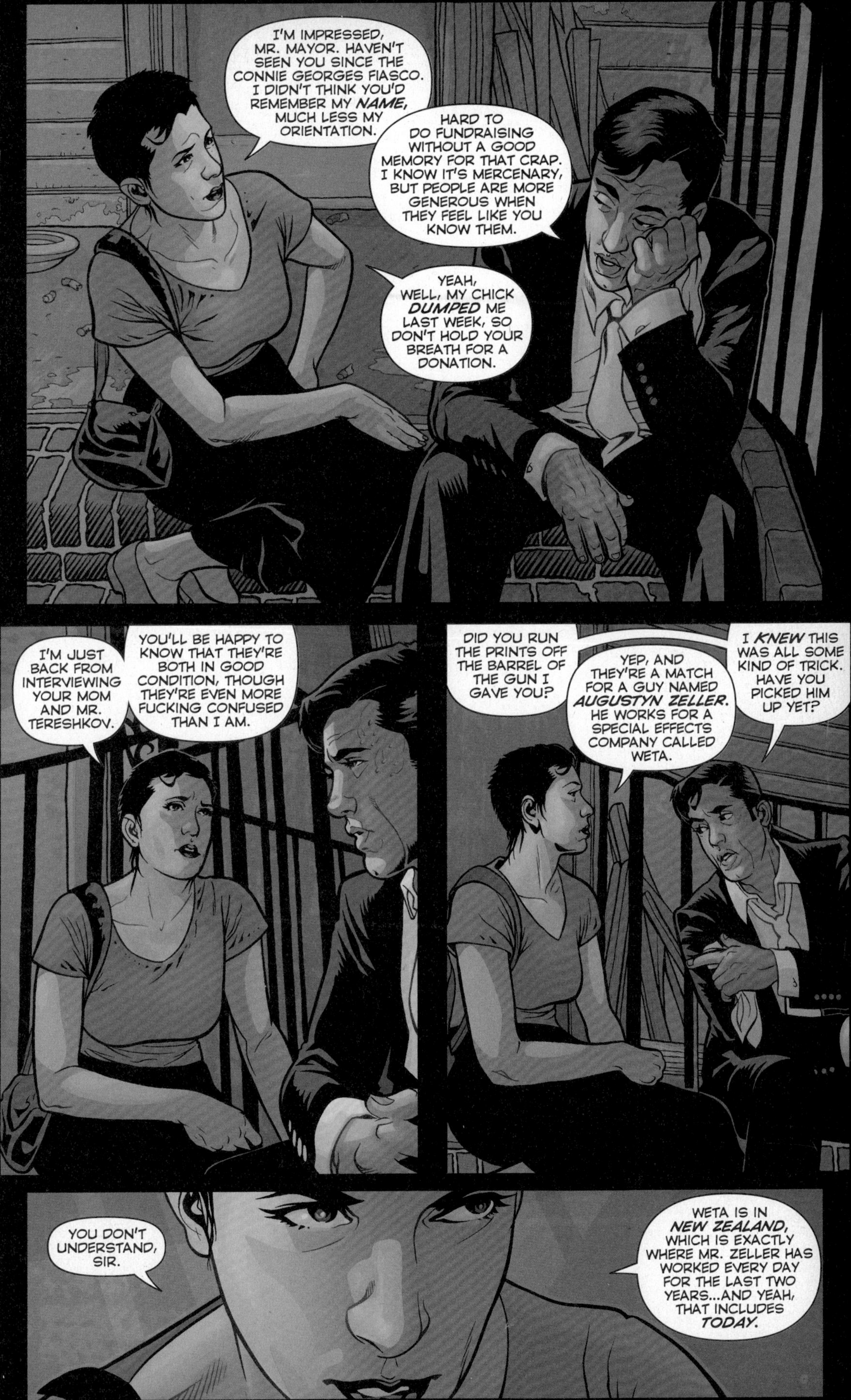
I'M IMPRESSED, MR. MAYOR. HAVEN'T SEEN YOU SINCE THE CONNIE GEORGES FIASCO. I DIDN'T THINK YOU'D REMEMBER MY NAME, MUCH LESS MY ORIENTATION.
HARD TO DO FUNDRAISING WITHOUT A GOOD MEMORY FOR THAT CRAP. I KNOW IT'S MERCENARY, BUT PEOPLE ARE MORE GENEROUS WHEN THEY FEEL LIKE YOU KNOW THEM.
YEAH, WELL, MY CHICK DUMPED ME LAST WEEK, SO DON'T HOLD YOUR BREATH FOR A DONATION.
I'M JUST BACK FROM INTERVIEWING YOUR MOM AND MR. TERESHKOV.
YOU'LL BE HAPPY TO KNOW THAT THEY'RE BOTH IN GOOD CONDITION, THOUGH THEY'RE EVEN MORE FUCKING CONFUSED THAN I AM.
DID YOU RUN THE PRINTS OFF THE BARREL OF THE GUN I GAVE YOU?
YEP, AND THEY'RE A MATCH FOR A GUY NAMED AUGUSTYN ZELLER. HE WORKS FOR A SPECIAL EFFECTS COMPANY CALLED WETA.
I KNEW THIS WAS ALL SOME KIND OF TRICK. HAVE YOU PICKED HIM UP YET?
YOU DON'T UNDERSTAND, SIR.
WETA IS IN NEW ZEALAND, WHICH IS EXACTLY WHERE MR. ZELLER HAS WORKED EVERY DAY FOR THE LAST TWO YEARS...AND YEAH, THAT INCLUDES TODAY.

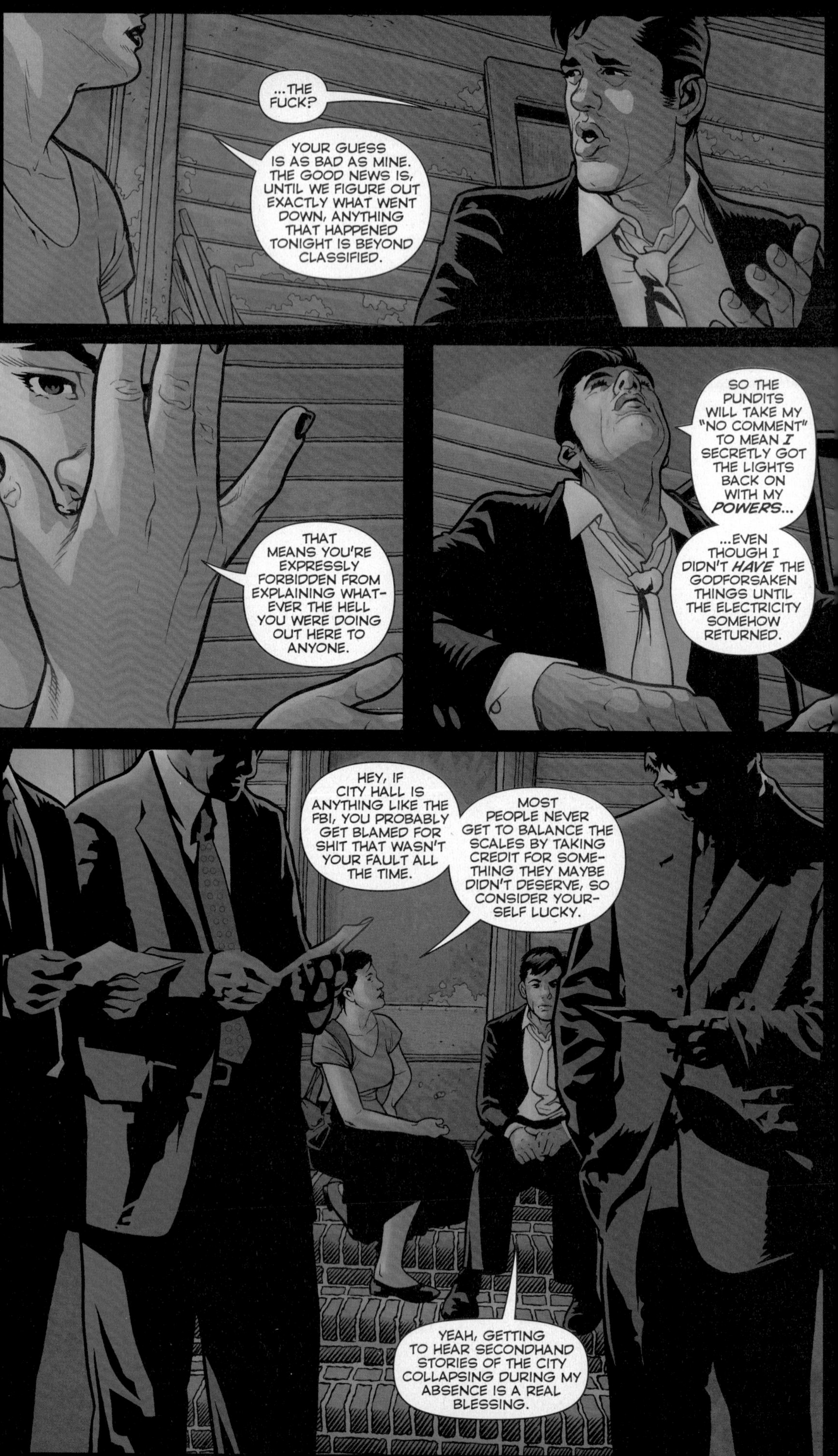
...THE FUCK?
YOUR GUESS IS AS BAD AS MINE. THE GOOD NEWS IS, UNTIL WE FIGURE OUT EXACTLY WHAT WENT DOWN, ANYTHING THAT HAPPENED TONIGHT IS BEYOND CLASSIFIED.
THAT MEANS YOU'RE EXPRESSLY FORBIDDEN FROM EXPLAINING WHAT-EVER THE HELL YOU WERE DOING OUT HERE TO ANYONE.
SO THE PUNDITS WILL TAKE MY "NO COMMENT" TO MEAN *I* SECRETLY GOT THE LIGHTS BACK ON WITH MY ***POWERS...***
...EVEN THOUGH I DIDN'T ***HAVE*** THE GODFORSAKEN THINGS UNTIL THE ELECTRICITY SOMEHOW RETURNED.
HEY, IF CITY HALL IS ANYTHING LIKE THE FBI, YOU PROBABLY GET BLAMED FOR SHIT THAT WASN'T YOUR FAULT ALL THE TIME.
MOST PEOPLE NEVER GET TO BALANCE THE SCALES BY TAKING CREDIT FOR SOME-THING THEY MAYBE DIDN'T DESERVE, SO CONSIDER YOUR-SELF LUCKY.
YEAH, GETTING TO HEAR SECONDHAND STORIES OF THE CITY COLLAPSING DURING MY ABSENCE IS A REAL BLESSING.

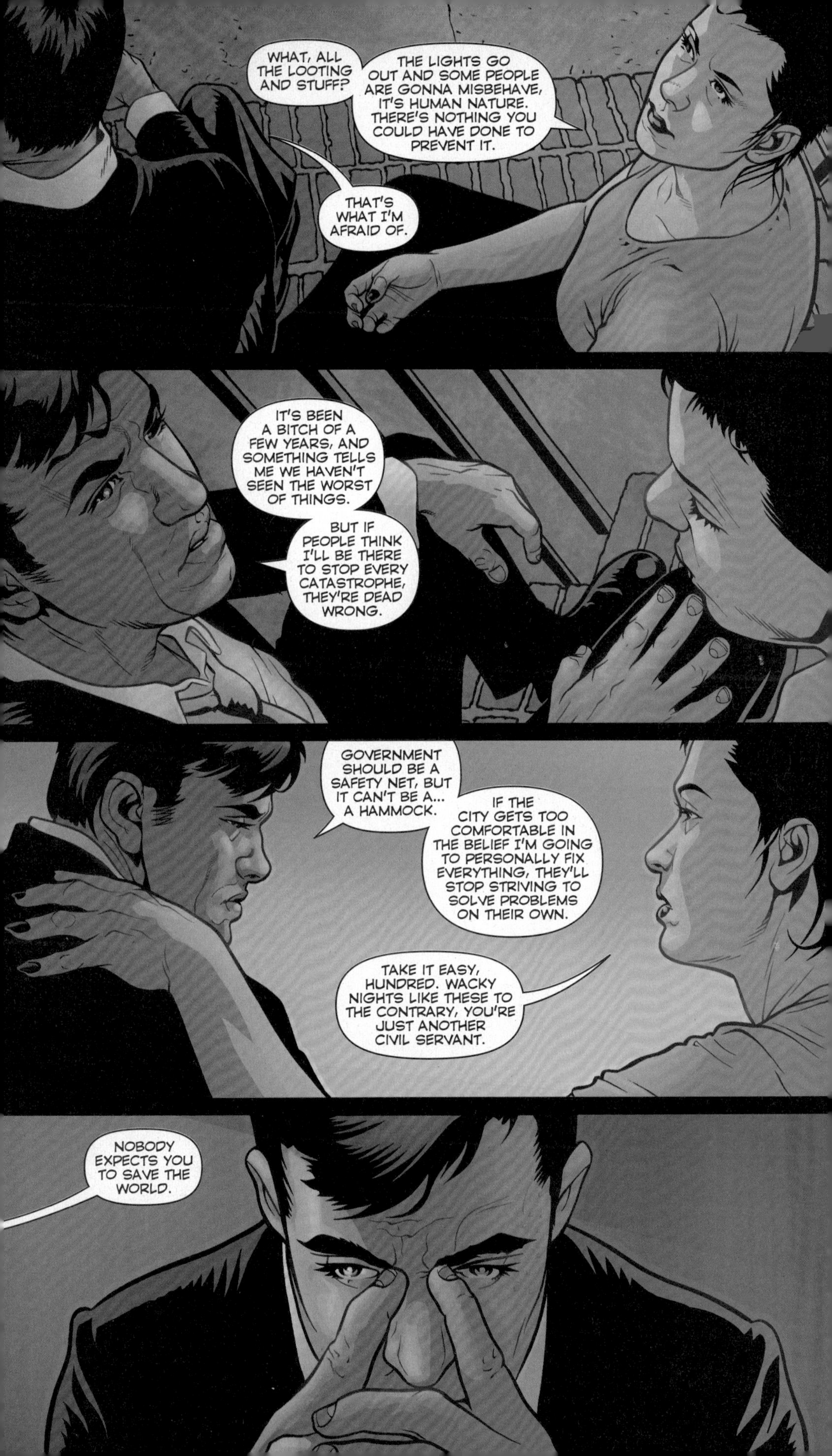
WHAT, ALL THE LOOTING AND STUFF?
THE LIGHTS GO OUT AND SOME PEOPLE ARE GONNA MISBEHAVE, IT'S HUMAN NATURE. THERE'S NOTHING YOU COULD HAVE DONE TO PREVENT IT.
THAT'S WHAT I'M AFRAID OF.
IT'S BEEN A BITCH OF A FEW YEARS, AND SOMETHING TELLS ME WE HAVEN'T SEEN THE WORST OF THINGS.
BUT IF PEOPLE THINK I'LL BE THERE TO STOP EVERY CATASTROPHE, THEY'RE DEAD WRONG.
GOVERNMENT SHOULD BE A SAFETY NET, BUT IT CAN'T BE A... A HAMMOCK.
IF THE CITY GETS TOO COMFORTABLE IN THE BELIEF I'M GOING TO PERSONALLY FIX EVERYTHING, THEY'LL STOP STRIVING TO SOLVE PROBLEMS ON THEIR OWN.
TAKE IT EASY, HUNDRED. WACKY NIGHTS LIKE THESE TO THE CONTRARY, YOU'RE JUST ANOTHER CIVIL SERVANT.
NOBODY EXPECTS YOU TO SAVE THE WORLD.

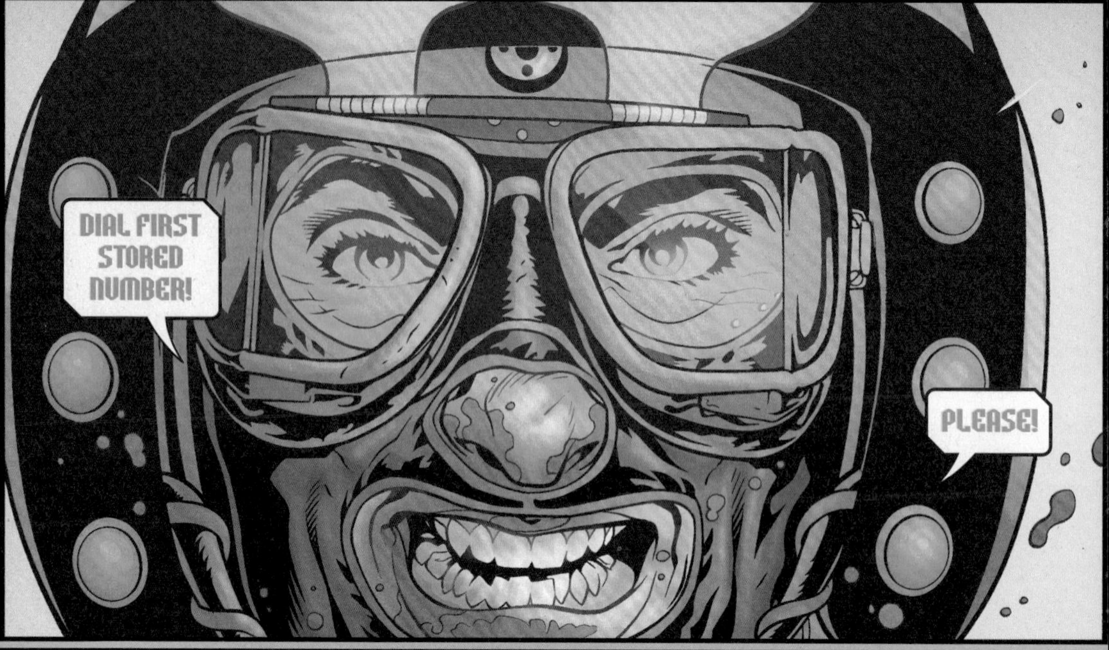

DIAL FIRST STORED NUMBER!
PLEASE!

TUESDAY, SEPTEMBER 11, 2001

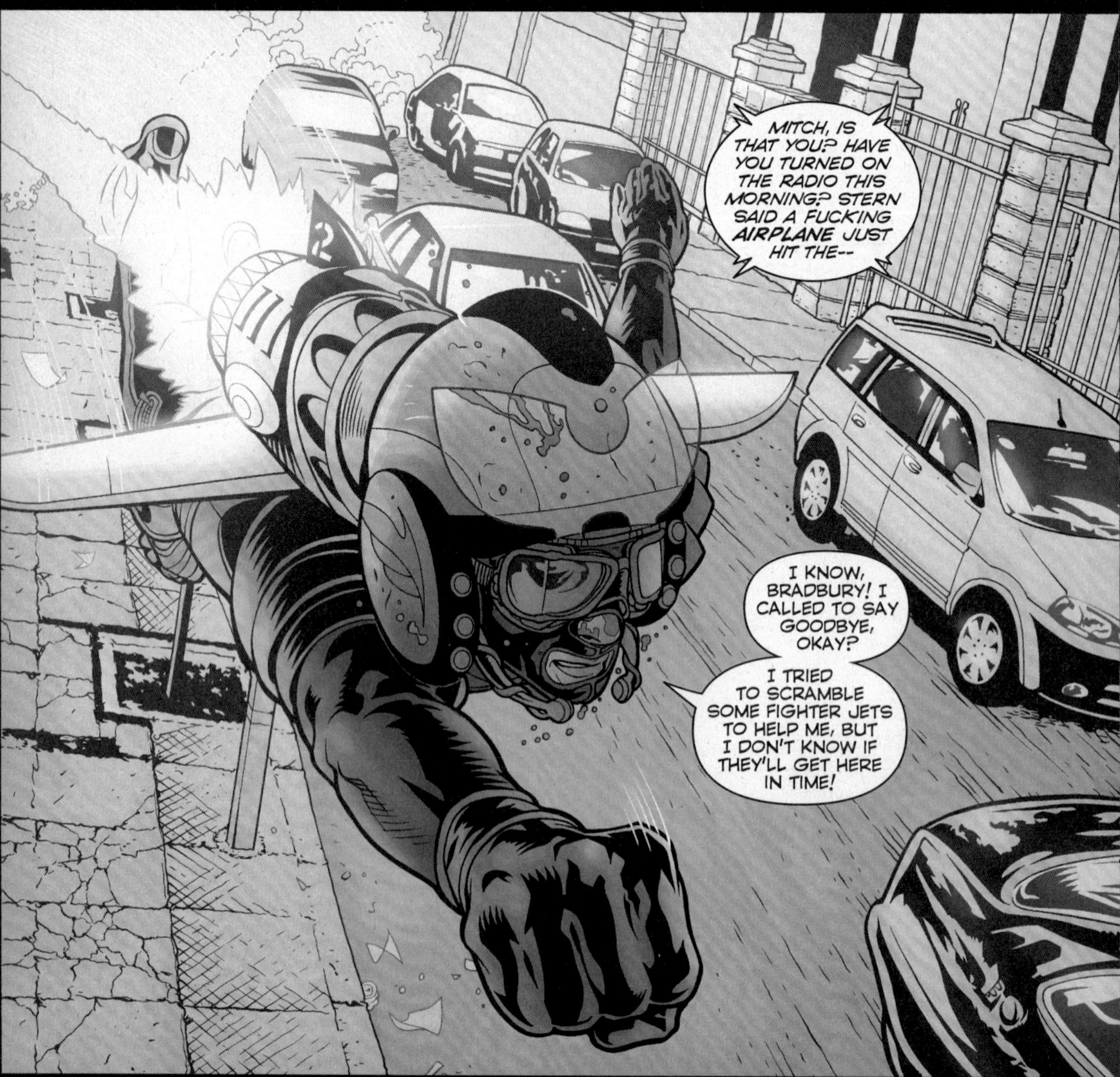

MITCH, IS THAT YOU? HAVE YOU TURNED ON THE RADIO THIS MORNING? STERN SAID A FUCKING AIRPLANE JUST HIT THE--
I KNOW, BRADBURY! I CALLED TO SAY GOODBYE, OKAY?
I TRIED TO SCRAMBLE SOME FIGHTER JETS TO HELP ME, BUT I DON'T KNOW IF THEY'LL GET HERE IN TIME!

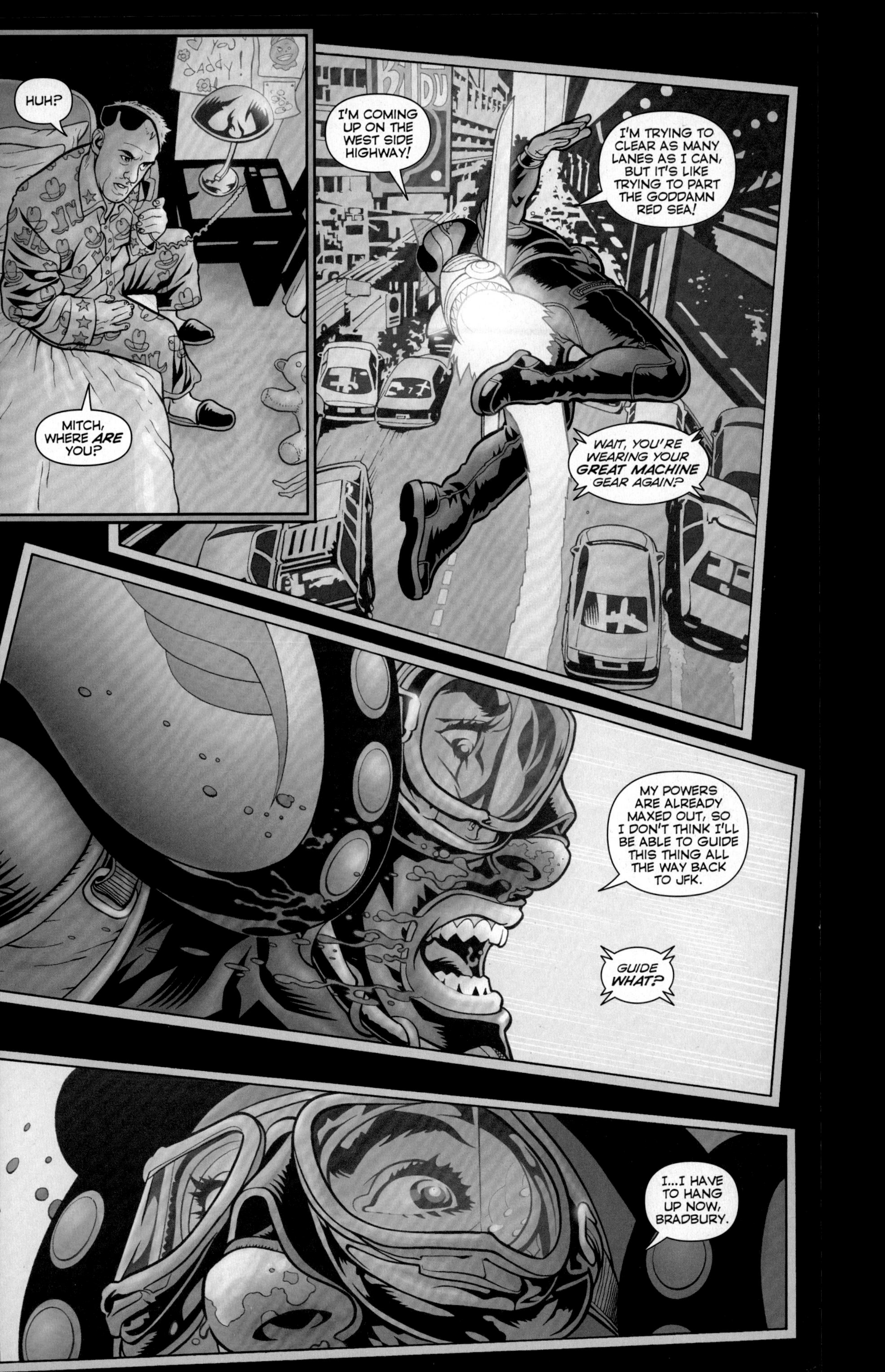

HUH?
MITCH, WHERE *ARE* YOU?
I'M COMING UP ON THE WEST SIDE HIGHWAY!
I'M TRYING TO CLEAR AS MANY LANES AS I CAN, BUT IT'S LIKE TRYING TO PART THE GODDAMN RED SEA!
WAIT, YOU'RE WEARING YOUR ***GREAT MACHINE*** *GEAR AGAIN?*
MY POWERS ARE ALREADY MAXED OUT, SO I DON'T THINK I'LL BE ABLE TO GUIDE THIS THING ALL THE WAY BACK TO JFK.
GUIDE ***WHAT?***
I...I HAVE TO HANG UP NOW, BRADBURY.

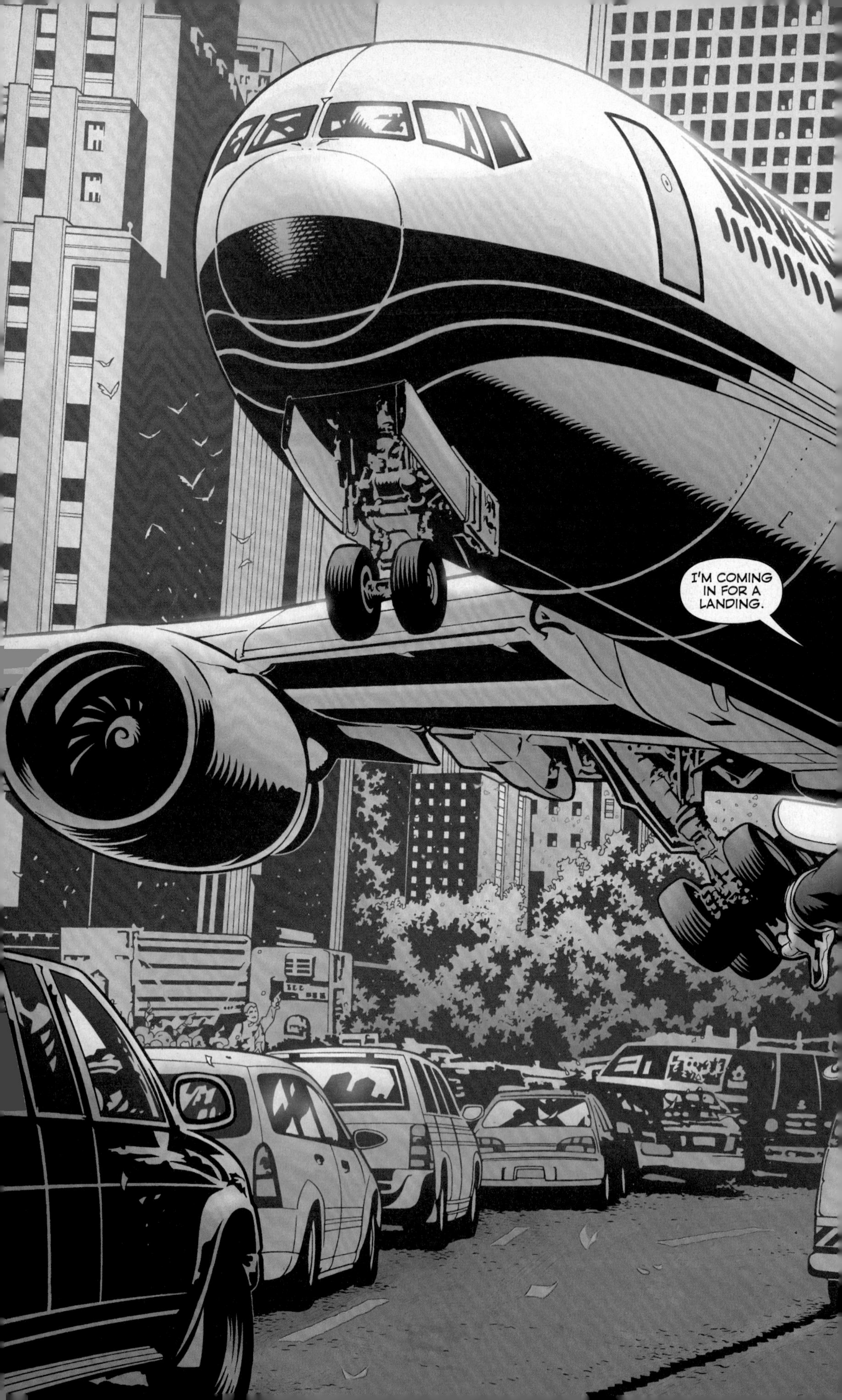
I'M COMING IN FOR A LANDING.

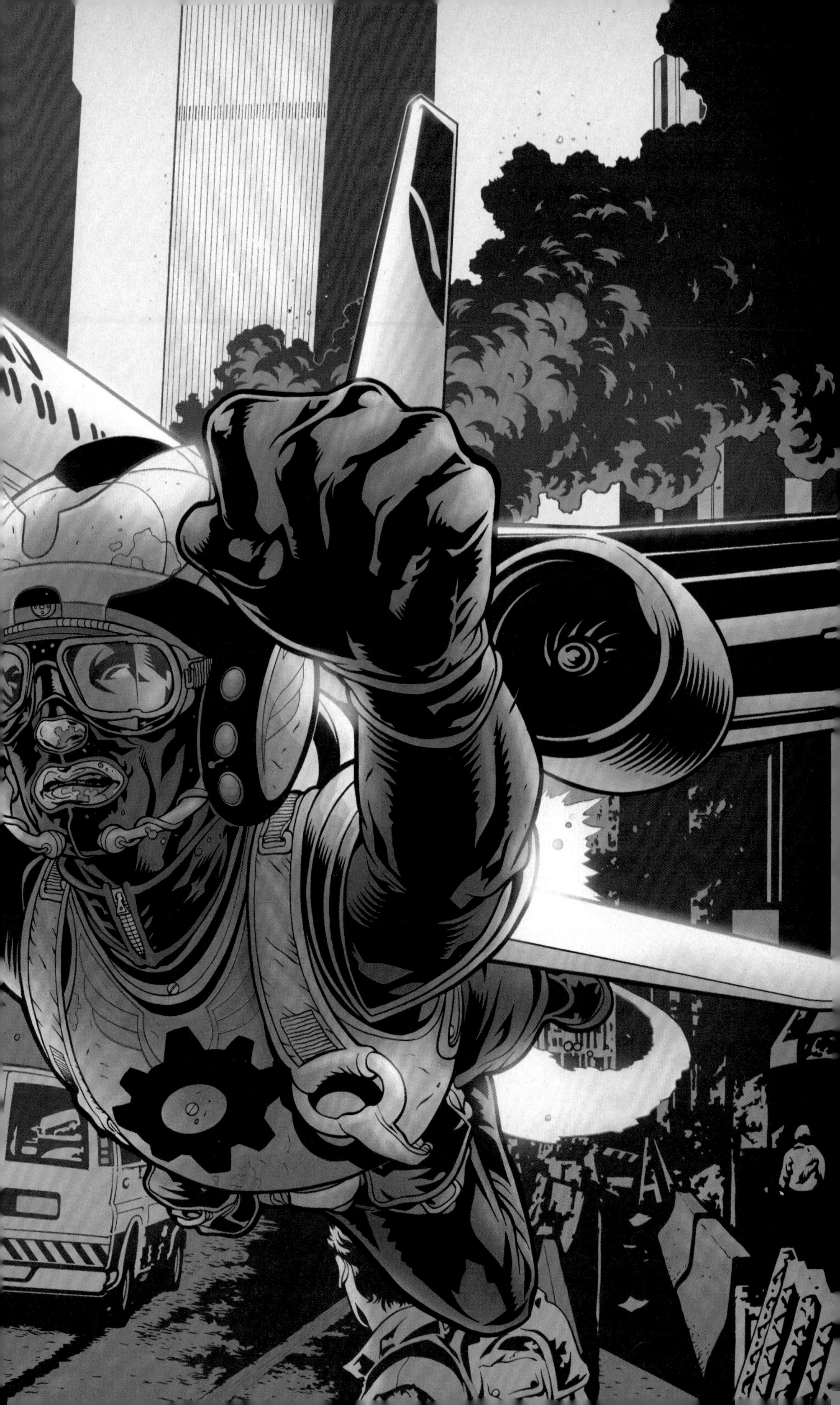

Chapter 5
Inside the Machine

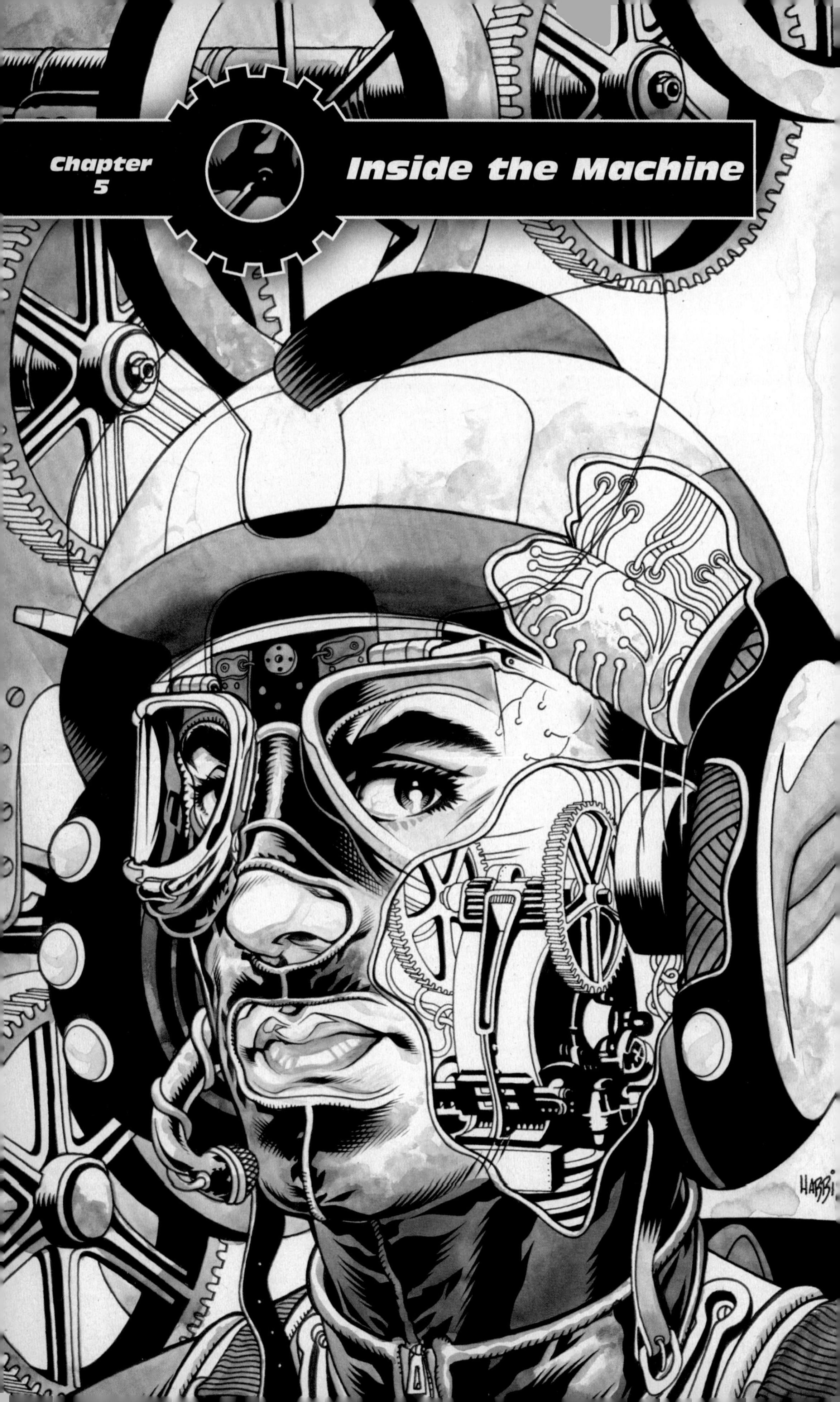

Introduction by Brian K. Vaughan

Comic books made by more than one creator are often derogatively referred to as "assembly-line books," implying that each stage of the work is dispassionately passed from one craftsman to the next in order to churn out product as quickly as possible. And while EX MACHINA does hit stands with shocking regularity, the above description doesn't capture our process in the least.

All of the artists behind this series are close friends, and it's sometimes hard to tell where one person's job starts and another's ends. My scripts often begin with a brilliant visual idea suggested by penciller and co-creator Tony Harris during one of our regular phone calls. While Old Man Harris and I are gabbing, our inker (first the amazing Tom Feister, now the equally talented Jim Clark) might catch a small continuity error in one of the previous issue's unfinished pages, which I'll try to address in the dialogue with the help of letterer extraordinaire Jared K. Fletcher. Meanwhile, J.D. Mettler will be e-mailing all of us his incomparable colors, getting input about setting the mood for a particular scene with a specific palette. This complex cross-country network is constantly being guided from the WildStorm offices by the tireless Ben Abernathy and Kristy Quinn.

And those are just the names you see in the credit box. Each month, our team is ably assisted by countless more people, whether it's the dedicated cast of actors Tony shoots for photo reference or the government sources who are kind enough to supply me with the inside scoop on life in City Hall. Our production is bigger and more complicated than many independent films, but everyone involved feels a responsibility beyond our individual contributions to the series, and I think it makes for a unique kind of book that feels like the work of one unified vision.

EX MACHINA has always suggested that the behind-the-scenes story is infinitely more interesting than the one the public gets to see, so it's only fitting that we finally reveal the secret inner workings of our "machine."

I hope you agree it's a great one.

- Brian K. Vaughan
Los Angeles, 2007

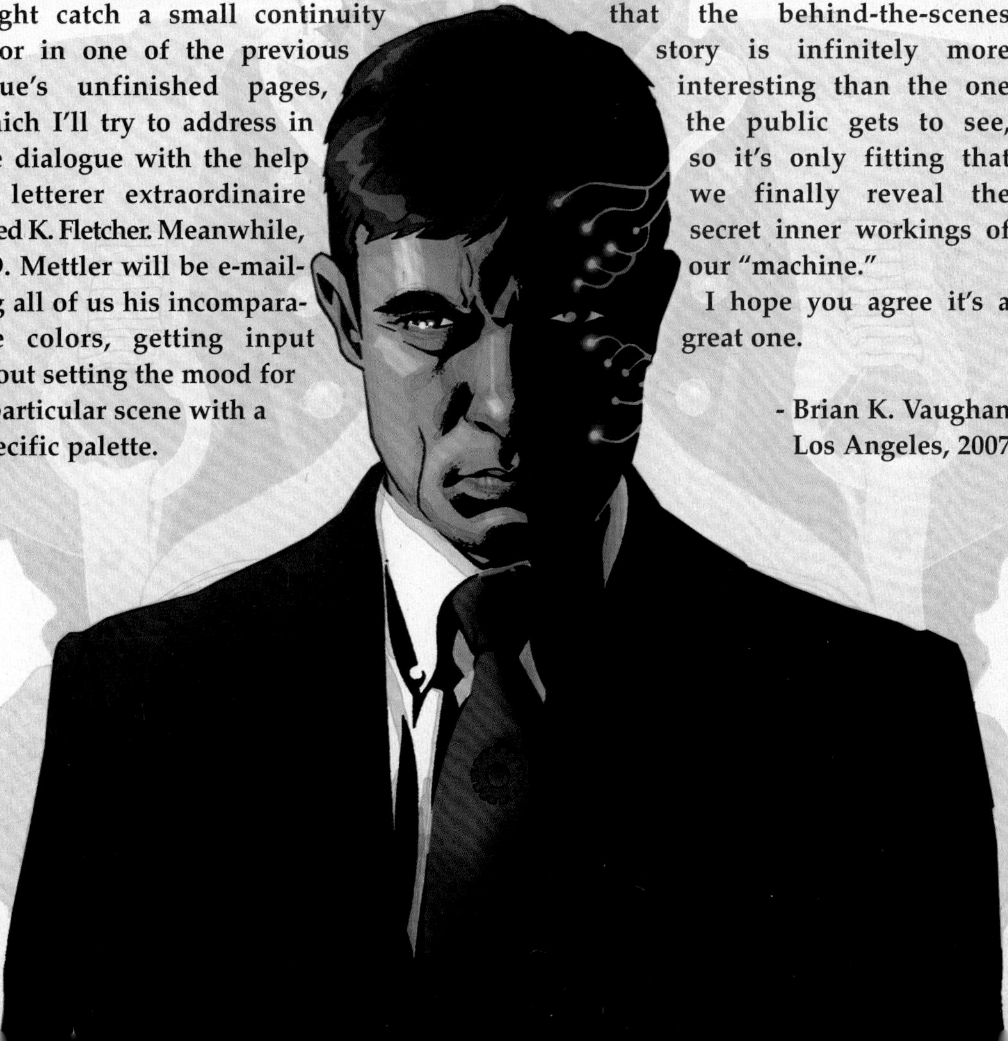

Inside Process:
Interior page showcase

Tony Harris is always experimenting with different techniques to push himself as an artist and excel at his craft. On his covers, he typically adds a "graywash" layer to the board following the inking stage, to add a little more depth to the finished piece. For a few issues of EX MACHINA, he experimented with this technique on the interiors as well.

What follows are the opening six pages to EX MACHINA #23, featuring script, pencils, gray-washed inks and color stages.

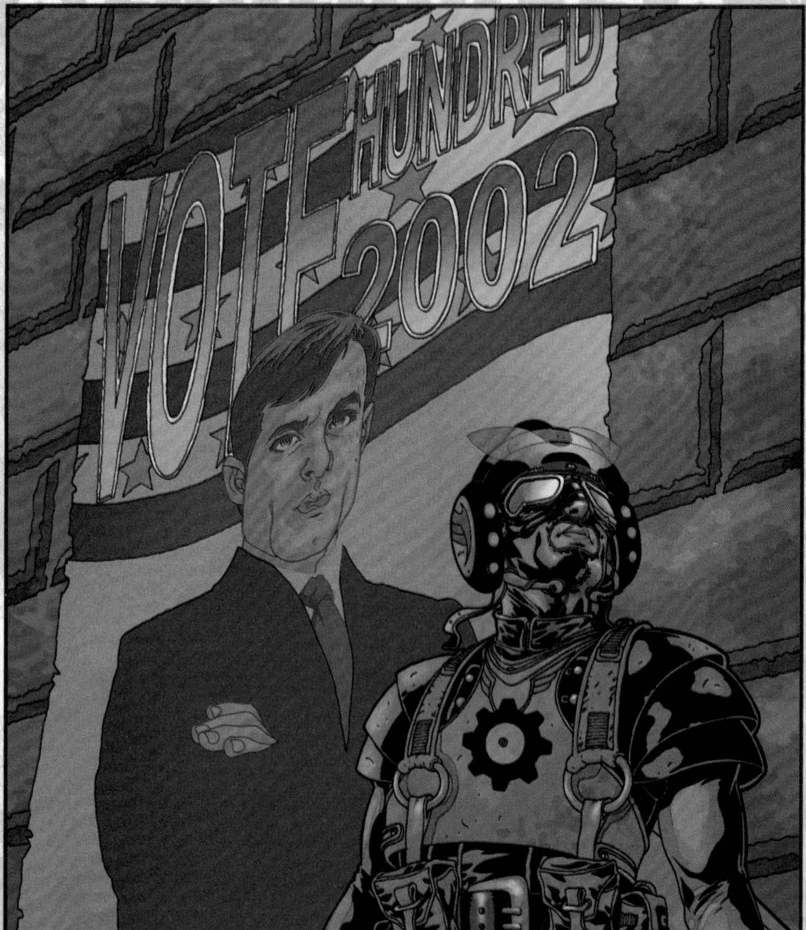
VOTE
HUNDRED
2002

This art was commissioned by *Wizard Magazine* for a piece they were doing on the Great Machine. When printed, they cropped out the background and just ran the free-floating figure.

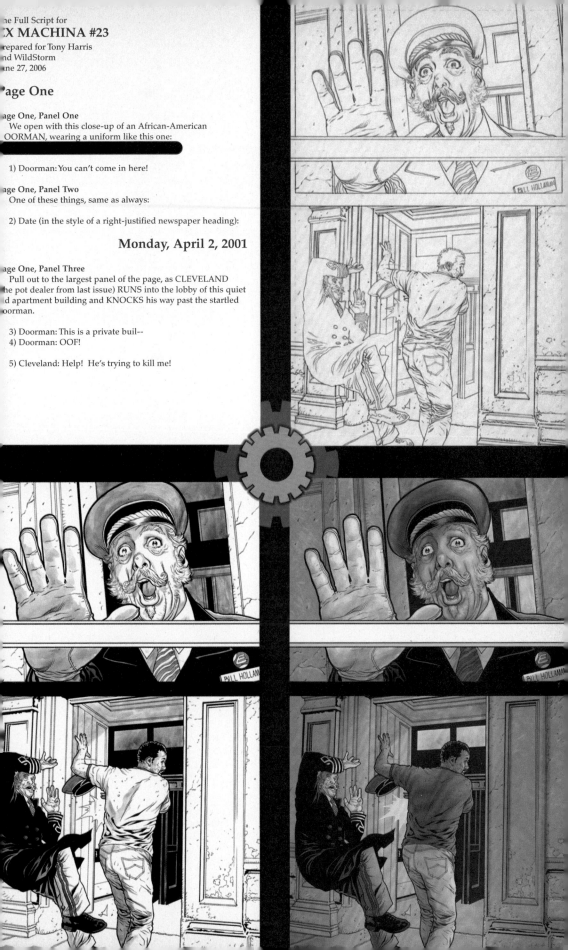

he Full Script for
X MACHINA #23
repared for Tony Harris
nd WildStorm
ne 27, 2006

age One

age One, Panel One

We open with this close-up of an African-American OORMAN, wearing a uniform like this one:

[redacted]

1) Doorman: You can't come in here!

age One, Panel Two

One of these things, same as always:

2) Date (in the style of a right-justified newspaper heading):

Monday, April 2, 2001

age One, Panel Three

Pull out to the largest panel of the page, as CLEVELAND he pot dealer from last issue) RUNS into the lobby of this quiet d apartment building and KNOCKS his way past the startled oorman.

3) Doorman: This is a private buil--
4) Doorman: OOF!

5) Cleveland: Help! He's trying to kill me!

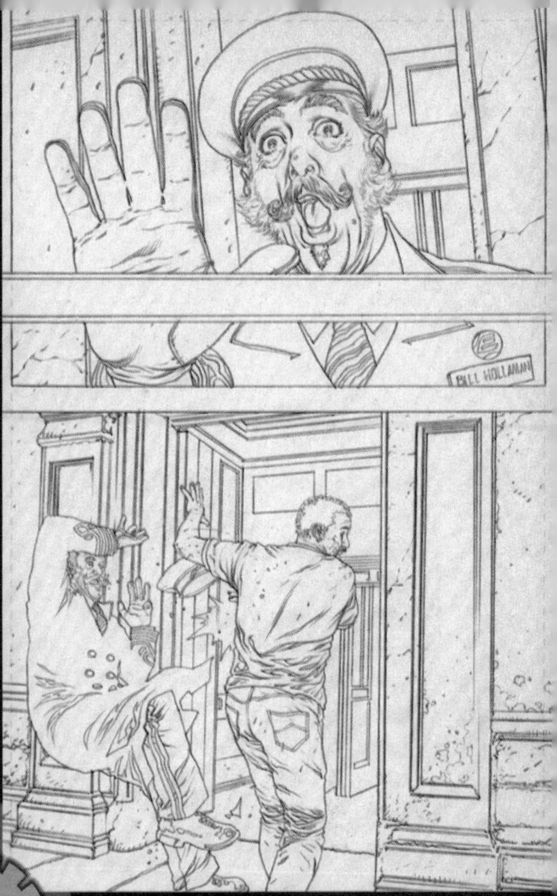
BILL HOLLAMAN

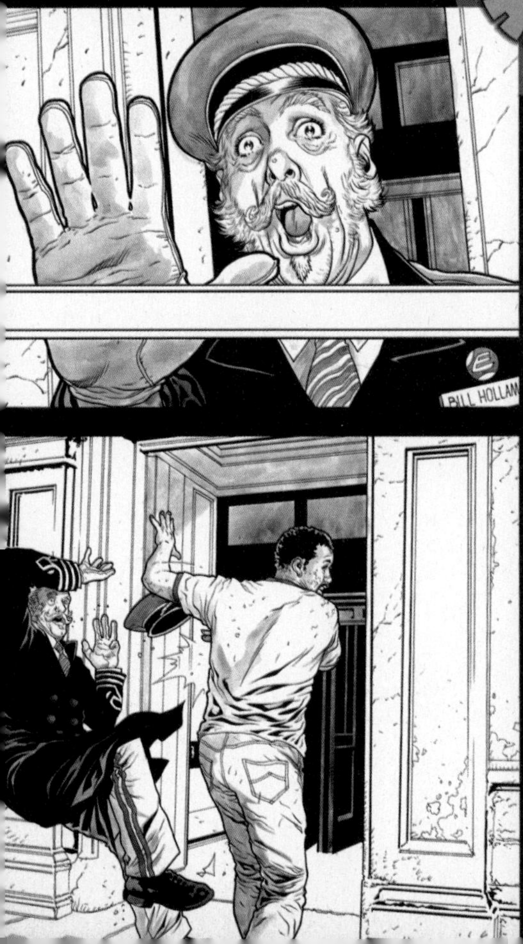

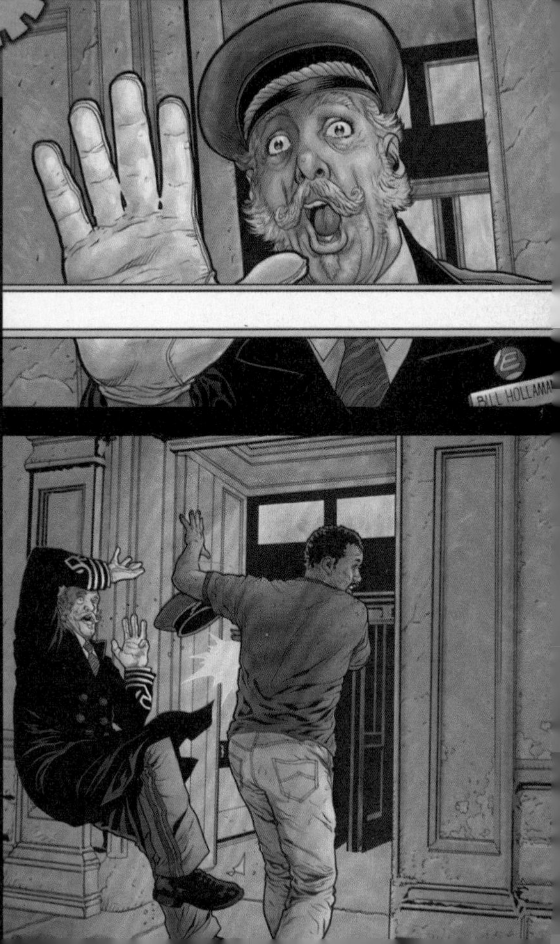

Page Two

Page Two, Panel One
Cut to the revolving door entrance to this old apartment building, as the helmeted GREAT MACHINE runs inside. He left his busted jetpack in the cab, so he's wingless here.

1) Great Machine (small font, whispering): Where did he go?

Page Two, Panel Two
Pull out to the largest panel of the page for a shot of the Great Machine and the doorman, as the floored doorman points at a nearby STAIRWELL DOOR.

2) Doorman: Say again?

3) Great Machine: Where the hell did he go?

4) Doorman: Stuh… stairwell.

Page Two, Panel Three
Change angles on the two men, as the Great Machine runs for an old elevator with an "OUT OF ORDER" sign on it.

5) Great Machine (small font, whispering): -koff- -koff- Thanks.

6) Doorman: Don't bother, man!
7) Doorman: That elevator hasn't worked in years!

Page Two, Panel Four
Push in on the Great Machine, as he gives a little half-smile.

8) Great Machine (GREEN FONT/BALLOON): I think I can coax her out of retirement.

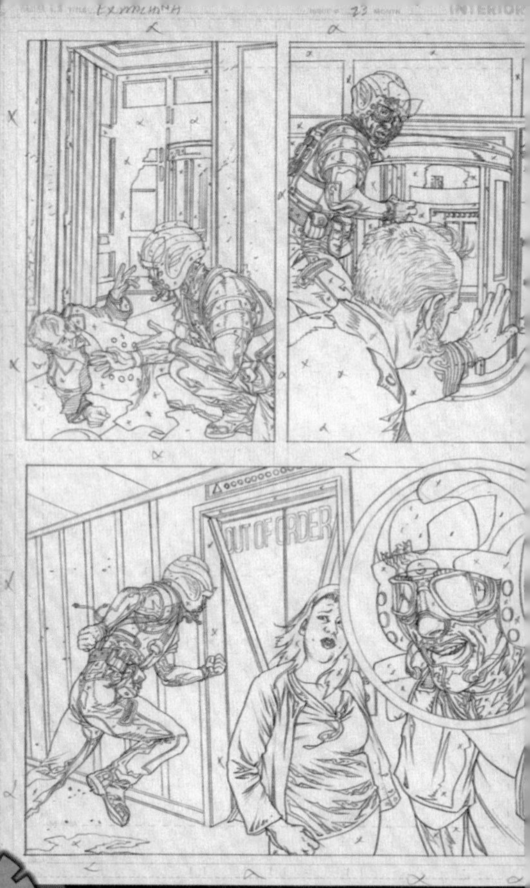
OUT OF ORDER

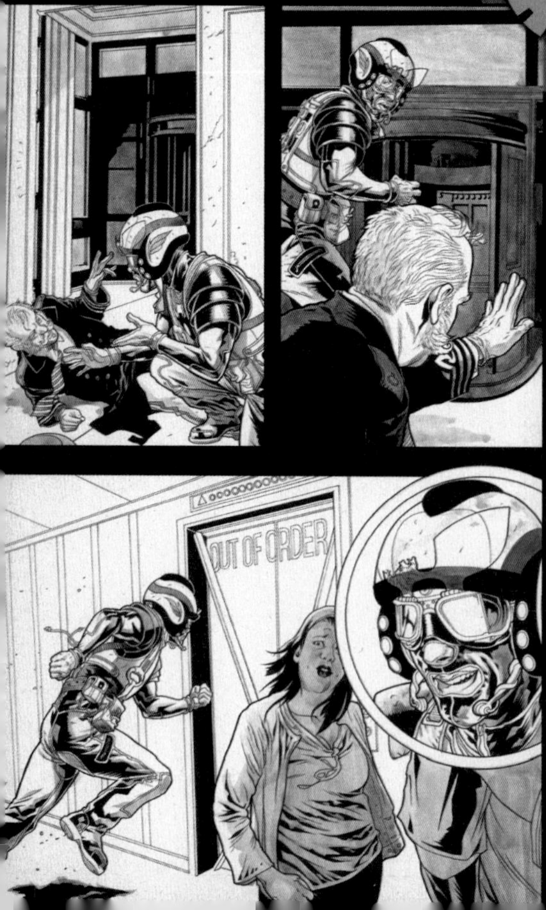
OUT OF ORDER

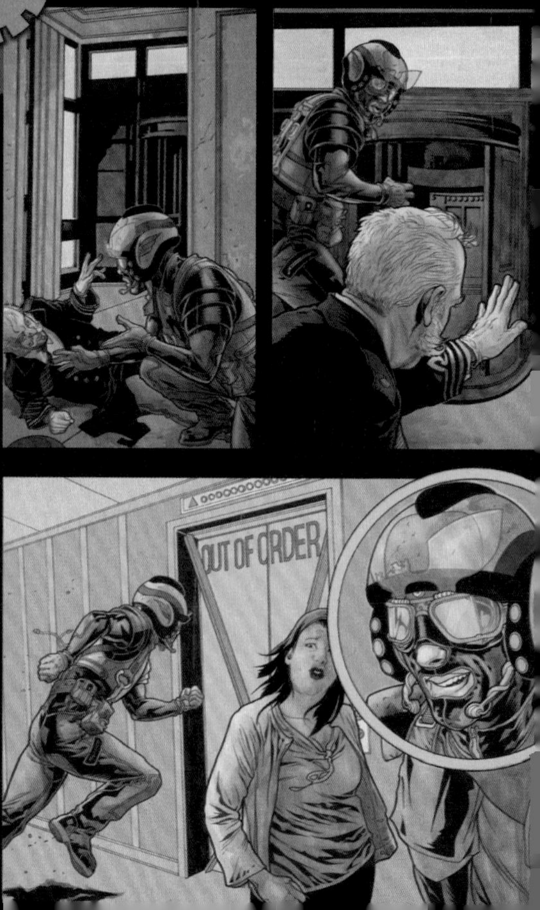
OUT OF ORDER

Page Three

Page Three, Panel One
Cut to the Great Machine's warehouse hideout (from [Sp]rouse's special) where KREMLIN is talking into a microphone, [w]hile BRADBURY listens in behind him.

1) Kremlin: Mitchell, let him go!
2) Kremlin: No pusher boy is worth dying for!

Page Three, Panel Two
Cut onto the roof of the apartment building, where the Great [M]achine bursts out of a roof-access door.

3) Great Machine: You stick with a job until it's finished, [K]remlin.

4) Electronic (tailless): But Bradbury says there is deli getting [ro]bbed two blocks from you! Those people need you more than--

Page Three, Panel Three
Pull out to the largest panel of the page. We're in the fore-[g]round with Cleveland, who is RUNNING at us, right for the [E]DGE of the five-story building's roof!

5) Great Machine: Cleveland, don't!

Page Three, Panel Four
Push in on the Great Machine, who yells:

6) Great Machine: You'll never make it!

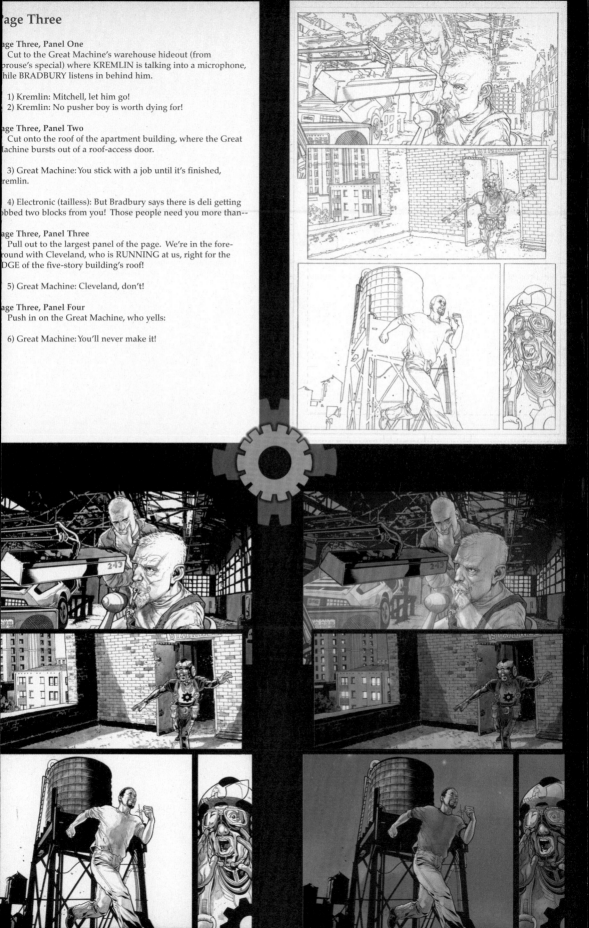

Page Four

Page Four, Panel One
Cut to Cleveland, who LEAPS over a wide alleyway towards another roof across the way.

1) Cleveland: Eat dick!

Page Four, Panel Two
We're behind the Great Machine, looking over his shoulder, as he watches Cleveland LAND safely on the other roof.

2) Great Machine: Son of a…

Page Four, Panel Three
Change angles on the Great Machine, as he RUNS as fast as he can, preparing to jump just like Cleveland did.

3) Great Machine (small font, whispering): My legs are machines, my legs are machines, my legs are…

Page Four, Panel Four
Change angles for this largest panel of the page, a cool-ass shot of the wingless Mitchell JUMPING across the wide alleyway. Maybe we're down in the alley, looking up at him as he makes the leap? Whatever looks coolest, man.

No Copy

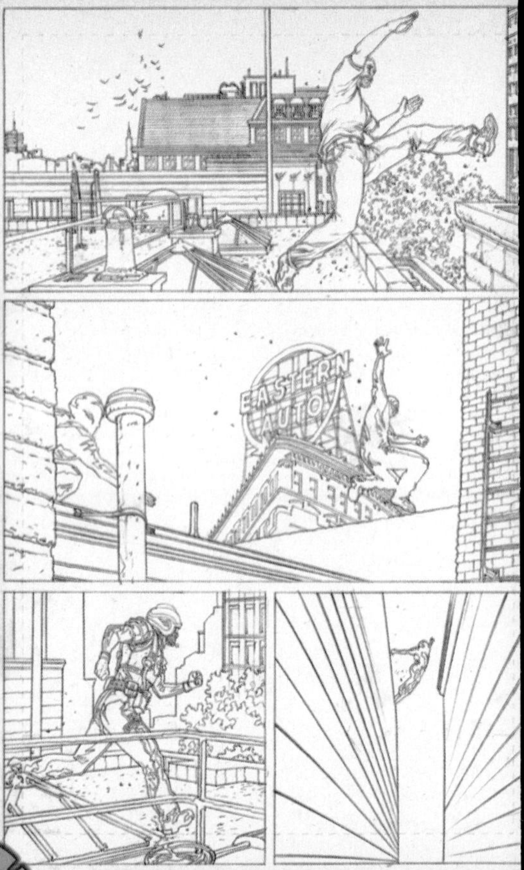
EASTERN
AUTO

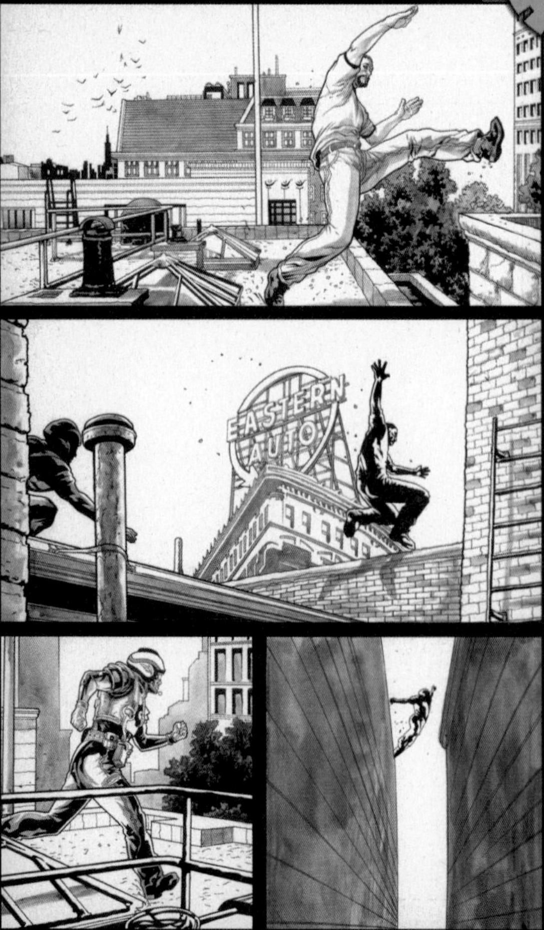
EASTERN
AUTO

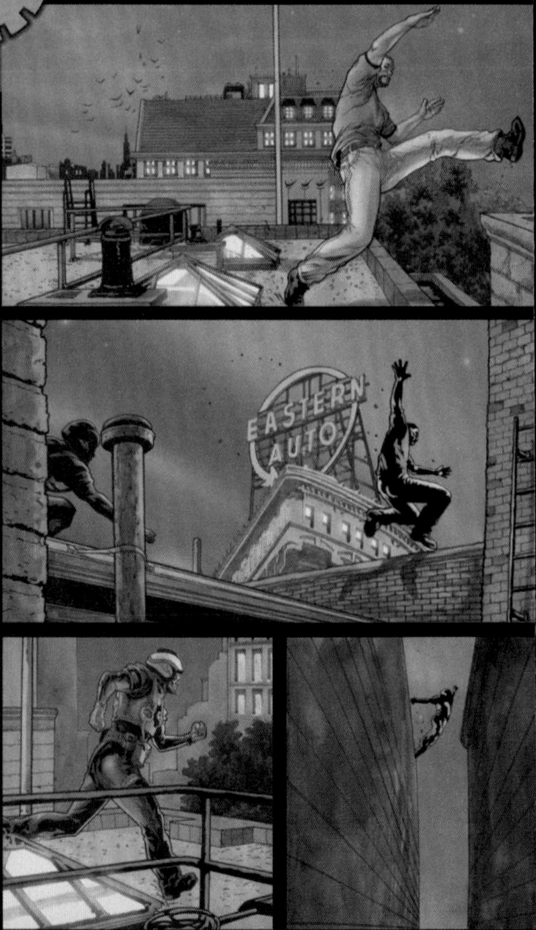
EASTERN
AUTO

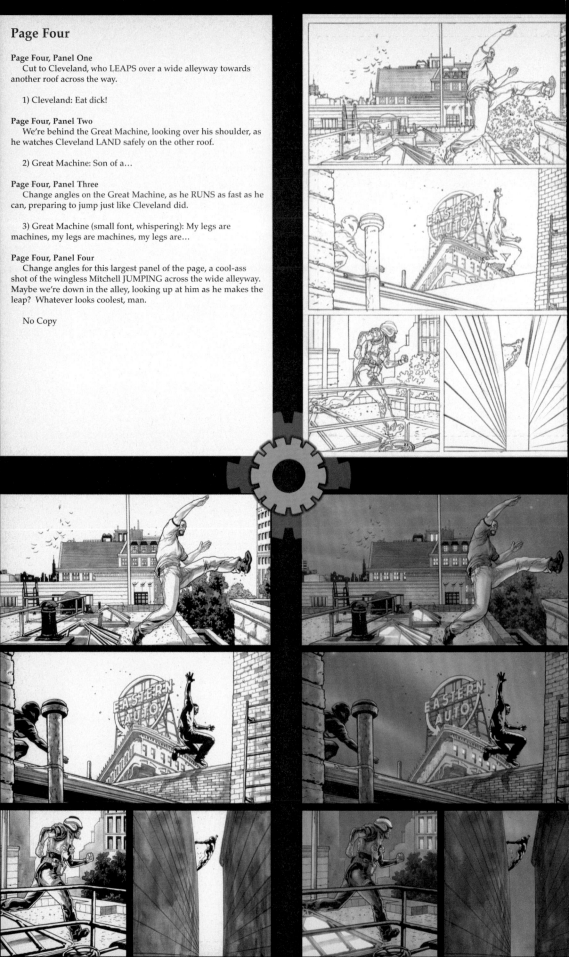

Page Five

Page Five, Panel One
Push in, as the Machine just MISSES the roof, and narrowly CATCHES the edge of it with his arms.

1) Great Machine: UNF!

Page Five, Panel Two
Pull out to a shot of both men, as Cleveland looks down at the Machine (holding on for dear life), and aims the RAYGUN he stole at his face.

2) Cleveland: Dude.
3) Cleveland: Stop. Fucking. *FOLLOWING ME!*

Page Five, Panel Three
Push in tight on the Great Machine, as his scars begin to GLOW beneath his goggles.

4) Great Machine (GREEN FONT/BALLOON): Voltage spike.

Page Five, Panel Four
Pull out to the largest panel of the page, as the raygun in Cleveland's hand suddenly EXPLODES in a burst of sparks, electrocuting him..

5) SFX: KZZZAXXXX

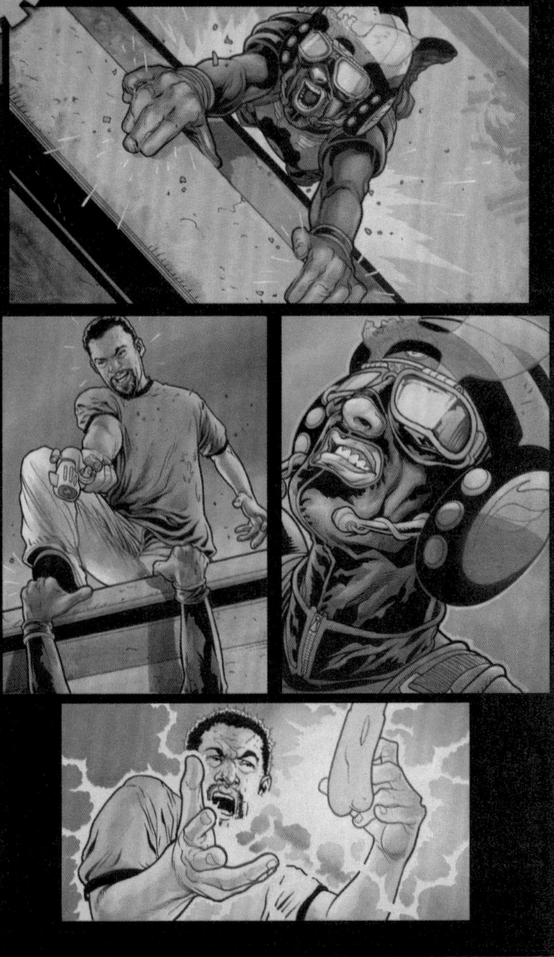

Page Six

Page Six, Panel One

We're with Cleveland's fallen body in the foreground of this shot. In the background, the Great Machine PULLS himself up onto the roof.

1) Cleveland: Nnn...!

Page Six, Panel Two

Pull out to the largest panel of the page for a shot of both men. The Great machine is standing over the groggy Cleveland, as Mitchell pulls out a pair of HANDCUFFS from one of his pouches.

2) Great Machine (small font, whispering): Cleveland Severtson, I'm placing you under citizen's arrest.

3) Cleveland: All this for a little grass?

4) Great Machine (small font, whispering): An apartment-full is hardly a little. Besides, you sell to children.

Page Six, Panel Three

Push in on the two men, as the Great Machine handcuffs Cleveland.

5) Cleveland: No, I sell to rich folk! I can't control who they give their shit to.

6) Cleveland: Look, I'm not a rapist! I've never murdered anybody! You can't send me to prison!

7) Great Machine (small font, whispering): I'm not. I'm sending you to the cops.

Page Six, Panel Four

This is just a shot of the exhausted Great Machine, as he matter-of-factly says:

8) Great Machine: I can't control who they give their shit to.

9) Great Machine: -koff- -koff-

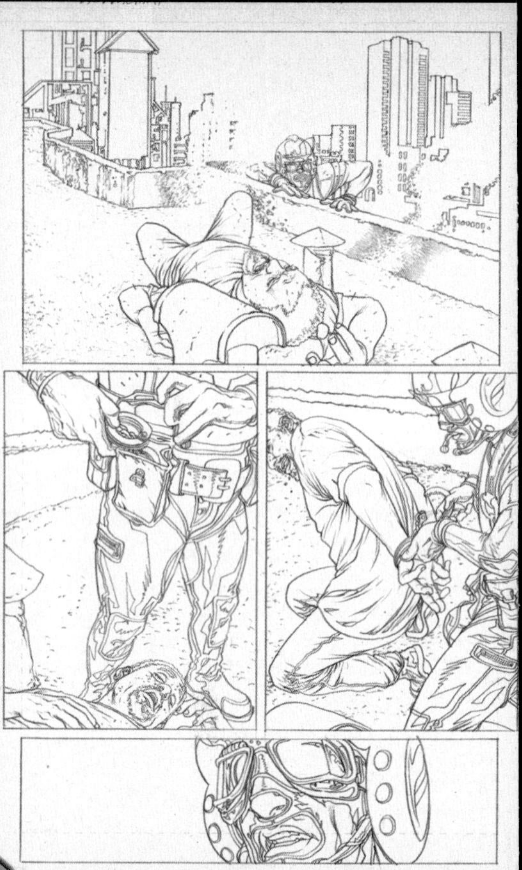

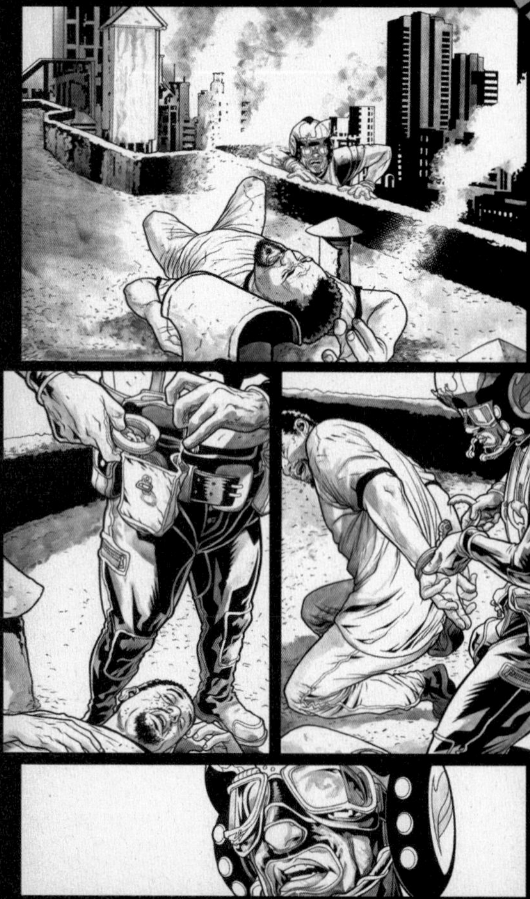

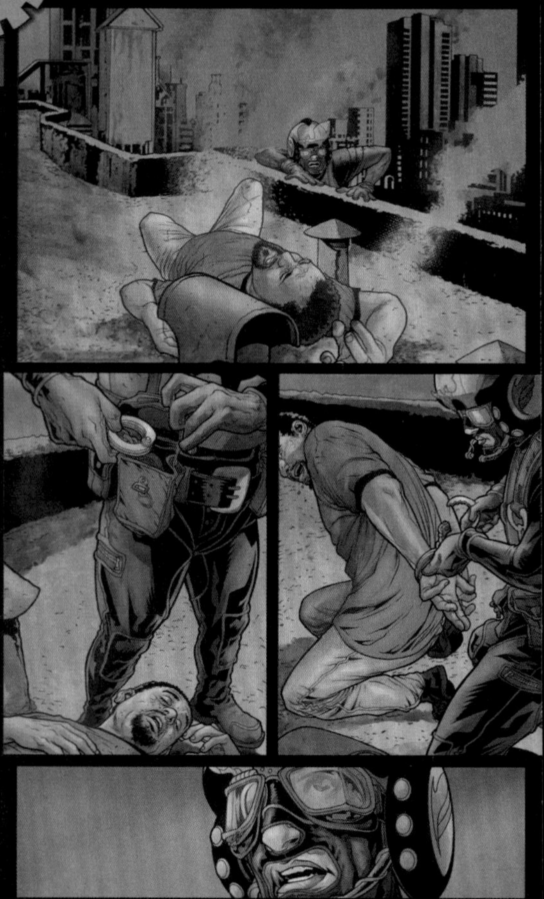

Inside the Covers

Tony Harris is an Eisner-winning cover artist from his STARMAN days—and in 2006, he was again nominated for "Best Cover Artist." What follows is an Inside look into Tony's cover creation process, as he pencils, inks and colors every cover on his own, with notes from the old man himself.

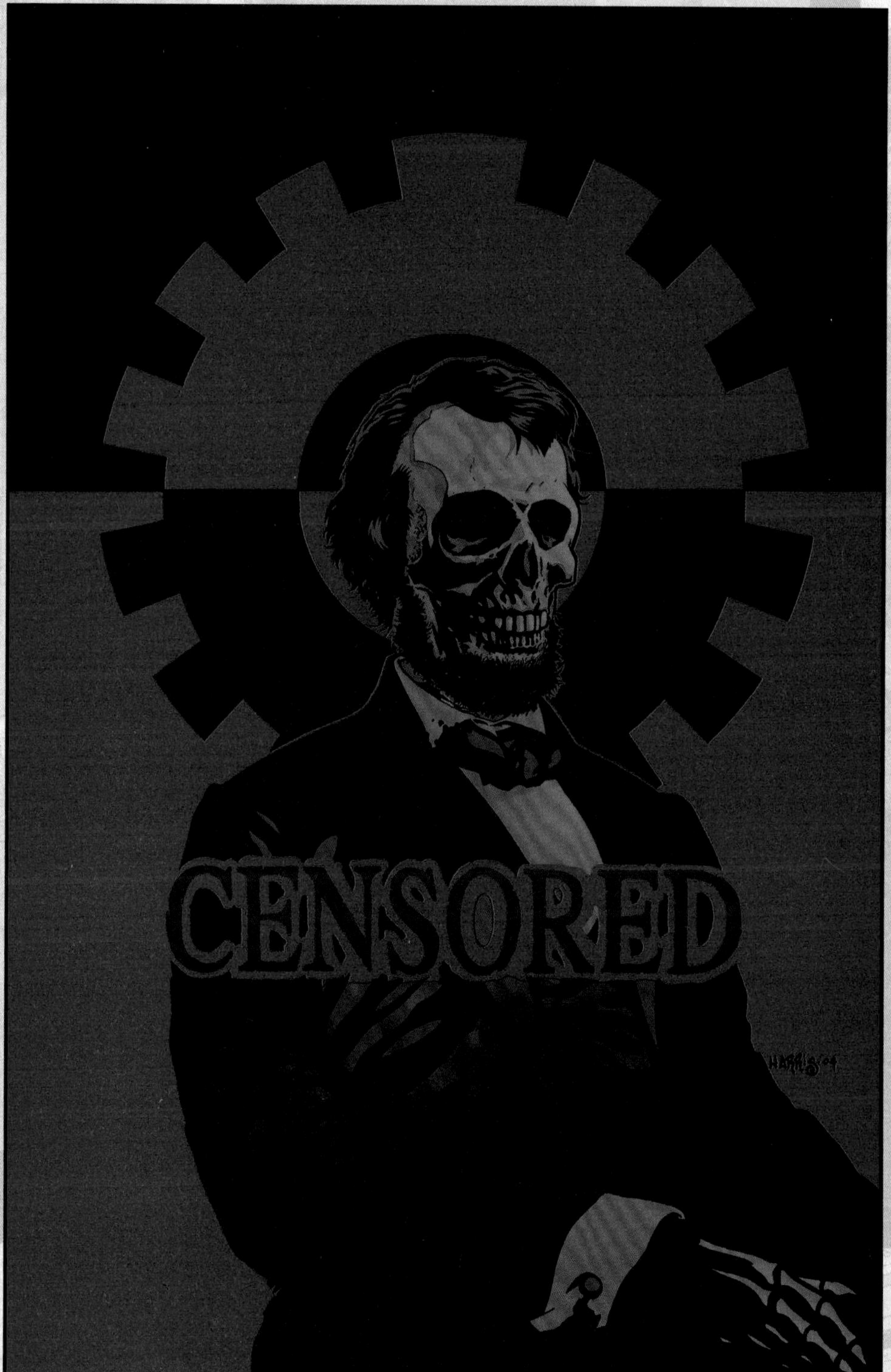
CENSORED
HARRIS/04

#1

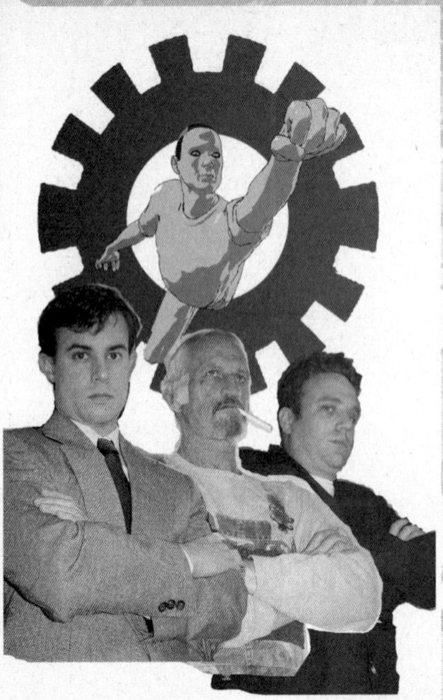

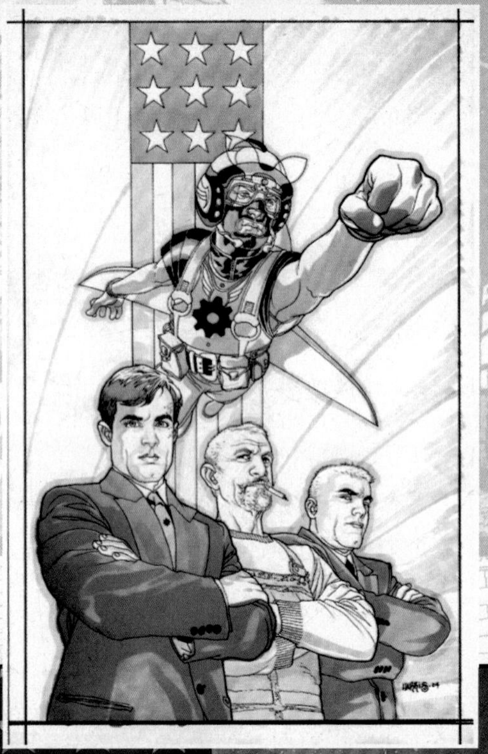

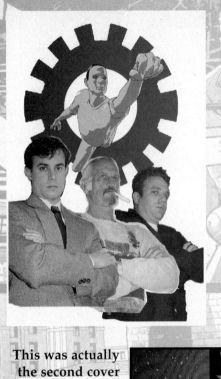

This was actually the second cover produced for the first issue. (More on that in a moment!) But the team felt the first version I did (which was eventually used as the cover to #4) wasn't powerful enough to be issue one's cover. I have to say, in hindsight, I agree.

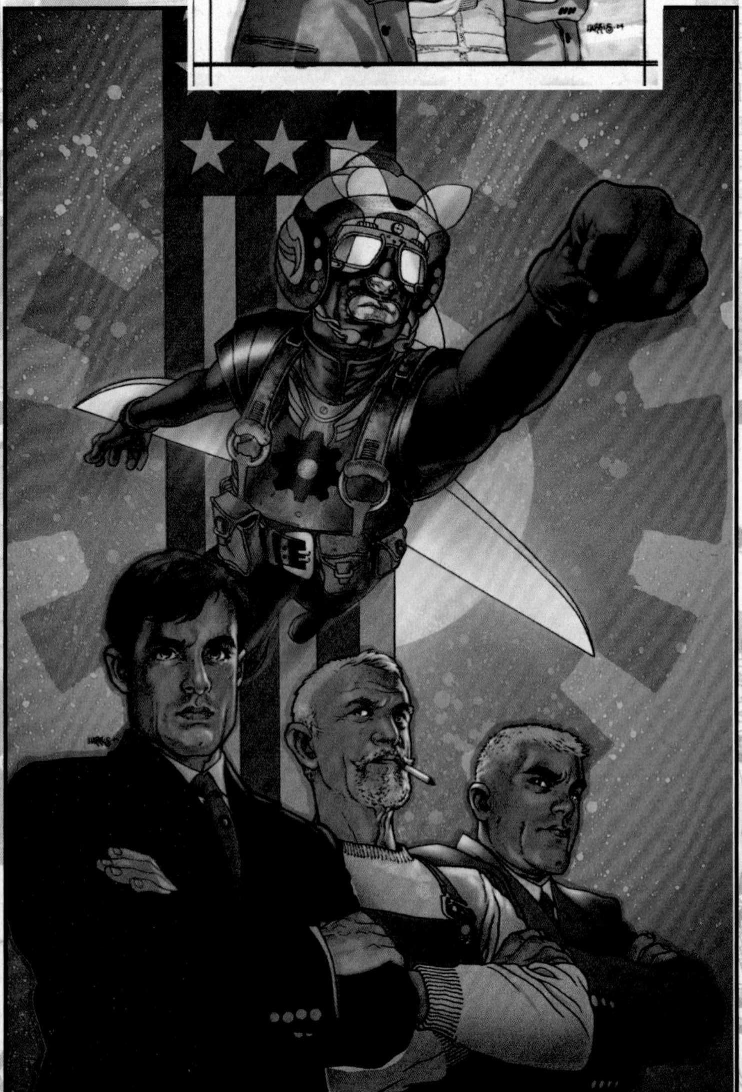

#4

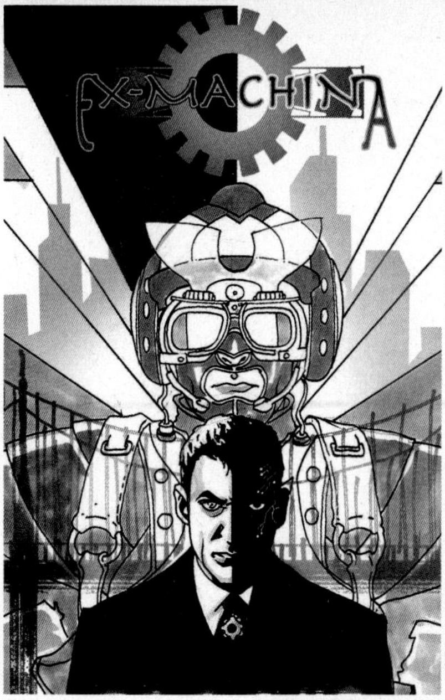
EX-MACHINA

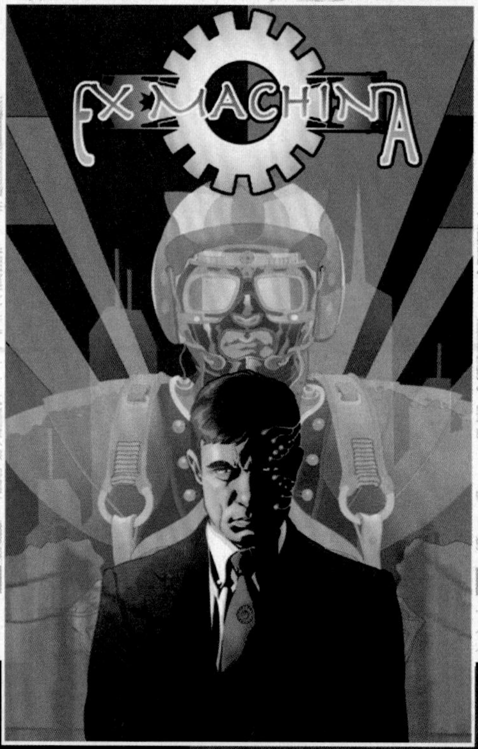
EX-MACHINA

This is the final cover for issue #4. As mentioned, this was originally the first issue cover.

My initial thoughts were to include a single bold word that would encompass the story inside. Later, we decided not to do this because it would fight with the logo and cover copy. I did, however, get to do this with the Lincoln cover to issue #2—effectively, as can be seen on page 105!

The ghosted city here was done totally digital and does not appear on the original. Note the super-ghosted Brooklyn Bridge at the bottom.

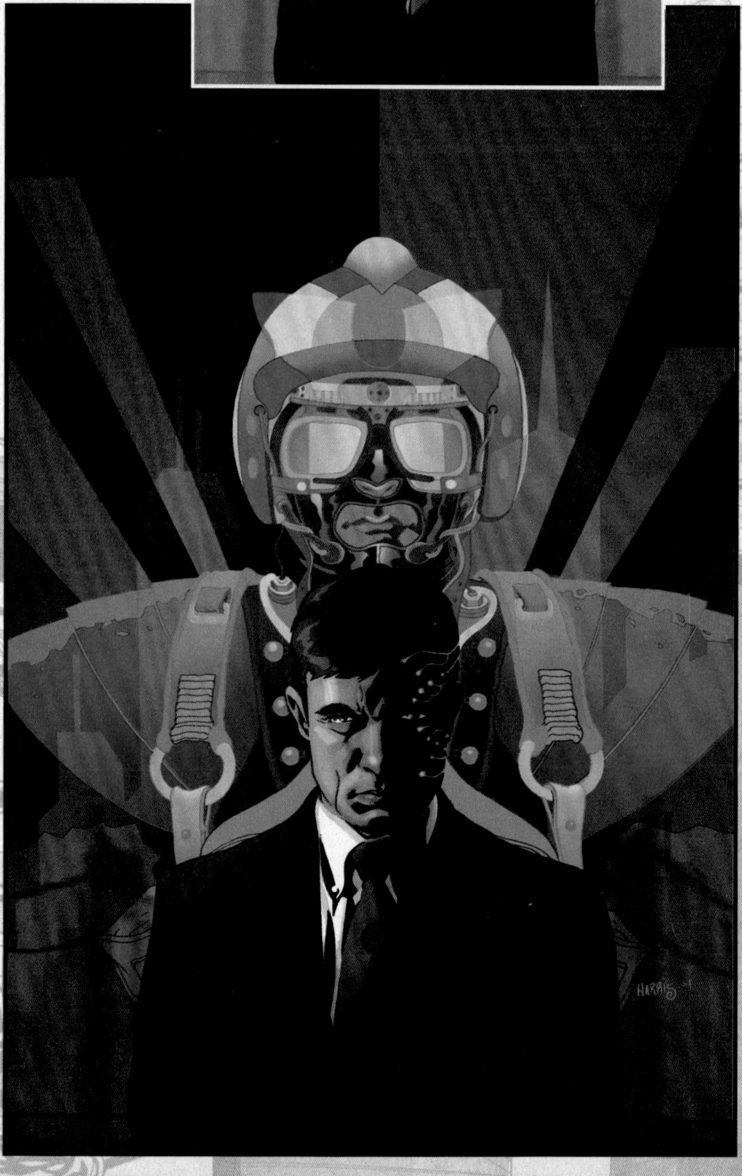

#5

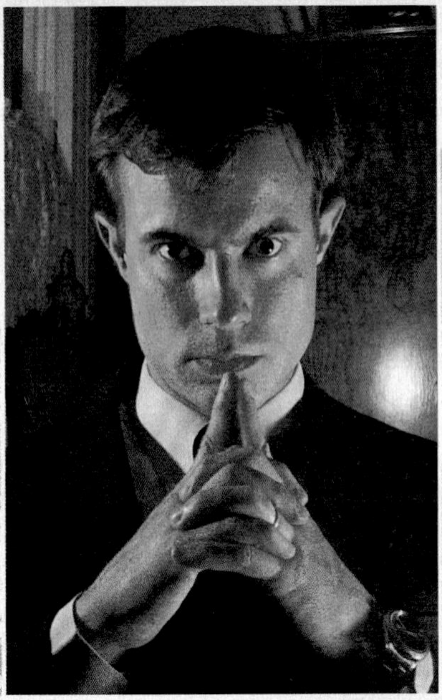

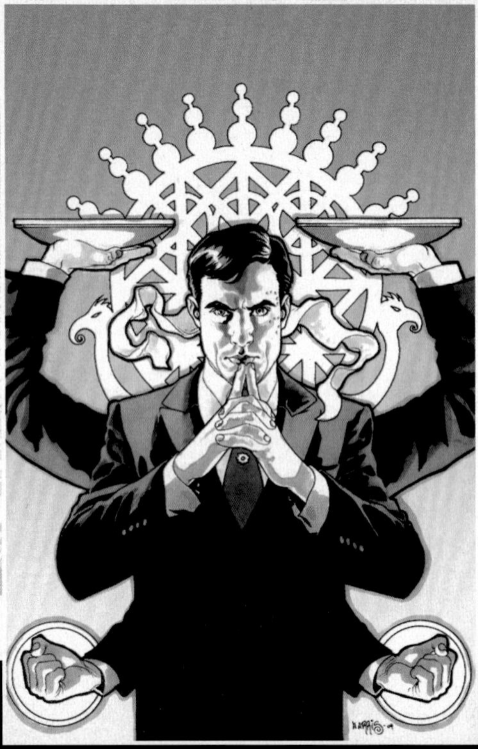

Here is my model for Mitchell Hundred, Jimmy Hill. He can have such an intense look when he's lit right. For this design I wanted to riff on Mitchell's multi-tasking as the Great Machine and the Mayor. So this cover represents the balance of Force (bottom pair of hands), Deliberation (middle pair), and the Scales of Justice (top pair).

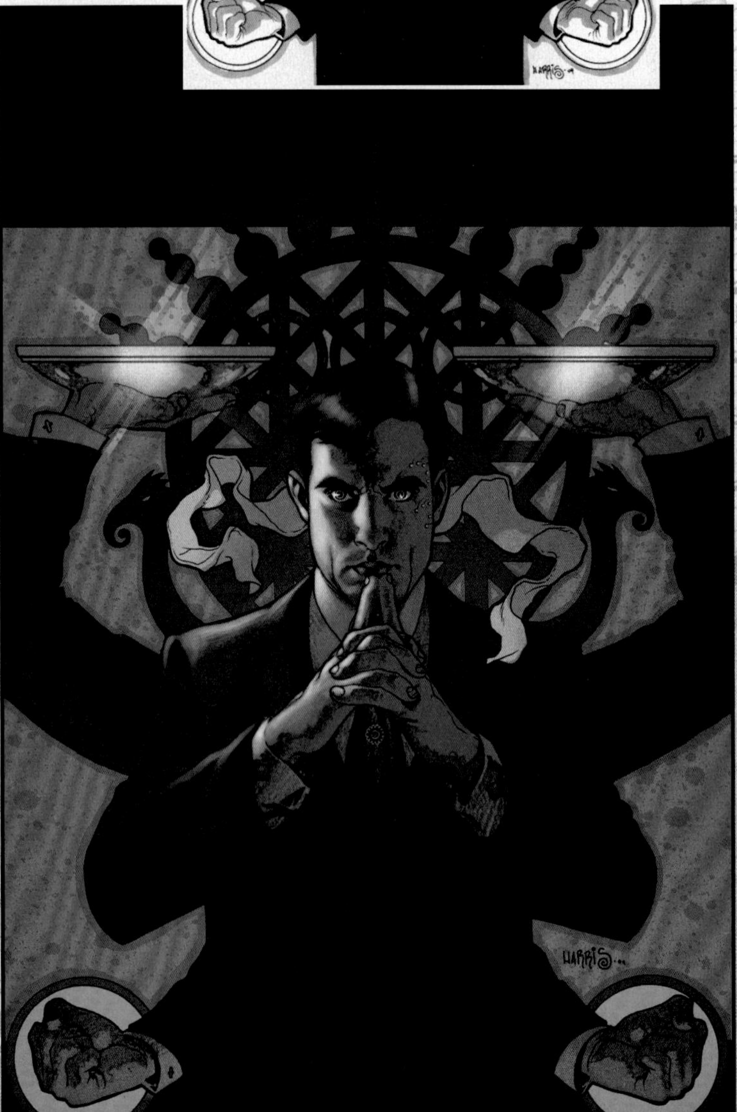

#12

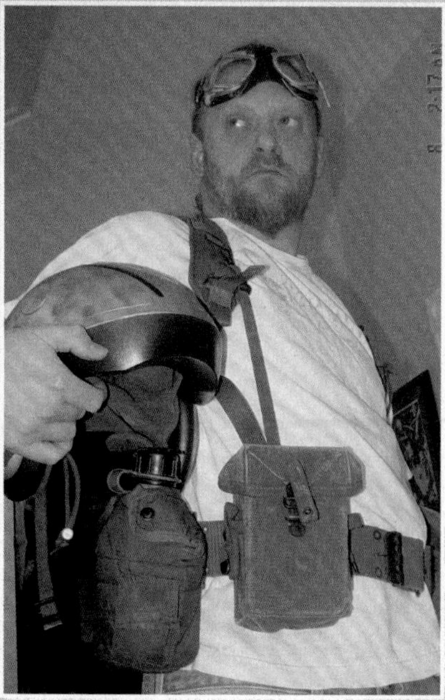

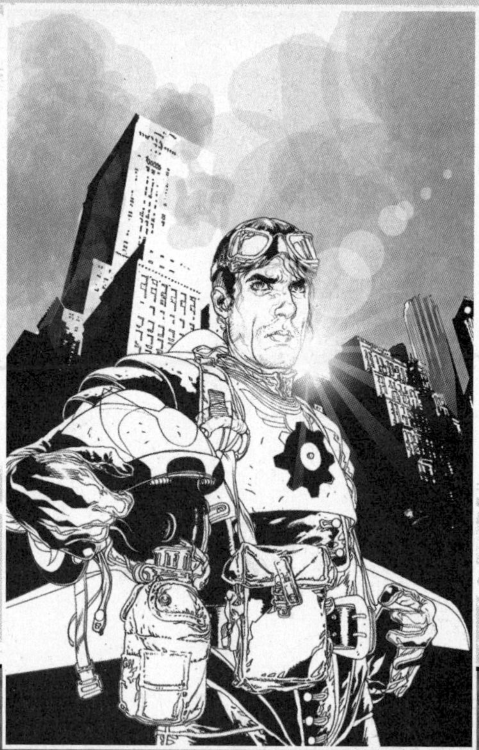

I used a shot of myself here because Jimmy wasn't available. I later shot his head and inserted it, then added the skyline as an afterthought. I really wanted to play with how matted down and sweaty his hair would be under that mask and helmet on a summer day. I thought it all worked out quite well.

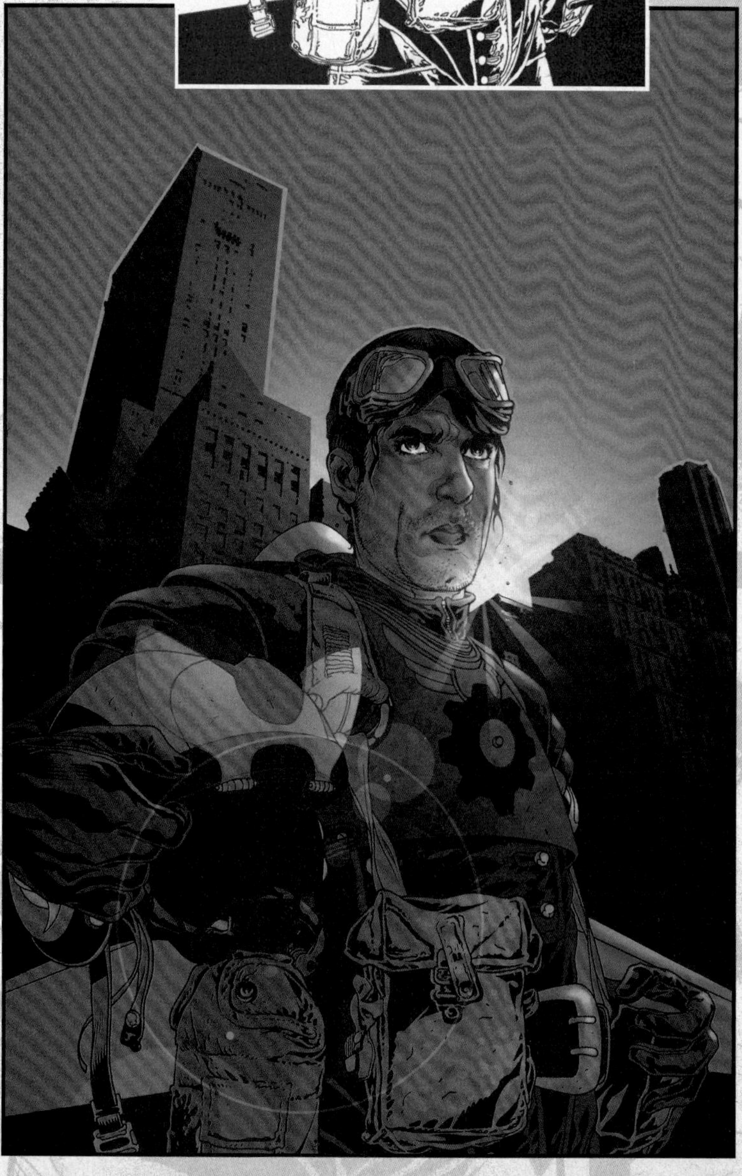

#29

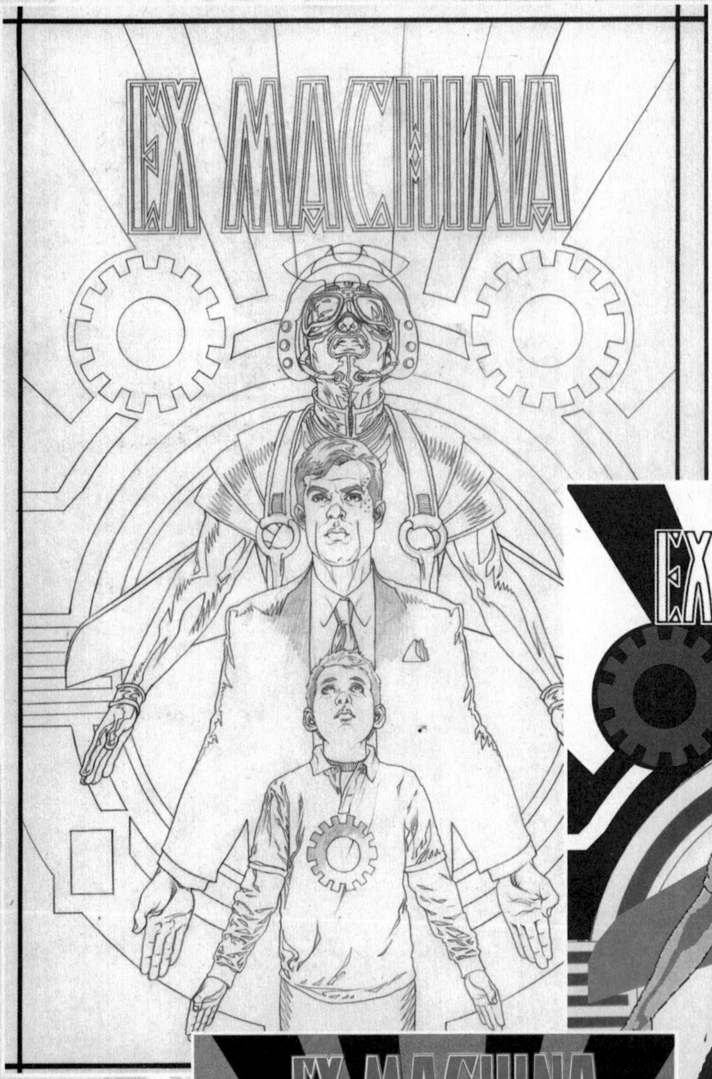
EX MACHINA

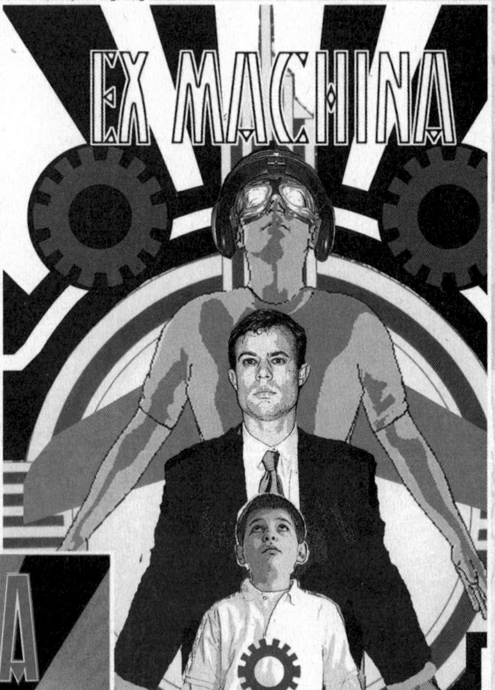
EX MACHINA

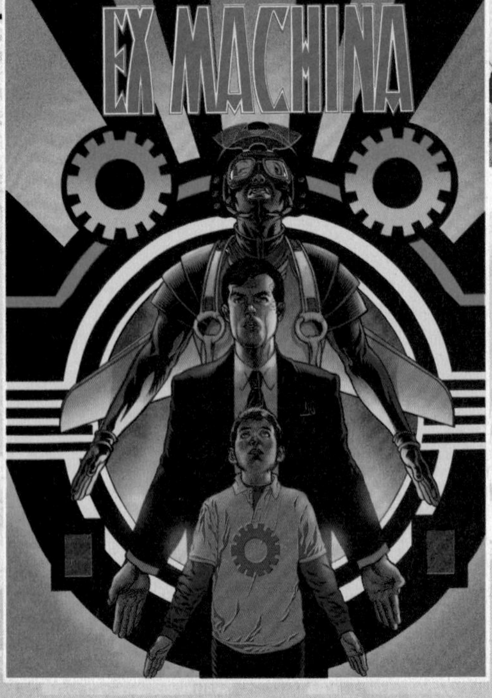
EX MACHINA

This might be my favorite EX MACHINA image to date. I got lucky with the design flowing properly.

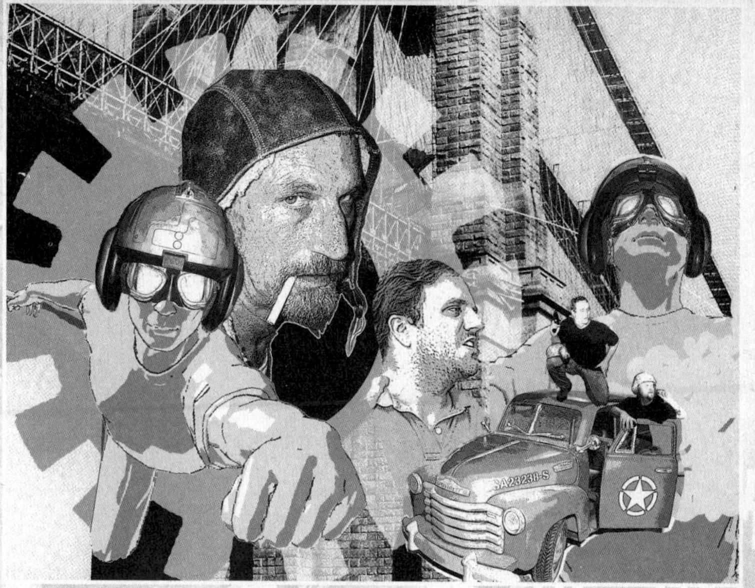

SA23238-S

I was worried when it was cut in two (to be the covers to the EX MACHINA SPECIALS) that they wouldn't work as well individually. But after some deliberation I removed the Brooklyn Bridge (pictured in the photo comp) and replaced it with the Statue of Liberty and the NYC skyline featuring the Twin Towers. Then it all came together with the addition of the field of stars. I was really pleased to hear that DC will be releasing a poster of this image!

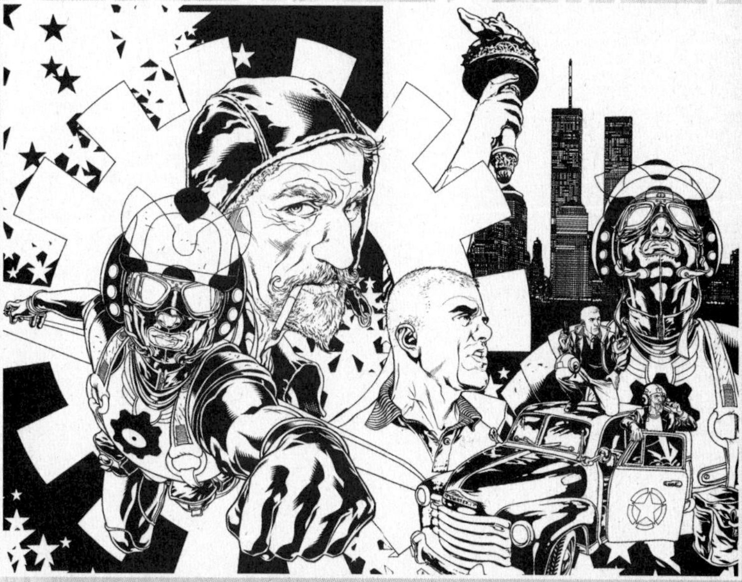

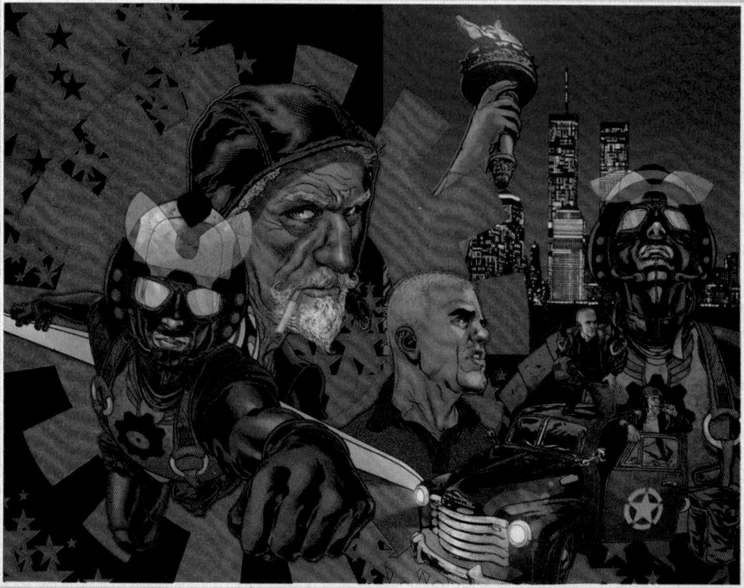

SPECIALS

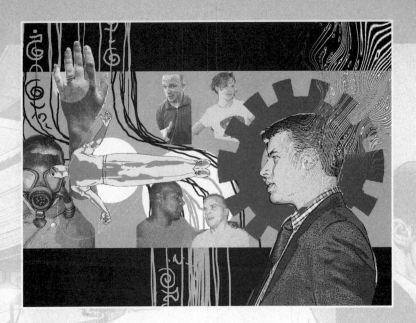

TAG

I used different Tarot Card titles to label the different characters and the issues dealt with in the story arc featured here.

The research and decision-making on this particular cover made it especially rewarding. Plus I got to play with my son's plastic rayguns I used as reference. The juxtaposition of hero and villain on the right side of the image was the cement that brought the whole design home for me.

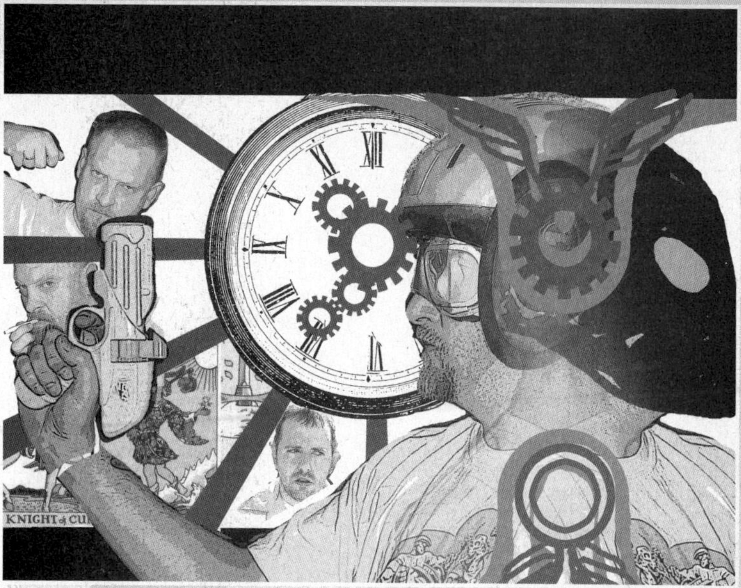

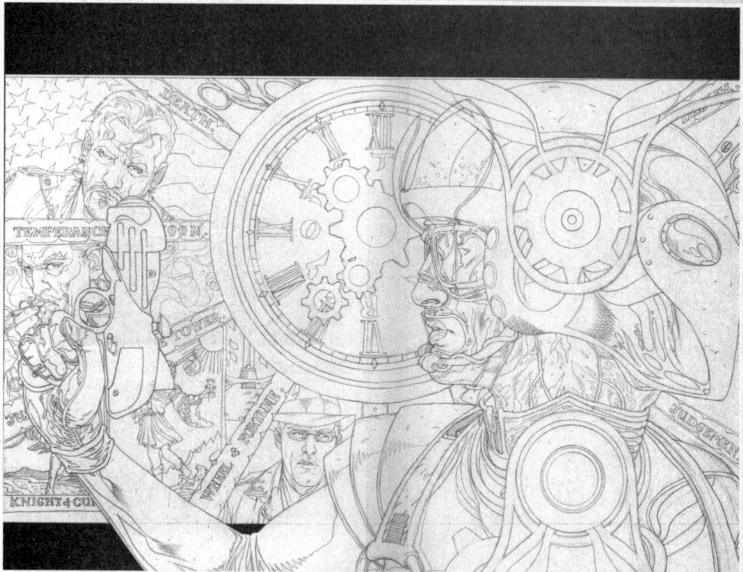
DEATH.
TEMPERANCE
JUDGEMENT

FACT V. FICTION

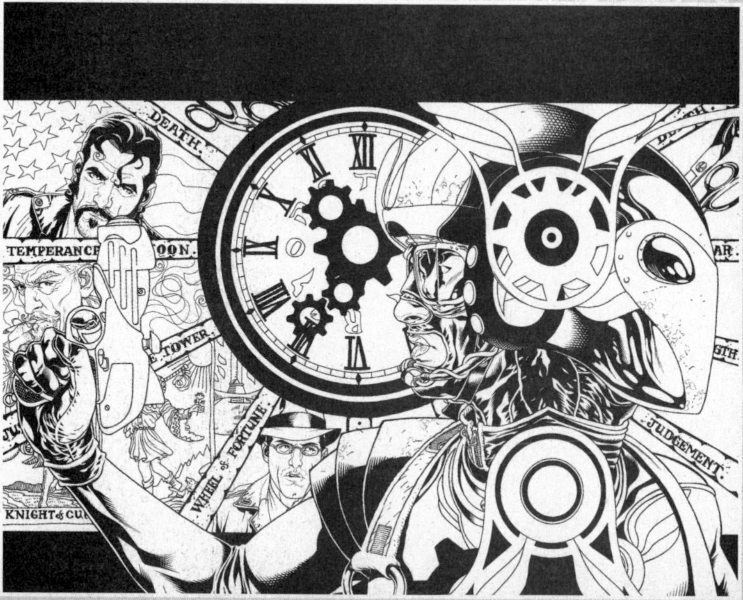
DEATH.
TEMPERANCE
WHEEL of FORTUNE
JUDGEMENT.

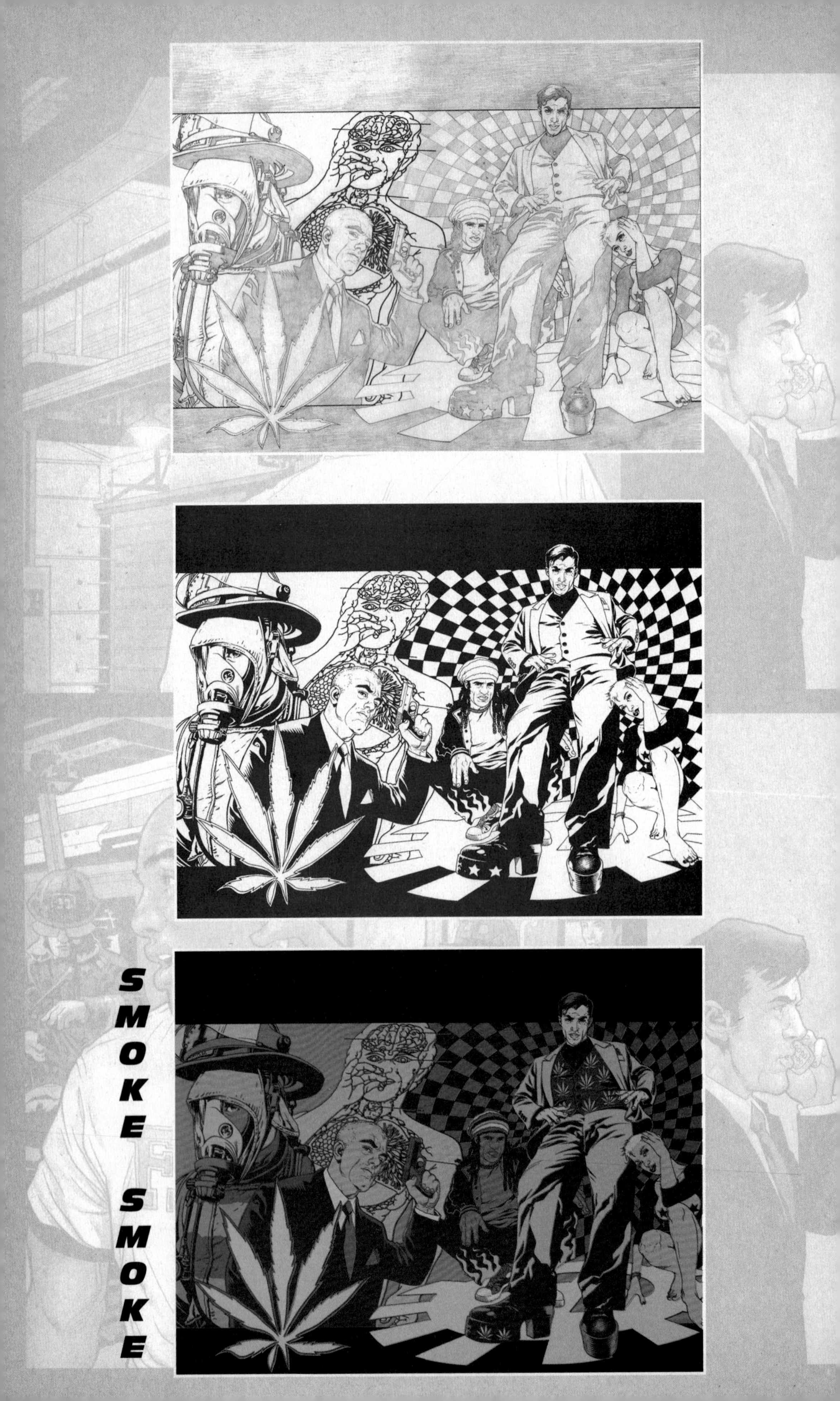
SMOKE
SMOKE

Ex Machina: Concepts & Photos

These were some 3-D images of the jet pack Brian Frey built. Originally, I wanted these commissioned so that I could do full turnarounds for photo ref while drawing the Machine in action. It proved to be too time consuming, so it was easier to just keep hard copies laying around and draw the jet pack freehand whenever needed. I did, however, create the entire cover to issue #10 digitally, using one of these images with a "skin" painted on.

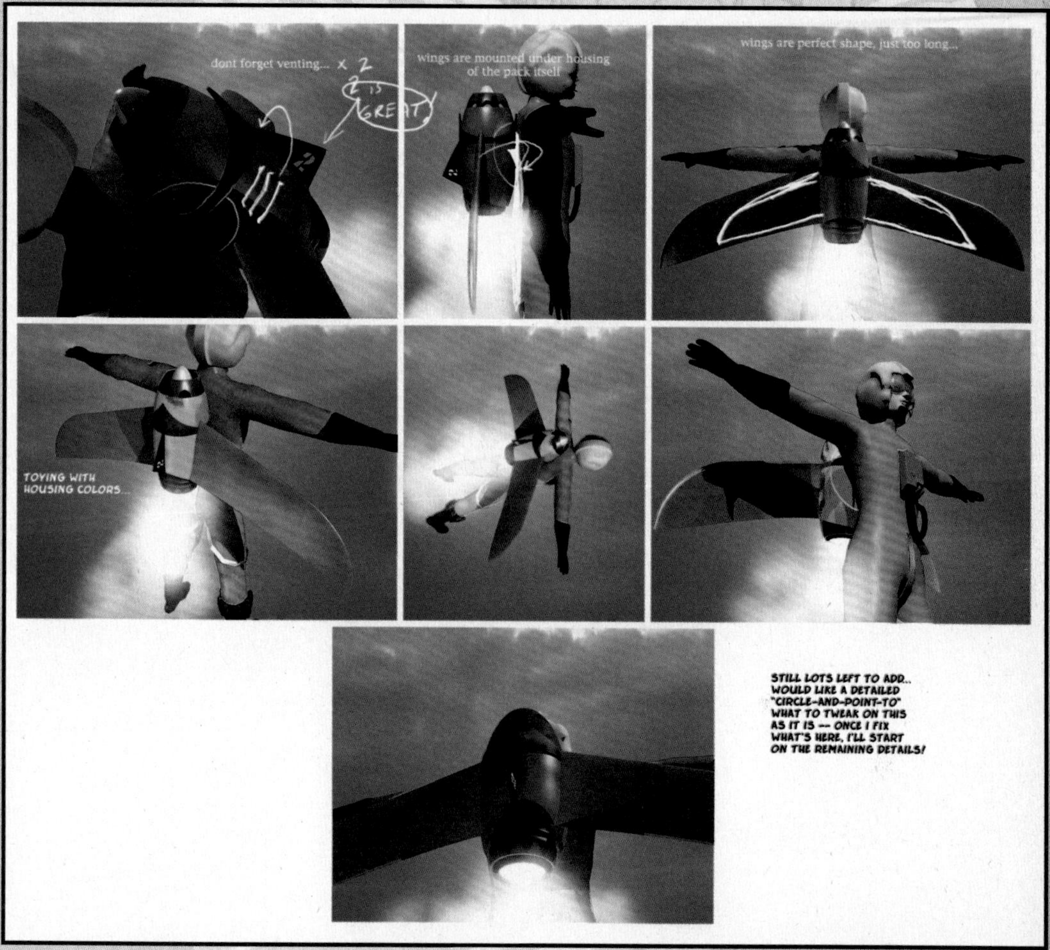

dont forget venting... x 2
2 is GREAT
wings are mounted under housing of the pack itself
wings are perfect shape, just too long...
TOYING WITH HOUSING COLORS...
STILL LOTS LEFT TO ADD... WOULD LIKE A DETAILED "CIRCLE-AND-POINT-TO" WHAT TO TWEAK ON THIS AS IT IS -- ONCE I FIX WHAT'S HERE, I'LL START ON THE REMAINING DETAILS!

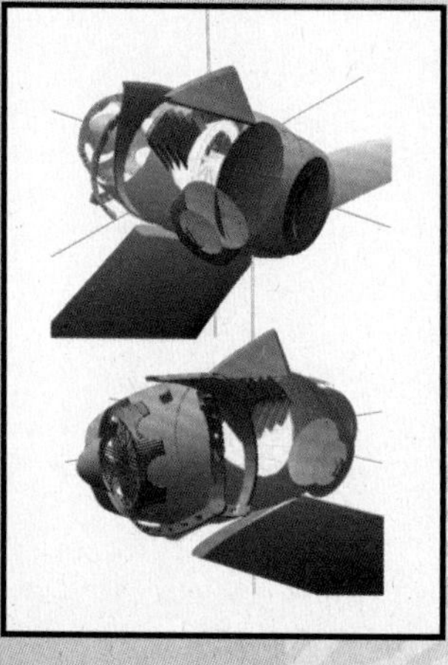

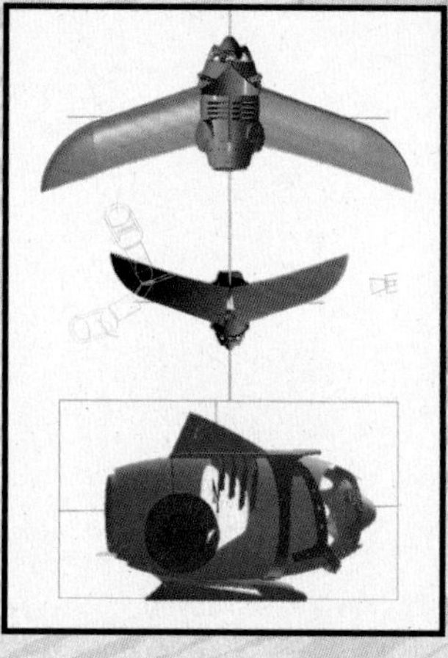

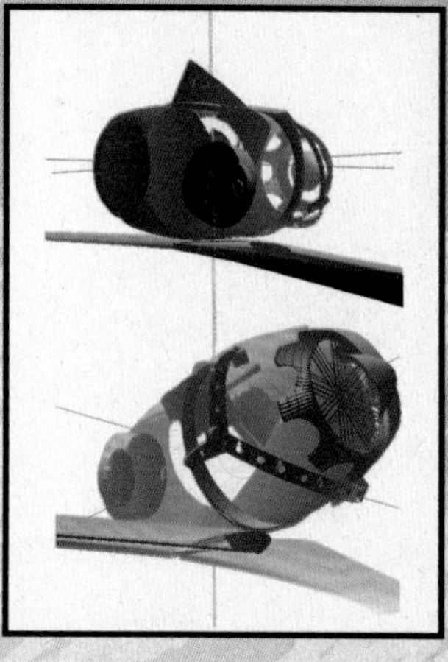

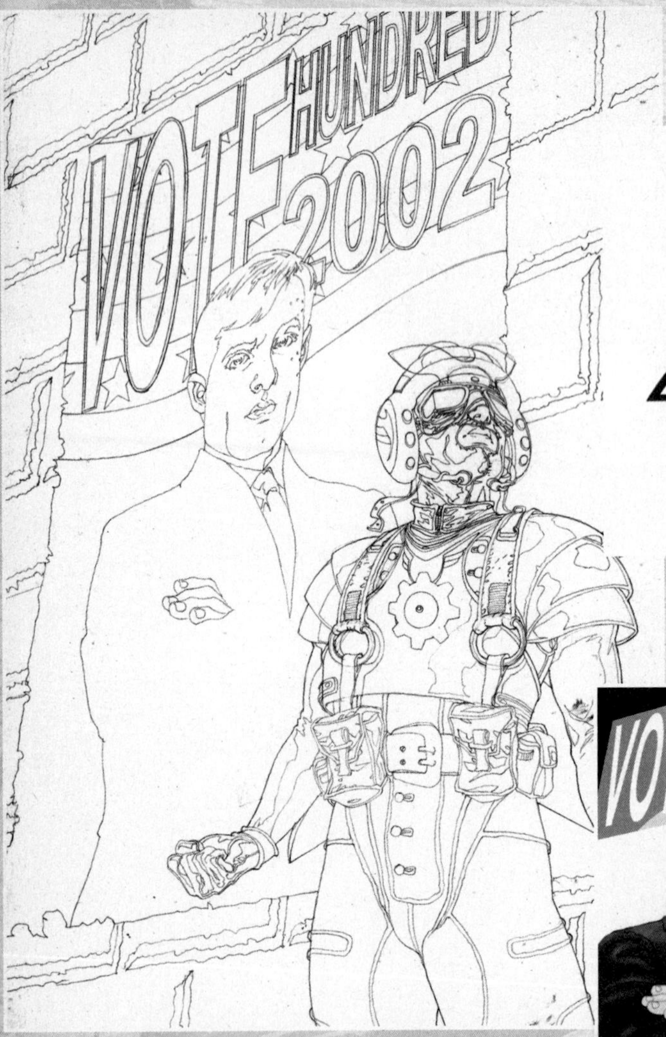
VOTE
HUNDRED
2002

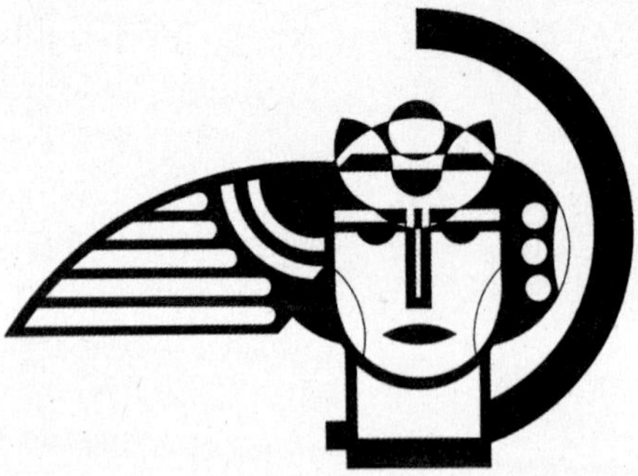

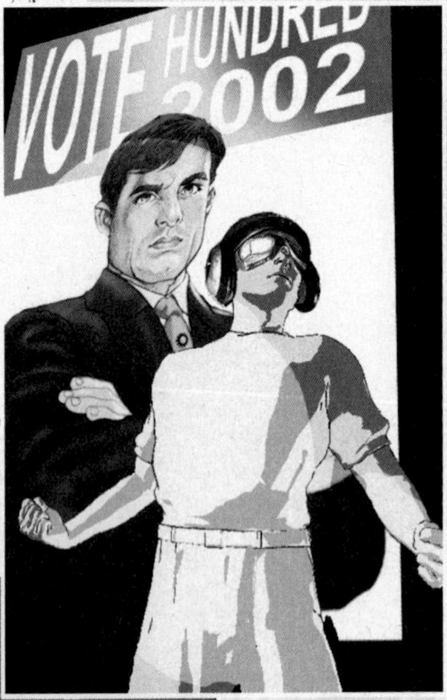
VOTE
HUNDRED
2002

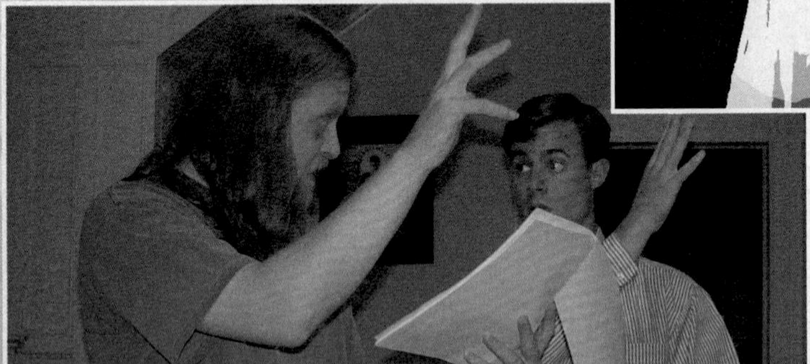
15 7:29AM

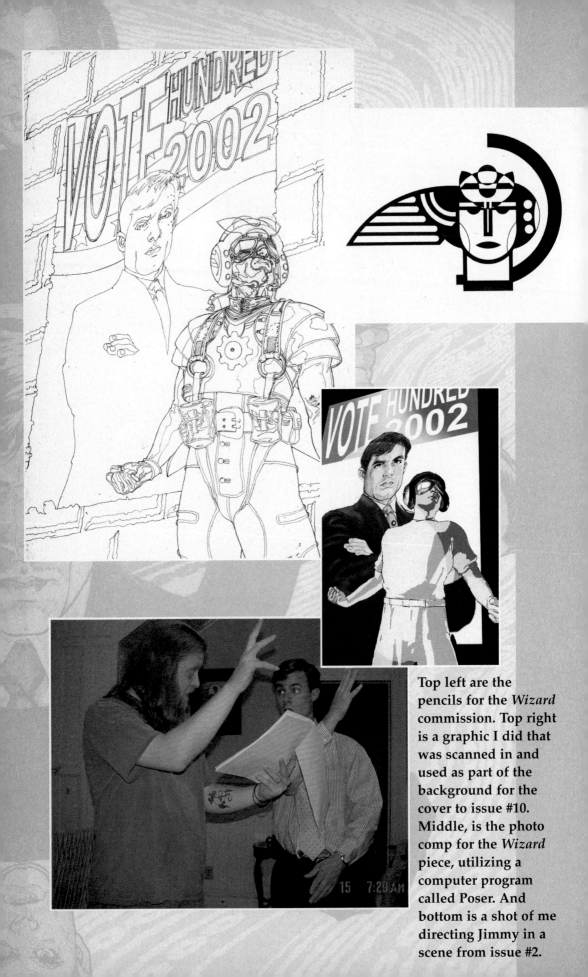

Top left are the pencils for the *Wizard* commission. Top right is a graphic I did that was scanned in and used as part of the background for the cover to issue #10. Middle, is the photo comp for the *Wizard* piece, utilizing a computer program called Poser. And bottom is a shot of me directing Jimmy in a scene from issue #2.

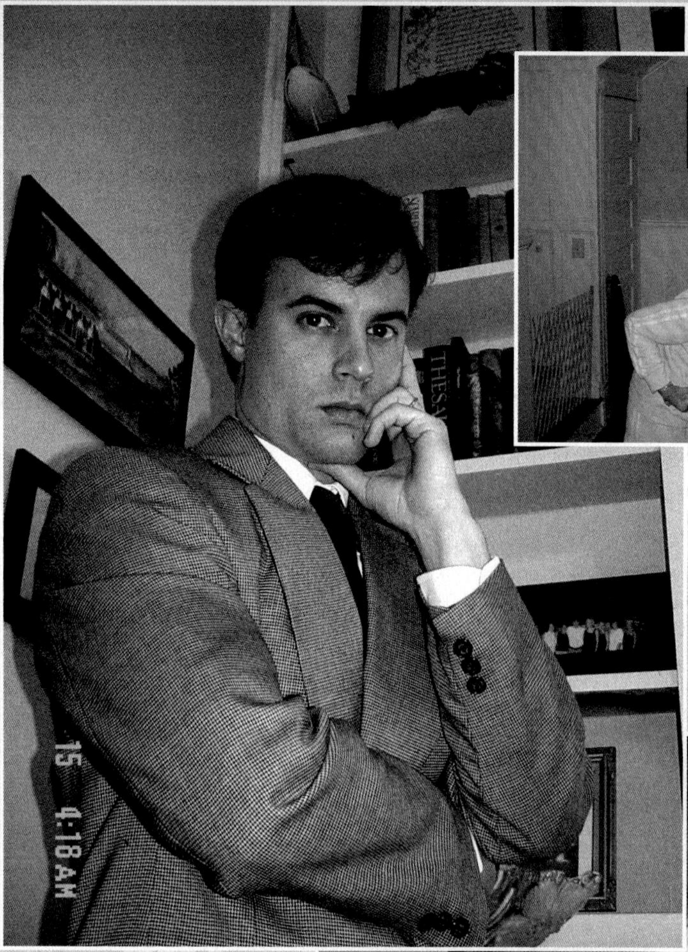

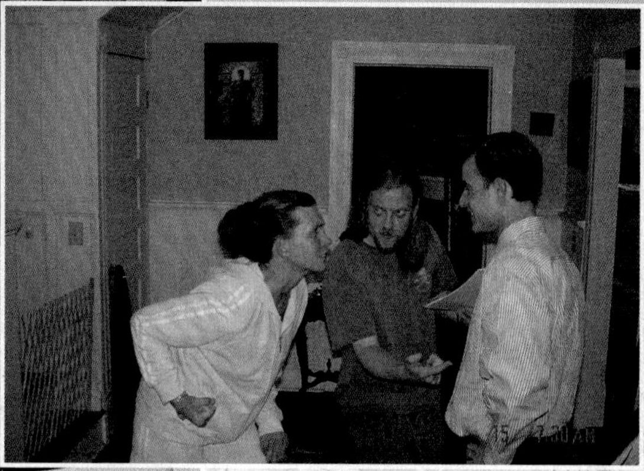

Jimmy Hill and Greta O'Dell (Commissioner Angotti) rehearsing the rooftop beating the Great Machine takes from Angotti in issue 2. At the bottom is Kremlin's aviator cap.

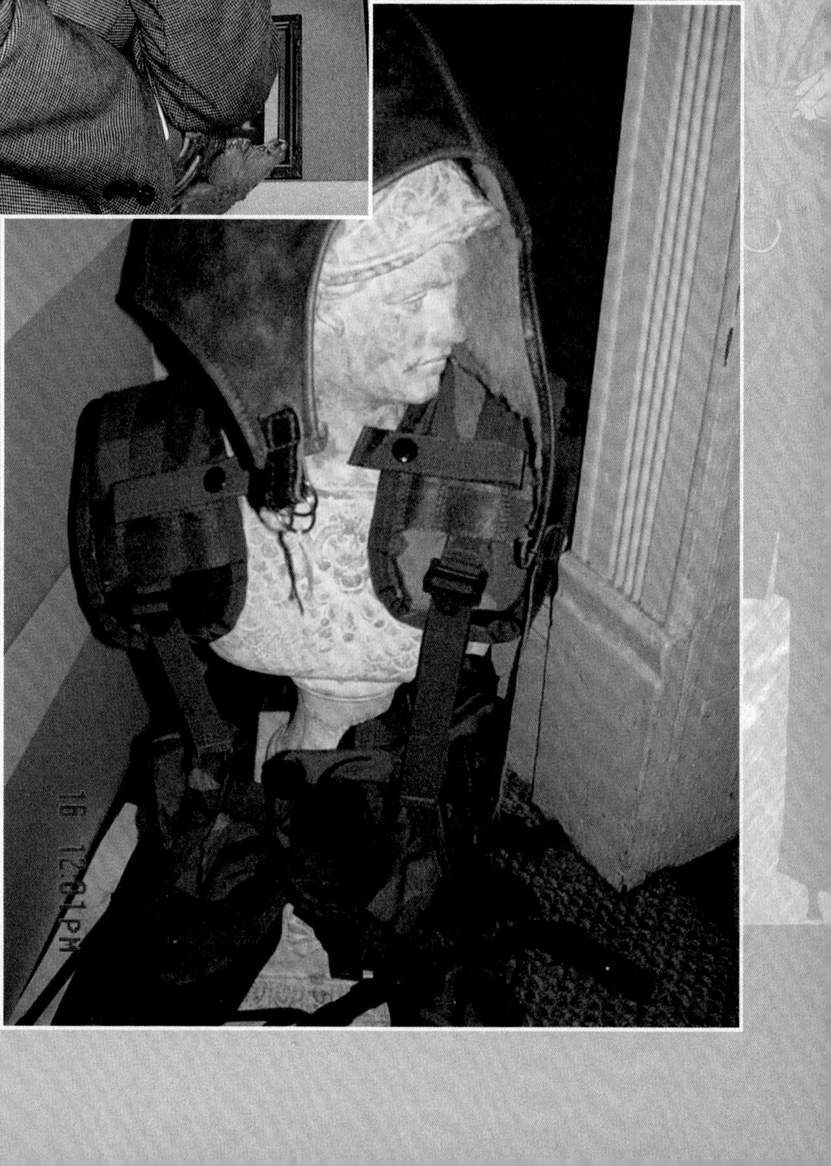

Afterword by Tony Harris

There's an old saying that goes, "I'm my own worst critic." That would totally be true in my case—except for the fact that I have a wife and two children. My wife and kids, specifically my son, are my worst critics. I wouldn't have it any other way. There is an honesty to their comments that makes them pure; the kind of honesty that you can only get from those closest to you.

Back when I was drawing STARMAN for DC Comics, my editor was the legendary Archie Goodwin. Aside from the honor of working for Archie, I also felt he was the single best editor I've ever worked for. He had the same honesty about my art that my wife has. Each month when it was time for me to do the painted cover on the book, I would submit anywhere from one to three sketches for approval. Generally I would try to let Archie know—in a roundabout way—which of the sketches I was leaning toward, without tempering his input. Now here's where it gets interesting. My wife sees everything I do before it goes out the door, in every stage from sketch to pencil, ink or paint. In the four years I worked for Archie, my wife always picked the sketch that Archie would ultimately choose. Every time.

Every single time.

As an artist, it is so important to trust in your ability, your skill. But equally important are the people you surround yourself with. Your confidants. Over the years I have shared studio space with other artists, writers, painters, and friends. They came and went, and sometimes I moved on. These days, my trusted friends, co-workers, and confidants are the guys I work with on EX MACHINA. I can honestly say this is the best collaboration I've experienced in 19 years of working in comics. And as much as I never thought it would happen again, I found in Ben Abernathy the same feeling of trust and comfort that I remember fondly from the years I spent working under Archie Goodwin.

Then there is Brian K. Vaughan. What can I say that everyone else already hasn't?

It's all been said so I won't repeat it. But I can speak to what it's like to work with him. I've been blessed to work with a lot of talented writers, but this working relationship is the truest collaboration I've experienced. I came to EX MACHINA on the back end of Brian's deal with WildStorm, so it was a shock and surprise that he was so open to what I had to say and what I had to show him. The Great Machine went from being a typical superhero with a cape to the leather clad, jetpack-wearing, helmeted gimp we all love today. And once I was on board, I had some other ideas, too. I went to Brian with them and much to my surprise he liked them. I gotta say I wasn't used to that from writers; a lot of them are very guarded when it comes to their scripts and they want drawn exactly what was written. Brian wants that too, but he also wants his script interpreted. He wants to collaborate. Lucky me.

Guess who else I trust? You. I really don't have a choice. Team Machina put a book about politics in your hands, and you all "got" it. You made it fly. And all of us on the team immediately got it, too. I think that's why we all signed on so quickly. A lot of people didn't think it would work, so I wonder: how's that working out for them now, do you think?

I had hoped to give you all a special treat with this book. An inside look at the Machine. How it works, and how we work. Hopefully we did that, and right now you are twice as excited about EX MACHINA as you were before you read this. The funny part is, we just arrived at the halfway point! I realized this the other day when I started working on issue 28. We have so much more to come—so many more great stories and hopefully some creative leaps in the art. My point is, we are just getting warmed up and the future looks bright. Thanks so much for making it possible to see my dreams come true on such a great project.

- Tony Harris, 2006

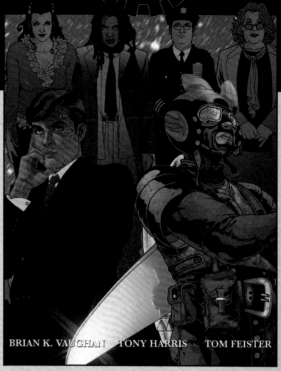

CHECK OUT MORE EXCITING WildStorm TITLES

AMERICAN WAY

RIDLEY • JEANTY

DESOLATION JONES: MADE IN ENGLAND

ELLIS • WILLIAMS III

A MAN CALLED KEV

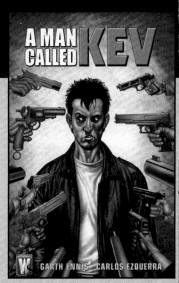

ENNIS • EZQUERRA

RED MENACE

**BILSON •DEMEO
BRODY • ORDWAY
VEY**

STORMWATCH: PHD

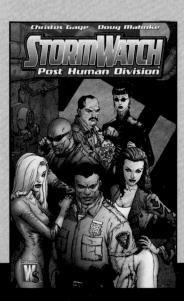

GAGE • MAHNKE

WELCOME TO TRANQUILITY

SIMONE • GOOGE

SEARCH THE GRAPHIC NOVELS SECTION OF

WWW.WILDSTORM.COM

FOR ART AND INFORMATION ON ALL OUR BOOKS!